The Cowpens Staff Ride and Battlefield Tour

by
Lieutenant Colonel John Moncure

Combat Studies Institute
U.S. Army Command and General Staff College
Fort Leavenworth, Kansas 66027-6900

FOREWORD

Staff rides provide officers and other students of military history with the opportunity to obtain important insights into military operations and to study the effects of technology in combat, concepts of leadership, and how men have fought and endured in battles. *The Cowpens Staff Ride and Battlefield Tour*, by Lieutenant Colonel John Moncure, offers a staff ride guide on a critical Revolutionary War battle. The guidebook examines the war from a strategic perspective, looks at the campaign as an operational event, and provides the backdrop to the tactical battle. The author has gathered operations orders, dispatches, and numerous eyewitness accounts to allow each visitor to reconstruct the events that occurred at the Cowpens.

January 1996

Jerry D. Morelock
Colonel, Field Artillery
Director, Combat Studies Institute

CONTENTS

Maps	v
Introduction	vii
I. An Overview of the American Revolution	1
II. The Campaign in the Carolinas, 1780–1781	17
III. "This Unexpected Event": Annihilation at the Cowpens	43
IV. The Staff Ride	71
Appendix A. Order of Battle	91
B. Documents Pertaining to the Campaign Leading to the Cowpens, 1 November 1780 to 17 January 1781	95
C. Documents Pertaining to the Battle of the Cowpens, 17 January 1781	121
D. Correspondence Pertaining to the Campaign of the Cowpens, 1 December 1780 to 20 January 1781	161
E. Miscellaneous Writings Pertaining to the Campaign of the Cowpens	187
Bibliography	199

Lieutenant Colonel John Moncure

Lieutenant Colonel John Moncure, U.S. Army, is the American liaison officer at the French Cavalry School. He is a graduate of the U.S. Military Academy, has an M.A and Ph.D. in Modern European History from Cornell University, and is a USACGSC graduate. He has been regimental adjutant and squadron executive officer in the 3d Armored Cavalry Regiment and a troop commander in the 11th Armored Cavalry Regiment. At the U.S. Military Academy, he taught history. He prepared this work while serving as professor of military studies at Davidson College in Davidson, North Carolina. He is also the author of *Forging the King's Sword: Military Education Between Tradition and Modernization—The Case of the Royal Prussian Cadet Corps* (New York: Peter Lang, 1993) and has written articles for *Army*, *Military Review*, and *The Assembly*.

MAPS

1. Principal battle sites of the American Revolutionary War 3
2. The southern theater of operations 1780–81 18
3. Situation, 20 December 1780 to 14 January 1781 25
4. Situation, 14 January 1781 30
5. Situation, 15 and 16 January 1781 32
6. Situation, 17 January 1781 33
7. Situation, 18 January 1781 34
8. Initial dispositions, 0700, 17 January 1781 49
9. British advance, 0710, 17 January 1781 53
10. Skirmish line withdraws, 0720, 17 January 1781 54
11. British attack and militia withdrawal, 0730, 17 January 1781 55
12. Continental Line withdrawal and British attack, 0740, 17 January 1781 57
13. Continentals' counterattack, 0745, 17 January 1781 59
14. Envelopment and destruction, 0750, 17 January 1781 61
15. Staff ride vantage points 1–12 73

INTRODUCTION

The renowned Field Marshal Count Helmuth von Moltke, chief of the great German General Staff and architect of the three campaigns that permitted the unification of Germany in 1871, believed fervently that war, to be understood, must be dissected and the parts examined. To that end, he directed not only that a section of the General Staff devote its energies exclusively to the study of military history but that all General Staff officers, drawn from the cream of the Prussian officer corps, travel to battlefields, study the plans made by the commanders, and relive the battles on the actual ground where the fighting took place. In this manner, Moltke believed, his officers could understand the interdependence of the commanders' plans, logistical considerations, morale factors, and so forth.

The staff ride, as the practice became known, has evolved into an institution in a number of armies. In the United States Army, officers in combat units frequently adjourn to nearby battlefields where one or more officers, tasked to provide a detailed study of the action, host a walking tour and analysis of the battle. Every branch school conducts staff rides for its students, and all ROTC cadets participate in staff rides as part of their professional military education requirements.

When I assumed my duties as professor of military history at Davidson College, I recognized that, while by training I was a European historian, I could not do justice to my students—most of whom were destined for commissioned service in the U.S. Army—without addressing some of the more important events in that Army's history. I was fortunate to discover the proximity of the Cowpens battlefield, about one and one-half hours southwest of the college.

During the first two years I taught at Davidson, I assembled documents containing eyewitness testimony to that battle. I believe this documentary record is critical for the use of students studying the battle if they are to understand and empathize with the participants. I gave the documents to my students before we gathered for trips to the battlefield. It occurred to me that, while many exciting histories of the battle exist, none of them had been written to facilitate a staff ride to the battle site. Students need to relive the terror, the exultation of the troops, and the self-doubt and sometimes unreflectiveness of the battlefield commanders, all in the full richness of the officers' own language. Even the excellent accompaniments to Civil War battlefields prepared by Jay Luvaas and Harold Nelson provide only excerpts of that testimony. Consequently, as part of the staff ride narrative, I assembled this collection of eyewitness accounts and dispatches for my students. The three chapters that precede the narrative serve only as glue to help students assemble the body of material more coherently. While I have consulted many detailed studies and determined (in cases where authorities disagree) how I believe events occurred, I do not pretend to supersede current scholarship. Likewise, as I laced the sometimes contradictory narrative accounts and dispatches into my analysis, I kept in mind that some eyewitness accounts were in fact written long after the dead were buried and could be colored by the dimness of an old man's memory or by the deliberate distortions of a man with a grudge to bear or a reputation to protect.

I have organized three chapters to focus on the discrete components of the war. In order to place the campaign in the Carolinas in context, chapter one addresses the Revolutionary War in its strategic context—how military planners determined to prosecute the war to achieve its political goals—and relates the principal events of the war. In order to provide the environment for the Battle of the Cowpens, chapter two discusses operational issues and narrates the campaign. The third chapter focuses on the tactical aspects of the battle on that cold morning in January 1781. The fourth chapter I have included as a guide for the staff ride. The leader of a staff ride could use it in conjunction with the narrative chapters and appendix or let it stand alone as a guide to a study of the campaign and battle.

A close reading of the documents in the appendixes will highlight a number of interesting aspects of this battle and, by extension, of combat in general that I do not address in the narrative. For instance, I am struck by remarkable differences between the correspondence in the two armies. The Cornwallis-Tarleton correspondence is timely and reveals the freedom and even deference that Major General Charles Cornwallis awarded his protégé, Lieutenant Colonel Banastre Tarleton. As for the American commander, Major General Nathanael Greene, the graceful strategist, worried about his unit and lectured its commander on matters his tactical better knew perfectly well how to address. Brigadier General Daniel Morgan, one of the recipients of this advice, impatiently strained at the bit but calmly assured his superior that he was taking the care that Greene demanded. The fact that the American correspondence always overlapped in time must have confused matters immeasurably.

I have given short shrift to the manifest logistical problems experienced during the campaign. Guilty of concentrating on the tactical dimensions of battle, as are many historians, I understand full well that great military leaders dwell on far less romantic concerns. From the pitiable description of Sergeant Major William Seymour to the repetitive discussion of forage, shoes, and tents in the correspondence, it seems clear that Greene's deployment in December 1780 was motivated primarily by logistical considerations, as was Morgan's proposal to invade Georgia and his plea to rejoin the main army.

Finally, I recognize that the assembled evidence derives mainly from American sources. While Tarleton and Mackenzie provide us a spirited and informative dispute, the British rank and file are silent, as are most of the officers. Obviously, American sources are more readily obtainable for me, but they are from the mouths of American veterans trying to justify pensions—and perhaps embellish their personal exploits—after a popular war. The British sources, with a characteristic predilection for understatement anyway, downplay events all the more in the wake of the unsuccessful war. Moreover, although British casualties were far higher than the American ones, with many of the captives remaining in America after the war, these men were ineligible for pensions and had little incentive to make public the record of their military actions against their newly adopted country. Finally, the few Legion cavalry who escaped consisted primarily of Loyalists who either removed to Canada after the war or would have been unlikely to trot out their memories of service against the United States. I trust careful readers will be able to weigh this shortcoming as they evaluate the evidence.

I owe a debt of gratitude to a number of talented people without whose patient efforts this work could not have been completed. Foremost among them are the fine staff of the Cowpens National Battlefield. In particular, Patricia Ruff and Bill Kianos showed me every kindness and offered helpful suggestions that I have incorporated throughout these pages.

I prepared this manuscript far from the rich source materials I needed to complete it. Were it not for the determined and cheerful efforts of the staff of Davidson College's E. H. Little Library to honor my near-impossible requests, I could never have finished. Leading their efforts were Dr. Mary Beatty, Sharon Byrd, Jean Coates, Ellen Giduz, Cindy Pendergraft, Kelly Wood, and Suzy Yoder. With dedication and expertise, they ferreted out obscure sources from the most unlikely places.

I am very grateful to Mr. Donald Gilmore of the Combat Studies Institute for the professional expertise he brought to bear in editing this manuscript.

I am also deeply indebted to Lieutenant Colonel Leonid Kondratiuk and the Historical Services Division of the National Guard Bureau for providing the funds with which this guide was printed.

To several noted scholars, I owe a debt of thanks: Colonel Robert Doughty at the United States Military Academy and Professor Russell Snapp of Davidson College read an early version of the narrative and corrected several points of style and historical fact that would surely have proved embarrassing to me.

My wife Anne accompanied me on my first visit to the Cowpens. She understands my compulsion to write and supported my efforts to complete this work. Without her gentle prodding, this book would have remained a working manuscript.

Finally, I dedicate this work to my students, especially the ROTC cadets of Davidson College, for whom it is written.

I. AN OVERVIEW OF THE AMERICAN REVOLUTION

A mysterious chemistry of Enlightenment political theory[1] and the North American colonial frontier experience, sparked by the economic and political repercussions of the French and Indian War (1754–63), finally exploded into revolution at the village green in Lexington, Massachusetts, on 19 April 1775.[2] Although the dispute between American colonists and the British Parliament over taxation was most vexing to Bostonians who made their livelihood from relatively unrestrained trade prior to the 1760s, broader principles were sufficiently pressing to elicit supporters (admiringly called patriots, critically labeled rebels) from all thirteen colonies, albeit not in equal proportions. The clash pitted a portion of the colonial civilian population against the armed might of one of the greatest maritime powers of the time.

To suppress this dispersed and largely unorganized "rabble," the English king sent to the colonies three competent professional soldiers: Major Generals Sir William Howe, Sir Henry Clinton, and Sir John Burgoyne.[3] They brought with them additional regular British troops and regiments leased from the Hessian elector, many trained and experienced in fighting a form of European warfare characterized by rigid discipline, efficient concentration of combat power, and extensive logistics and administrative regulation. For these British officers, battle was more akin to a minuet than a brawl.

Their colonial opponents, however, had little military experience. Men such as George Washington, Philip Schuyler, Israel Putnam, and Daniel Morgan had served as militia officers during the French and Indian War; others had served in paid provincial units (such as Rogers' Rangers).[4] What the bulk of American men knew of the army and of war, they had learned in their periodic militia drill on the village commons. As the American Revolution loomed on the horizon, many of these military organizations suffered from neglect.[5] Still, shortly after the fighting began, the New England colonies all managed to raise numbers of regiments based on the geographical location of the militia.[6] At the instigation of the Massachusetts

Provincial Congress, these forces (some 30,000 strong) were gathered around Boston as the New England Army. In 1775, they became the basis of the Continental Army. Only in time, and with the expert and perceptive advice of General Baron von Steuben,[7] was the Continental Army to develop the battle-worthy stamina and skill expected of European forces.[8]

Strategic Considerations

In order to maintain the thirteen colonies as British possessions, the king needed to subdue the population and reestablish loyalty (or at least obedience) to the Crown. The theater for this operation was daunting in scale: it contained a population of a bit over 3 million settlers dispersed over almost 800,000 square miles. Lord North sought to divide the Colonies by applying economic sanctions to the most rebellious of them.[9] British military objectives were fourfold: separate the New England colonies from the others by seizing the Hudson River north to Lake Champlain; isolate the "bread basket" colonies of Pennsylvania and Maryland; control the southern populace by holding Charleston,[10] Georgetown, and the line of the Santee River; and, finally, blockade the entire American coast to prevent an influx of arms from abroad (see map 1). As New England was the center of revolutionary sympathy, it logically became the first priority. A number of military historians claim that this strategy would have worked if the British had possessed adequate forces in the hands of resolute commanders. This observation is only partly accurate. The large army of British regulars, Loyalists, and Hessian mercenaries, a fleet, and 10,000 sailors indeed were sufficient to destroy the Continental Army, but British commanders never manifested the will to win, and they squandered their resources, especially time, until the war was beyond recovery.[11] Whether an overwhelming tactical victory would have won the war, however, is open to conjecture.[12]

To achieve independence, the Americans needed to eject all British troops—the symbol of the Crown's rule—from the Colonies. The Continental Congress would have been delighted had King George III granted the colonies their freedom,[13] but as this bounty was not forthcoming, and as the strength of Britain lay in its considerable

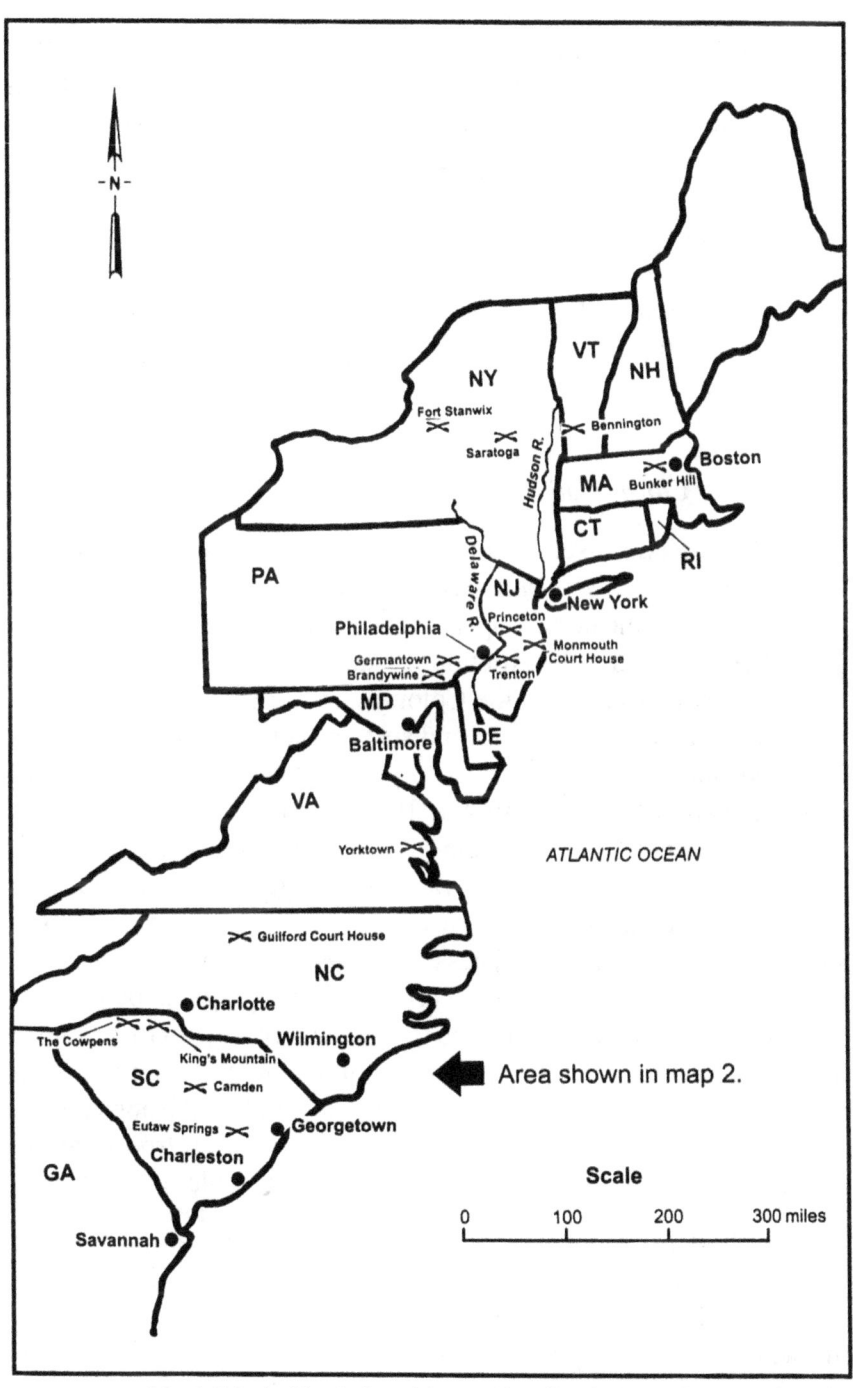

Map 1. Principal battle sites of the American Revolutionary War

army and fleet, the Americans could not hope to bring their oppressor to his knees. As historian Russell Weigley has noted, "Washington's was a generalship of military poverty."[14] Often necessity breeds inventiveness, and in this case, circumstances led the American commander to several brilliant feats of maneuver. While he was obliged on occasion to face a major British army, he adopted early a strategy of attrition, at once harassing British detachments while avoiding battle to preserve his own strength. American diplomats in Paris, meanwhile, sought intervention from England's traditional foes before General George Washington could be trapped by the king's troops.[15]

Operational Considerations

Both sides addressed a number of operational issues. Britain's most obvious weakness in its effort to subdue the rebellion was the distance of the theater of operations from the home country. To project power across the Atlantic, Britain required adequate troops to occupy key locations in the Colonies, sufficient transport vessels to carry them across the ocean and sustain them (for seven years, as it turned out), and a battle fleet to protect these extended lines of communication.[16] Although the British possessed these assets, America was not England's sole focus of attention. Increased pressure from England's colonial rivals and traditional continental foes stretched the country's assets to the limit.[17] The American rebels sought to exploit this weakness by engaging privateers and the fledgling American navy to prey on British shipping and by encouraging the French to join them. The British, in turn, sought to minimize the troop burden by raising Loyalist units in the colonies. This measure, effective at least in the sense of the number of troops raised, eased the burden of recruitment and transportation of troops across the Atlantic, but it did not resolve the resupply problem.

Still, the British were capable of projecting substantial force to their American colonies. As Washington observed, "The amazing advantage the Enemy derive from their Ships and the Command of the water, keeps us in a State of constant perplexity and the most anxious conjecture."[18] Sea power gave the British the advantage of lateral communications; although their armies may have been farther apart than those of their colonial opponents, movement by sea was usually much faster (though subject to seasonal storms) than by land. Thus, the British army in Boston could evacuate the city in the spring of 1776, retire to Canada, and reappear in New York later that year. Furthermore, once at sea, the army could strike any unguarded coast without telegraphing its intentions with advanced guards, lines of communications, or any of the other indicators upon which a defending army might rely for intelligence.

The British also hoped to take advantage of a mixed Tory-rebel population. Conventional wisdom divides loyalties in the American Revolution into three roughly equal groups: the rebels, the Tories, and the indifferent. British commanders occasionally demonstrated sensitivity to the advantage of wooing the uncommitted; more often they (like Cornwallis in New Jersey and Tarleton in the Carolinas) inflamed the population by their cruelty. The British succeeded, however, in arming and organizing numbers of Tories into effective units that fought beside regulars in several battles.[19] The British strategy of pacification of the population entailed the widespread occupation of colonial territory—first major cities, then the surrounding countryside.

The British command struggled with a problem often manifesting itself in pacification operations: there was no central point of resistance. The British could not identify a single objective the seizure of which would yield decisive results. No single American city held the strategic importance of a London or Paris. The capture of Boston, New York, Philadelphia, and Charleston failed to affect the American resolve significantly. Defeating but not destroying the American armies—both Continental and militia—also frustrated British hopes to turn the tide. In no small measure, this circumstance was a deliberate strategy of the American commander, who realized that time favored his cause. At the same time, since America was not vital to British national interests, the war was not universally popular in Parliament.[20] Thus, the British suffered simultaneously an inability to end the war quickly to their satisfaction and inadequate political resolve to continue it indefinitely.

The dispersion of patriot forces and centers of gravity was not always advantageous to rebels. Washington was troubled from the outset with the problem of how to defend the same vast, sparsely populated land the British found so difficult to conquer. Unable to defend all places, he determined to fortify the most critical points, maintain a field army to counter regular British forces, and raise militia for local defense in the absence of the main army. The vast defenses at West Point on the Hudson River served as the best—and most successful—fortifications. The Continental Army became the Americans' regular force. Militia units and guerilla bands ranged from useless to lethal. Although Washington did not perceive guerrilla warfare as decisive, some militia units conducted effective guerrilla operations: the exploits of Colonel Francis Marion of South Carolina, for example, earned the colorful leader the sobriquet "Swamp Fox."

The unequal struggle played itself out in phases that the British would measure differently from the Americans. In the American view, the first successful year of war was characterized by the transformation of a popular armed New England mob into a conventional army that ejected the British from Boston. In its second phase, the Americans suffered defeat and near disaster as they were ejected from New York. As a consequence of this experience, Washington evolved a better understanding of the nature of the contest. Wintering at Morristown, he launched the celebrated and much romanticized raid across the Delaware that characterized his operations in the north for the remainder of the war. In 1779, American attention followed the British to the south. Sometimes successful, often disastrous, and frequently savage meetings between American and British regulars and militia resulted in the British decision to leave the Carolinas and concentrate in Virginia where, in October 1781, Cornwallis surrendered to Washington's combined Continental-French army.

From a British perspective, the war could be divided almost as it was planned. Only the outcomes distinguished the plan from the historical narrative. The experience at Bunker Hill led the administration in London to realize that "a rap on the colonial knuckles" would not end the conflict.[21] Planning for a war would only then begin in earnest. After the evacuation from Boston, Howe concentrated his military might on the middle colonies, focusing his effort first on New York and then Philadelphia. Once the British lost the disastrous campaign culminating at Saratoga, they turned to the south, the purported center of Tory support. A campaign to wrest the Carolina highlands from rebel control ended in failure and withdrawal to Yorktown, where the main British army finally surrendered.

Conduct of the War

When Washington assumed command of the veterans of Bunker Hill on 2 July 1775, he busied himself immediately with securing additional volunteers. Enlistments for most of the force that had fought at Bunker Hill ended on 1 December 1775 (some had enlisted until 1 January 1776), forcing the general to address himself almost immediately to the issue of recruitment. He suggested that Congress enlist the Continental Army from a broader geographic base. He further recommended a standard organization of twenty-six infantry regiments (each of 728 men), rifle and artillery units, standard uniforms, and Congressional control over commissions. The Continental Congress accepted all these recommendations.[22] Furthermore, in the implementing order of 1 January 1776, Washington established a basis for discipline without which no regular force could long survive.

During the winter of 1775–76, the British were besieged in Boston. When Washington acquired from Colonel Henry Knox fifty-nine guns taken at Fort Ticonderoga, he was able to invest the city in a textbook siege. In spite of expirations in short-term recruits, the stranglehold on the main British army in Boston remained firm. As a result of the American army's persistence, Howe evacuated Boston on 17 March 1776, removing his troops to Halifax.

Lord George Germain, appointed in 1776 to be secretary of state for the American Colonies, was convinced of the need to protect the Loyalists south of Virginia, whom he believed to exist in large numbers. He approved of a southern expedition, with Clinton in command and Cornwallis as his second. Loyal Scots living in western North Carolina, who detested the Whig eastern aristocrats, swept down from the hills to show their strength in Wilmington, but failed to rouse the population. Finding no support of the kind he had been led to expect in North Carolina, Clinton sailed to Charleston, which he also failed to take.

Returning to the campaign plan, Howe determined to take New York, which Washington had spent the summer fortifying for winter quarters. After an unsuccessful effort to persuade Washington to disperse his army in exchange for pardons, Howe finally attacked New York's 19,000 rebel defenders with 32,000 troops. Outflanked, Washington was forced to withdraw from Long Island, up to Manhattan, and finally to Peekskill. British troops took New York and chased Washington into New Jersey but could not crush his rapidly dwindling force.

After Washington's defeat in New York, patriot morale was at a low ebb. Most of the enlistments were expiring, and few veterans intended to renew their commitment. Washington planned a daring move to rally their flagging spirits. In December, he sallied forth with 2,400 troops across the Delaware River and defeated a Hessian brigade at Trenton, New Jersey, the day after Christmas, 1776.[23] Stung and angered, Cornwallis attempted to catch Washington in New Jersey before the rebel general could escape back across the Delaware. Again Washington demonstrated remarkable skill, ambushing the British rear guard at Princeton on 2 January 1777. Upon these brilliant victories was built Washington's reputation as a tactical commander. With his stature secure in Congress, Washington was able to forge the Continental Army into a much more effective instrument. The militia forces prospered as well. Later that winter, the ranks of patriots swelled, as Cornwallis carried out a vicious campaign of subjugation in New Jersey.

The mission of the rebel northern army, commanded by Major General Horatio Gates, was to guard the Great Lakes and the Hudson River arteries. Howe, in line with the first phase of the British strategic plan, determined to split the rebellion by severing the New

England head from the southern body by way of a three-pronged attack: from the north by Burgoyne, from the west by Lieutenant Colonel Barry St. Leger, and from the south by Howe himself. As a preliminary move (and following the second point of the British program), he sailed up the Chesapeake Bay, landed at Head of Elk, Maryland, and marched on Philadelphia. He defeated Washington at the Brandywine River and entered Philadelphia on 26 September 1777. An American counterattack at Germantown proved ineffective.

Burgoyne's force began on schedule but suffered horribly from the harsh environment and from the harassment of the militia forces opposing him. At Bennington, Vermont, rebel Brigadier General John Stark smashed a large reconnaissance party. St. Leger was stymied at Fort Stanwix. And Burgoyne was stopped at Saratoga by an insubordinate but brilliant General Benedict Arnold.[24] Washington wintered at Valley Forge, Pennsylvania, where his army suffered from great physical privations but enjoyed the expert, if sometimes comical, guidance of the drillmaster, Major General Friedrich von Steuben.

In May 1778, Howe was relieved at his own request and replaced by Clinton, who promptly moved through New Jersey to New York. Seeing an opportunity to sting the British again, Washington fell on Clinton's rear guard at Monmouth Court House on 28 June 1778. Poor planning and execution by Major General Charles Lee threatened the outcome of the battle. Washington, however, personally rallied the Continentals, relieving Lee in a rare storm of oaths.[25] The Continental Line withstood several violent assaults before nightfall, and both armies camped on the field. Fighting a tactical draw, the Continental Line had proved it could match the British regulars in open battle. Both armies were stunned by the outcome; they would not meet again until Yorktown in 1781.

As a consequence of the Continental Army's successes, France joined the war, encouraged by the American prospects for eventual victory. The French admiral sent to support the American cause, Comte d'Estaing, arrived off the Delaware capes just after the battle at Monmouth Court House. Although his command was far more powerful than the British fleet in New York, d'Estaing was cautious and failed to bring his advantage to bear before sailing off to Martinique for the winter. Thus, Washington realized no immediate military advantage as a result of the French intervention. However, d'Estaing's presence in the Caribbean together with a Spanish fleet in Havana (after Spain's entry on the American side in June 1779) forced Clinton to send 8,000 troops to the West Indies. These transfers weakened Clinton so severely that he never seriously challenged Washington's position at West Point, New York.

Although the entry of France into the war signaled a dramatic change in the chemistry of the struggle, the British commanders failed to reevaluate their strategy.[26] Clinton continued the strategic approach envisioned at the onset of hostilities. In November 1778, he sent Lieutenant Colonel Archibald Campbell to Savannah, which was captured. Later, joined by Major General Augustine Prevost,[27] he moved briefly into South Carolina, which proved as inhospitable as it had to Clinton two years earlier. Campbell soon returned to Georgia. Offsetting this failure, 2,400 British successfully defended Savannah against 5,000 troops brought there by the French fleet of d'Estaing.

Encouraged and still believing South Carolina to be a stronghold for Loyalists, Clinton invested Charleston with 10,000 men. He erected siege batteries in March 1780 and slowly closed in on the city until its defender, Major General Benjamin Lincoln, surrendered on 12 May.[28] In reaction to the terrible news of the fall of Charleston and its garrison of 5,000, Congress, against the wishes of Washington, selected Major General Horatio Gates for command in the south. Militiamen rallied around Gates, who moved against Clinton's field commander, Cornwallis, at Camden. There, the colonists suffered a terrible defeat on 16 August 1780. Emboldened by that victory, Cornwallis dispatched Major Patrick Ferguson with a force consisting exclusively of Tory volunteers to western South Carolina. Western settlers rallied to engage Ferguson at King's Mountain, where they destroyed his small force.

Given the difficulties the British faced in the south, some question exists as to whether Clinton should have attempted such a bold move with so little force. The general, however, believed that the fall of Charleston obviated the problem of subjugation of the colony; he therefore directed his deputy to move into North Carolina as the situation permitted. Clearly Clinton erred in his judgment, but Cornwallis compounded the problem by expanding from his logistical base more rapidly than he was able to recruit additional Loyalist forces.[29]

Major General Nathanael Greene, Gates' replacement after Camden, sent Brigadier General Daniel Morgan with a small body of regulars and militia into South Carolina to rally the patriot inhabitants. In January 1781, Morgan met the infamous Tarleton and defeated him soundly. That battle was followed by an American flight ahead of Cornwallis, interrupted briefly at Guilford Court House, Hobkirk's Hill, and Eutaw Springs.[30] Although Cornwallis won these engagements, he realized that he could not subdue the evasive Greene in the Carolinas. Maneuvering for advantage, he collected his forces in August at Yorktown, in southern Virginia.

At Yorktown, the British could enjoy the advantages of lateral communications (Clinton was still in New York)—but only as long as Britain controlled the sea. Certainly, both British commanders recognized the potential for the French to seal Cornwallis in the Chesapeake. However, given d'Estaing's performance since his arrival off the American coast in 1778, they felt secure in accepting the risk to their lines of communications.

By staging in Staten Island, New York, Washington deceived Clinton into believing that New York was the theater for a new colonial offensive. Washington then stealthily departed through New Jersey for southern Virginia, accompanied by Lieutenant General Comte de Rochambeau's French reinforcements. The French fleet sealed off the British inside Chesapeake Bay, isolating them from free access to the sea and reinforcements from Britain or Clinton. The siege of Yorktown began in September with the American occupation of Cornwallis' abandoned outer redoubts. American and French troops and Admiral de Grasse's French fleet continued to tighten the stranglehold they held on Cornwallis. On 17 October, allied troops entered the town. Two days later, the British marched out of the fort as their band, defiant even in defeat, played "The World Turned Upside Down."

The war would last another two years, although a cease-fire ended hostilities in January of 1782. The Peace of Paris formally ended the American Revolutionary War, and the last British troops sailed from New York on 23 November 1783, over eight years after that brisk spring day in Lexington, Massachusetts.

NOTES

Chapter 1

1. In particular that of John Locke, *Two Treatises of Government*, 1690, and Montesquieu, *L'Esprit des lois*, 1748.

2. In that action, the British commander, General Gage, sent several hundred of his troops from Boston under Lieutenant Colonel Francis Smith to raid a rebel arms cache at Concord, some fourteen miles away. They were stopped by seventy rebels hastily assembled and commanded by Captain Jonas Parker. After scattering the rebels, the British moved on to Concord, where they burned the military stores. A large mob of angry farmers harassed the British withdrawal, and by the time the troops returned to the safety of Boston, 79 of their number had been killed and 147 wounded.

3. William Howe (5th Viscount Howe, 1729–1814), brother of Admiral Richard Howe, served brilliantly as a young officer in the French and Indian War. Sent again to America in 1775, he was present at Bunker Hill, Brandywine, and Germantown. He turned over his command to General Clinton in 1778 and returned to England. See Ira D. Gruber, *The Brothers Howe and the American Revolution* (New York: Atheneum, 1972). Sir Henry Clinton (1738–95) joined the army in 1757 and campaigned in Europe in the Seven Years' War. He commanded British force in America from 1778 to 1781. See William B. Willcox, *Portrait of a General: Sir Henry Clinton in the War of Independence* (New York: Knopf, 1964). Sir John Burgoyne (1723–92) purchased a commission in the Horse Guards in 1737. He campaigned in Portugal as a young officer and, in 1775 as a major general with three years' seniority, was sent to Boston. When the British evacuated Boston, he became deputy to the commander in Canada. After his disastrous defeat at Saratoga, he returned to England. See James Lunt, *John Burgoyne of Saratoga* (New York: Harcourt Brace Jovanovich, 1975), xiii, xiv, 3–11.

4. Other veterans included former British regulars Horatio Gates, Richard Montgomery, and Charles Lee, and colonial officers Artemas Ward, David Wooster, and Joseph Spencer. All these numbered among the first group of generals created by Congress. See Robert K. Wright, *The Continental Army* (Washington, DC: U.S. Government Printing Office, 1983), 8.

5. See John W. Shy, "A New Look at Colonial Militia," *The William and Mary Quarterly*, 3d ser., 20 (1963):179. The quality of the militias varied from colony to colony and from year to year. The frequency of their drill and their measure of attention varied directly with the level of tension with the Indians. See Jack S. Radabaugh, "The Militia of Colonial Massachusetts," *Military Affairs* 18 (Spring 1954):13, and E. Milton Wheeler, "Development and Organization of

Note: Appendixes referred to in the notes refer to those mentioned in this book.

the North Carolina Militia," *The North Carolina Historical Review* 61 (July 1964):314.

6. Wright, *Continental Army,* 15. By June 1775, the Massachusetts establishment, for instance, was planned to consist of twenty-three infantry regiments and one artillery regiment.

7. Von Steuben was neither a general nor a baron, but Benjamin Franklin, who discovered him, correctly identified the Prussian officer as ideally suited to Washington's need for a drillmaster. See Russell F. Weigley, *History of the United States Army* (New York: Macmillan, 1967), 63.

8. For a thorough description of the events leading to the establishment of the Continental Army, see Wright, *Continental Army*, 23–25. One of the first light infantry companies raised directly to serve in the Continental Army was a Frederick County, Virginia, unit commanded by Daniel Morgan.

9. Ira D. Gruber, "Britain's Southern Strategy," *The Revolutionary War in the South: Power, Conflict, and Leadership*, ed. W. Robert Higgins (Durham, NC: Duke University Press, 1979), 206, 207.

10. The names of a number of the towns have evolved since the Revolutionary War. Charleston, for instance, was then spelled "Charlestown," and Charlotte was often called "Charlotte Town." In all cases, I have used the modern spelling or name of the town.

11. See J. F. C. Fuller, *A Military History of the Western World*, vol. 2 (New York: Minerva Press, 1955), 277, and Vincent Esposito, ed., *The West Point Atlas of American Wars*, vol. 1 (New York: Praeger, 1959), 4. Dave Richard Palmer agrees that, until mid-1776, the British were "too weak to destroy the rebel army and thereafter Washington was too wily to catch." See Dave R. Palmer and James W. Stryker, *The Way of the Fox* (Westport, CT: Greenwood, 1975), 39. The number of British troops in North America grew from 7,000 in 1775 to over 52,000 in 1778. See Philip R. N. Katcher, *Encyclopedia of British, Provincial, and German Army Units 1775–1783* (Harrisburg, PA: Stackpole, 1973), 141.

12. See also Paul David Nelson, "British Conduct of the American Revolutionary War: A Review of Interpretations," *Journal of American History* 65 (December 1978):623–53.

13. This was not, of course, their original aim. The Continental Congress was reluctant to break with the Crown. Only after the storming of Fort Ticonderoga did Congress take its first concrete decision to wage war, on 25 May 1775. For a discussion of the formation of American strategy, see Palmer, *Fox*, 50–76.

14. Russell Weigley, *The American Way of War* (New York: Macmillan, 1973), 3. John Morgan Dederer notes a similarity in the strategic approaches of Wash-

ington and Mao Tse-tung in *Making Bricks Without Straw: Nathanael Greene's Southern Campaign and Mao Tse Tung's Mobile War* (Manhattan, KS: Sunflower University Press, 1983). Similarities certainly exist. Weigley's conclusion that Washington's weaker position led him to evasion is less exotic than Dederer's claim that Washington's thinking was revolutionary and, in the context of eighteenth century generalship, more palatable as well.

15. Elmer Bendiner describes the diplomatic efforts of Benjamin Franklin, John Adams, and John Jay in the capitals of Europe in *The Virgin Diplomats* (New York: Knopf, 1976).

16. For a discussion of the problems of provisioning the British army in America, see Edward E. Curtis, *The Organization of the British Army in the American Revolution* (New Haven, CT: Yale University Press, 1926), 81–134. The Ordnance Department owned transport vessels but contracted over 50 percent of its transatlantic shipments, 180, 181.

17. In R. Arthur Bowler, *Logistics and the Failure of the British Army in America 1775–1783* (Princeton, NJ: Princeton University Press, 1975). Bowler argues that the British failed to maintain dependable supply lines.

18. John C. Fitzpatrick, ed., *The Writings of George Washington*, 39 vols. (Washington, DC: Government Printing Office, 1931–44), viii, 470.

19. As many as 25,000 Tories served the British, Loyalists in 1779 and again in 1782 claimed that more Americans were serving under the King's colors than with rebel forces. See Lerenzo Sabine, "The Tory Contingent in the British Army in America in 1781," *The Historical Magazine* 8 (October, 1864):331. One Loyalist unit was the British Legion, commanded by Lieutenant Colonel Banastre Tarleton. Sabine lists thirty Loyalist officers in this unit, 358. W. O. Raymond, *Loyalists in Arms* (St. John, N.B.: Sun Printing, 1904), lists 25 officers and 341 rank and file for the Legion cavalry, 220.

20. On 14 January 1776, William Pitt thundered in the House of Commons: "I rejoice that America has resisted. Three millions of people, so dead to all the feelings of liberty, as voluntarily to submit to be slaves, would have been fit instruments to make slaves of the rest." See Robert Debs Heinl, Jr., *Dictionary of Military and Naval Quotations* (Annapolis, MD: United States Naval Institute, 1966), 9. The parallels between this aspect of the American Revolution and the United States' involvement in Vietnam are striking and paradoxical.

21. Palmer, *Fox*, 38.

22. Wright, *Continental Army*, 29–40.

23. Wounded at the battle were a future president, Lieutenant James Monroe, and Captain William Washington, who would command the American cavalry at the Cowpens four years later.

24. Daniel Morgan commanded a rifle regiment in the battle. Afterward, Burgoyne was alleged to have told Morgan, "My dear sir, you command the finest regiment in the world." See J. D. Bailey, *Some Heroes of the American Revolution* (Spartanburg, SC: Bond & White Printers, 1924), 12. Whether Burgoyne made this gracious remark is unknown; however, Morgan did play a crucial and valiant part in the American victory, and his Virginia rifles have been judged by the eminent military historian J. F. C. Fuller to be "the finest light infantry of the day," *Military History* 2, 293. Morgan figures prominently in Trumbulls' well-known portrayal of Burgoyne's surrender. See David Meschutt, "Portraits of Daniel Morgan, Revolutionary War General," *American Art Journal* 17, no. 3 (1985):38.

25. For an analysis of the Washington-Lee controversy, see John Richard Alden, *General Charles Lee Traitor or Patriot?* (Baton Rouge: Louisiana State University, 1951).

26. See William B. Willcox, "British Strategy in America, 1778," *Journal of Modern History* 19 (1947):97–121.

27. Major General Augustine Prevost (1723–86) was apparently the son of a Swiss officer who raised the Royal American Regiment (60th Foot). He was wounded as a major with Wolfe at Quebec and found himself in 1776 in command of British forces in east Florida. He returned to England in 1779. See Mark Mayo Boatner III, *Encyclopedia of the American Revolution* (New York: David McKay Company, 1976), 889.

28. Fighting skirmishes with militia units during the siege operations was Lieutenant Colonel Banastre Tarleton.

29. See Robert B. Asprey, *War in the Shadows* (Garden City, NY: Doubleday & Company, 1975), 105.

30. See chapter two for a more detailed analysis of this campaign.

II. THE CAMPAIGN IN THE CAROLINAS, 1780–1781

When Clinton sailed south, he hoped, as a preliminary step to the eventual subjugation of the colonies, to secure the broad base of operations denied him and his predecessors farther north. The campaign plan was simple enough. Operating from a secure base at Savannah, Georgia, Clinton would seize the key port of Charleston and then destroy the isolated pockets of resistance in the upcountry. The French fleet had the potential to disrupt communications from Charleston to Savannah, New York, and England, but this threat had yet to be realized since the fleet's arrival in American waters. As was the case throughout the war, the Americans reacted to British initiatives. Consistent with Washington's overall strategy, militia units harassed the British until regulars could hurry south to counter the threat.

The campaign that ensued in the Carolinas was characterized, on the one hand, by rapid movement of light troops, either regular or militia, and, on the other, by brutal guerrilla warfare of rebel and Tory bands. While both armies contained regular troops, terrain and tactics dictated the predominance of light fighters.[1] The Carolinas counted but two cities in the eighteenth century, Georgetown and Charleston. Beyond these ports, scattered settlements formed a loose network of frontier civilization having little in common with the coastal aristocracy.[2] The river network in South Carolina flowed generally southeast from the rugged hills around modern-day Spartanburg to the inhospitable swampland along the coast. The major water arteries—the Savannah, Santee, and Great Pedee Rivers—afforded rapid movement of supplies and troops by small boats only, and the vast pine woods in between could only be traversed slowly and painstakingly (see map 2).

Main armies were intended for decisive action on the battlefield, but getting them to it was a Herculean task. The baggage customary in an eighteenth-century army encumbered it on the march. An infantry regiment such as the 7th Royal Fusiliers, with an establishment of 477 men, required four wagons and sixteen horses by

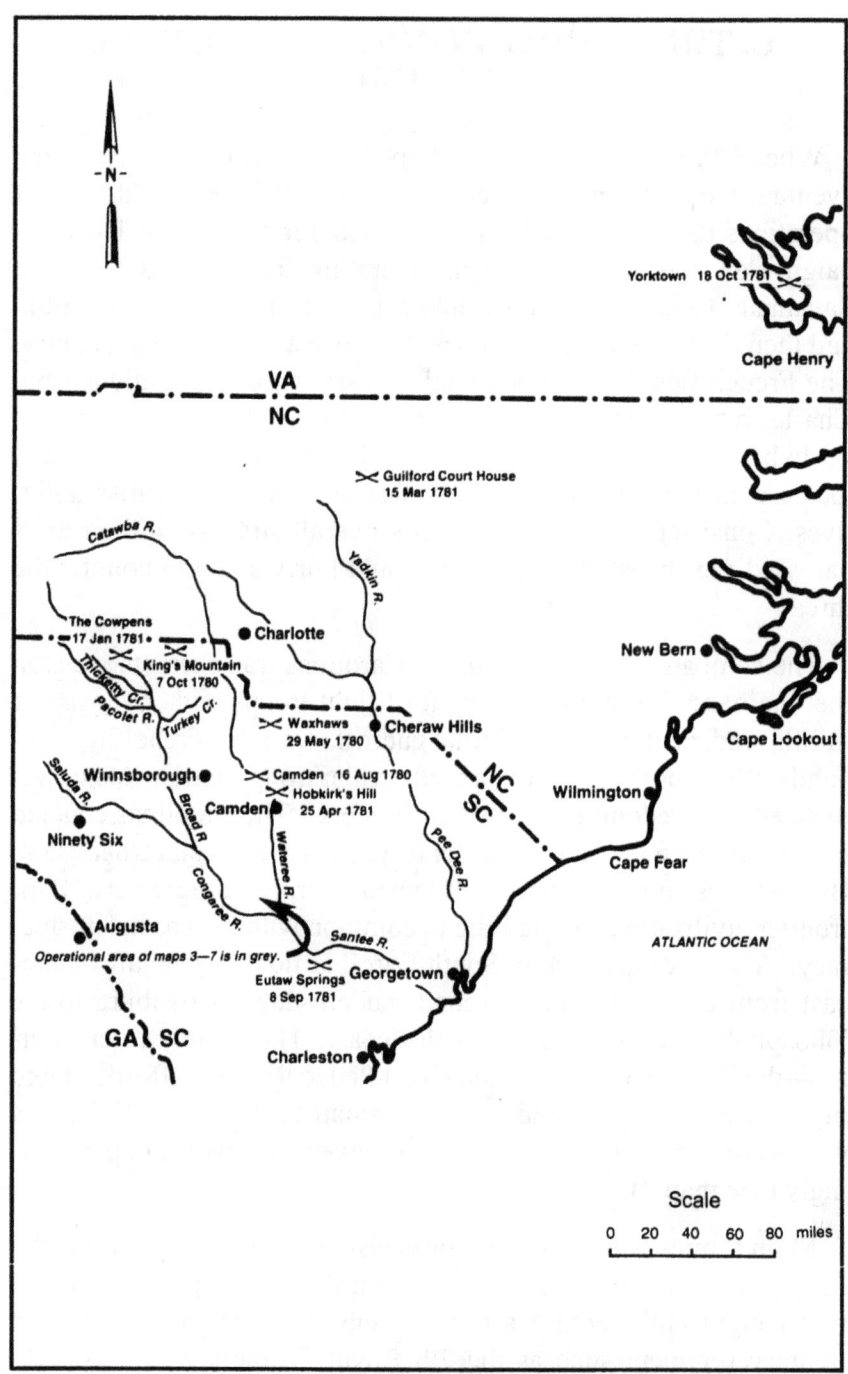

Map 2. The southern theater of operations, 1780–81

regulation and probably hired more on campaign.[3] A 12-pounder artillery piece weighed 3,200 pounds and required a team of twelve horses to pull it. Even Tarleton's light baggage became an issue as he raced to meet Morgan in the winter of 1780–81.[4]

On both sides, partisans who enrolled in provisional or militia companies could reasonably be expected to move as quickly as light infantry—which in many ways, they were. These units were raised because both sides suffered from too few regulars, and because the militia tradition was already well-established in the colonies. Since the partisans were not part of a regular establishment, commanders could not rely on their presence at a time of crisis.[5] And because the iron discipline and restraint customary in European armies of the day was foreign to these stubbornly independent frontiersmen, they were more likely to commit the sort of excesses forbidden (if still too often practiced) by regulars. The South Carolina militia, having seen action against Indians before and during the Revolution, had long been accustomed to unfettered brutality. Their traditional tactics were the ambush and the raid; their tools were rapid movement, terror as a psychological weapon, and rapid analysis of intelligence gained from scouts and spies. In accomplishing their mission to suppress Tory sentiment, they tended to use their customary methods.[6] One participant remarked that, when the army left, "it was now almost Fire & Faggot between Whig & Tory, who were contending for ascendancy[.] continued so till the 15th or 20th of May [1781]."[7] Reprisal and retaliation followed as passions became enflamed, and the conflict in the south resembled more a civil war than fighting according to the rules of organized warfare.

From the summer of 1778, the war in the north became a stalemate; the armed might of Great Britain had managed to secure the city of New York, while the Hudson highlands and New Jersey remained firmly in American hands. Using the only advantage he had, the Royal Navy, Clinton took his army south, where it could range through a supposedly friendly countryside without fear of detachments being ambushed by Washington's Continentals. By the time Clinton moved south, Savannah had been taken, and Prevost's St. Augustine garrison had moved north to assist in the recapture of

Georgia. Clinton saw Charleston as the logical target: Charleston was the seat of the colony, and its seaport facilities would be essential as a command and control and logistics base for the eventual subjugation of South Carolina, the taking of which would assist Prevost's efforts in Georgia. Lincoln, commanding the strong defenses that Brigadier General William Moultrie had successfully defended in 1776, unwisely concentrated his 5,000 troops in the city against the seaborne threat. Clinton arrived with 6,000 troops on 11 February 1780, delaying until 7 March to erect batteries on the Ashley River opposite the city. Finally reinforced by 4,000 additional troops, Clinton isolated the defenders by land and sea and snipped Lincoln's line of communications by sending Banastre Tarleton thirty miles up the Cooper River to crush a small band of American militia there. Over a month into the siege, Lincoln surrendered his force—including the entire Continental establishment of North Carolina, South Carolina, and Georgia. This may have been the greatest blow to the American cause in the war.[8]

With Charleston a secure logistics base, Clinton was able to send detachments to destroy the remaining opposition in the region. Tarleton, who had already proved himself to be an aggressive, ruthless, and decisive cavalry leader, chased down the rebels. Because the militia bands traveled light and were elusive, Tarleton's force was tailored to move faster than its opponents could run. The main component of his force was the Legion, an 800-man Loyalist force of light infantry and cavalry. In May 1780, Tarleton caught Colonel Abraham Buford's militia at Waxhaws and destroyed them, earning the frightening sobriquet "Bloody Tarleton."[9] With this success, Clinton returned to New York, hoping to catch Washington, now weakened from sending reinforcements south. Clinton appointed his deputy Cornwallis to sweep away the remaining detachments of partisans, secure the loyalty of South Carolina, and plan a campaign into North Carolina.[10] Cornwallis chased the remaining rebel bands, led by such heroes as Francis Marion and Thomas Sumter, into the swamps and backcountry. With the rebels on the run, long-suppressed Tories began to take their revenge. The rebellion in South Carolina, far from subsiding, became a vicious civil war.

As the British swept away the opposition, the Continental Congress reacted with alarm and sent more Continentals to the theater. Major General Baron de Kalb, one of a group of foreign adventurers and idealists drawn to the American conflict, was the first commander to come south to apply a tourniquet to bleeding Carolina. The Congress felt, however, that it was inappropriate for a foreigner to command a theater of the war. Against the advice of Washington, de Kalb was replaced by Gates who was considered to be the victor of Saratoga.[11]

Gates assumed command of about 4,200 Continentals and militia on 25 July 1780. Driven by local pressure to boost sagging morale and to preempt a British invasion of North Carolina, he immediately seized the initiative. When intelligence reports indicated that Cornwallis had left a detachment at Camden, Gates hurried his Continentals and militia there. In his haste, he almost overlooked his cavalry, which—surprisingly, considering the strength and reputation of Tarleton's force—he held as inconsequential in any case. As one sympathetic historian has observed, Gates intended to occupy breastworks and force an outmaneuvered British contingent to assault them. Thus, cavalry may have seemed unnecessary to him.[12] In any event, the Americans arrived bone tired and hungry only to discover that Cornwallis had returned. On 16 August, an inferior force of 2,200 British regulars scattered the North Carolina and Virginia militias and then outflanked the Delaware and Maryland regulars, killing their commander, de Kalb. Gates fled the field with the militia, discrediting himself in the process. Two days later, Tarleton defeated Sumter's South Carolina militiamen, killing 150 patriots and wounding another 300.

Having defeated both Gates and Sumter, Cornwallis had reason to believe that South Carolina was safe—but only for the time being. Clinton had left Cornwallis considerable latitude in his prosecution of the war. He had instructed only that South Carolina, and Charleston in particular, be safeguarded at all costs. Cornwallis, for his part, saw invasion of North Carolina as the only way to achieve Clinton's objectives.[13] To guarantee his recent successes, Cornwallis determined to move boldly into North Carolina. Sending a small detachment to Cape Fear to establish a closer logistics base, he continued his march north toward Charlotte and the main rebel army and directed Major Patrick Ferguson on a raid against partisans in the west. At King's Mountain in October 1780, Ferguson's Loyalists met partisans who had come down from the Tennessee hills. There, Ferguson was surrounded and his men killed at long range by accurate rifle fire from marksmen hidden in the woods below. This first setback for the British caused Cornwallis to retire from Charlotte to Wynnsboro, centrally located to enable him to cover South Carolina while he waited for Major General Alexander Leslie, sent south by Clinton, to arrive. Together, he thought, his and Leslie's troops could clear the Carolinas of rebels.

The victory at King's Mountain was not enough to save Gates' sullied reputation. He was relieved in December by Greene, who had always been Washington's selection for command in the south. Greene was a pudgy thirty-eight-year-old Quaker from Rhode Island. By most accounts, he was disavowed by the Society of Friends for having raised a company of militia in 1774. In fact, he and acquaintances had visited "a place in Connecticut of Publick Resort [a tavern] where they had No Proper Business." He was subsequently suspended.[14] He was not selected for captain by the men because, as a consequence of a limp, he cut a poor figure of an officer. Humbly, he served in the ranks until, in 1775, he was selected by the colonial assembly to command its contingent to the Continental Army.[15] He fought alongside Washington in every major action, earning his commander's highest regard. Greene confronted a mixed situation in the south: the conditions were desperate, morale in the army was low, and his predecessor had failed miserably; but, on the positive side, he had free rein and the financial authority and moral support of Congress to restore the army, and he held the unlimited confidence of the commander in chief. Nonetheless, he approached his task cautiously. To Congress, Greene wrote, "He [Greene] is conscious of his deficiencies, but if he is clothed with proper powers and receives the necessary support, he is not altogether without hopes of prescribing some bounds to the ravages of the enemy."[16] Despite the reputation he earned in the Carolinas, Nathanael Greene was a cautious, conservative commander.[17]

The new commander of the Southern Department managed to assemble just over 1,000 Continentals and militia of Gates' command.[18] The task Washington had assigned him was formidable. Five days after arriving in Charlotte, he wrote, "Nothing can be more wretched and distressing than the condition of the troops, starving with cold and hunger, without tents and camp equipage."[19] He addressed his formidable energy to the spirit of his army, creating in his headquarters an impression of determination and purpose. He appointed a new slate of staff officers, inspected formations, prepared to move the army, hanged a deserter, and demanded greater exertions from his commissary.[20]

Although outnumbered, Greene recognized his advantages at once and sought to capitalize upon them. With large (if scattered) numbers of militia and sympathizers in the west, he could keep well informed of Cornwallis' whereabouts. This asset enabled him to deviate from accepted rules of war. Although he could not defeat Cornwallis, he could nibble away at the British army, avoid destruction of his own force, and simultaneously attend to the dire logistical imperatives that overshadowed his operational plans.[21] To compensate for the lack of forage in Charlotte, he made the often-criticized decision to move his army to Cheraw Hill, where Colonel Tadeusz Kosciuszko had found adequate supplies.[22] This movement could have telegraphed the wrong message to patriots in the western Carolinas, as Cheraw Hill was farther from Cornwallis than Charlotte. However, Greene, by sending a detachment under Morgan into South Carolina, sought to make Cornwallis divide his forces as well.[23] Logistical considerations played an important role in the planning and outcome of the campaign. Difficulties in foraging may have forced Greene to seek a plan that allowed him to disperse his force sufficiently. While he realized Morgan's precarious position, he believed that intelligence gained from local patriots would keep Morgan sufficiently informed to avoid being surprised and to allow the army to combine quickly enough to defeat whatever force Cornwallis sent after him.

In his operational directive of 16 December 1780, Greene told Morgan to conduct a prudent campaign designed to call attention to itself. The order contained four critical components. First, Morgan was to raise such militia as could be found, in particular those led by brigadier generals Thomas Sumter and William Davidson (the latter of North Carolina). Second, he was to protect patriot settlements west of the Catawba River and "spirit up the people." Third, he was "to annoy the enemy in that quarter [the west]." And, finally, should Cornwallis snap at the bait, Greene directed Morgan to move to join with the main army. Paramount in the plan was the survival of Morgan's forces. The directive was clear and precise in its provisions yet gave the experienced Virginia rifleman adequate room for interpretation as the campaign developed.

Morgan's actions indicate clearly his method of achieving Greene's intent. Marching about fifty-five miles, he moved into South Carolina on 21 December 1780, arriving on the Pacolet River at Grindal Shoals on Christmas day (see map 3). There he encamped his army.[24] To shelter his men from the elements, he directed that huts be constructed. From this base, he sent raiding and foraging parties into the countryside to raise the western counties and attract Cornwallis' attention. Meanwhile, he sent word to Colonels Andrew Pickens and Sumter to join him. Lieutenant Colonel William Washington, with almost 300 horsemen, attacked Hammond's Store, killing and wounding about 150 Tories.[25] Colonel Hays of the South Carolina militia took fifty men to Fort William, where he chased the Tory garrison away and burned the fort. Reports of these forays led Cornwallis to fear for the safety of Ninety Six, which he considered to be the cornerstone of his defenses in the western part of the colony. Contrary to the impression left us by numerous authors,[26] Morgan was not a prey to be cornered on the Broad River by the huntsman Tarleton; Morgan was boldly teasing the British into a rash move.

For the first time in the southern campaign, and as a consequence of the British disaster at King's Mountain, the Americans had gained the initiative in the south. Now, Cornwallis could not direct his entire army against either wing of Greene's force without exposing Charleston to attack or the western region to intimidation. In response to

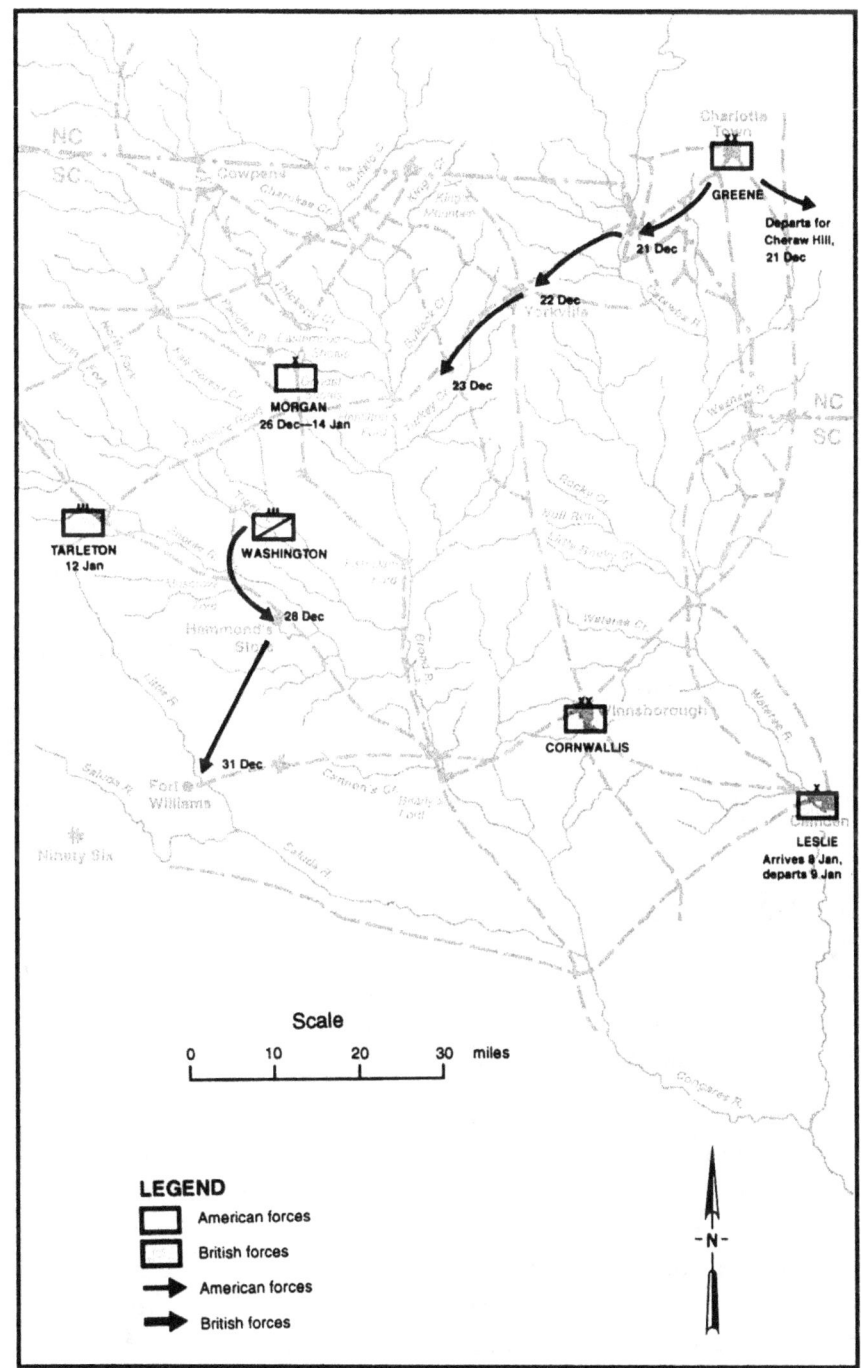

Map 3. Situation, 20 December 1780 to 14 January 1781

Morgan's foray into western South Carolina, Cornwallis directed his forces in three prongs, moving (in theory) within a day's march of each other toward the irritating rebels. Leading was Cornwallis' favorite, Tarleton.[27] Bringing up the heavy troops, artillery, and baggage, Cornwallis would march up the east bank of the Broad River with over 3,300 troops. Leslie would hurry to join the army with his 1,500 men. Tarleton's light force, leading the army, would fix the enemy, after which the regulars would destroy him. As the British forces marched only one day from each other, enemy contact with any prong could result in friendly forces coming to its support. The additional advantages of moving on separate axes were logistical. Parallel routes would reduce the length of the column and thus minimize the time required for the trail element to reach the front as it deployed for battle. Also, smaller columns would be easier to feed.

The British plans went awry almost immediately. Cornwallis' army soon became uncoupled as Tarleton moved with the swiftness his formation afforded him, and Leslie became mired in the swamps. Swollen rivers slowed the movement of all the columns. Additionally, Cornwallis lacked the urgency required of him to catch Morgan.[28] Although he urged Tarleton to ever greater exertions, his own movements portray a sense of frustration, perhaps at the slowness of his baggage-laden columns. Perhaps he assumed incorrectly that the swollen rivers that blocked him were a barrier to Tarleton as well. He also dallied, hoping that Leslie, who had landed in Charleston on 14 December, might catch up. But the dashing cavalry officer Tarleton saw no impediment; he swam his horses across the rivers and made rafts for the troops. While Cornwallis hoped Tarleton could fix and destroy Morgan, he knew the main army would be powerless to help.

In early January, both Tarleton and Cornwallis were within twenty-four-hours march of each other and placed generally *between* Morgan on the Pacolet River and Greene at Cheraw Hill. On 7 January, Tarleton's baggage caught up to him at Briarly's Creek, in the company of 200 recruits of the 7th Regiment, 50 dragoons, and a second 3-pounder. Hearing reports of reinforcements joining Morgan, Tarleton applied for and received permission to retain the escort.[29] But the swollen rivers plagued Cornwallis' march and inhibited combination by the two commanders. Thus, Cornwallis failed to control Tarleton in a coordinated move that would have combined the three formations against Morgan. Cornwallis' otherwise reasonable calculations violated the fundamental requirement that components of an army be synchronized.

Morgan also found the going difficult. He complained that "Forage and provisions are not to be had." And yet he feared the consequence of leaving the country in search of more hospitable campaigning grounds.[30] Greene authorized him to seek provisions as far south as Ninety Six, which put even greater distance between their two forces.[31] Without realizing it, Greene, by this direction, may also have led Cornwallis to fear for the safety of Loyalists in the area, thus causing the British general to spur on Tarleton to find Morgan.[32] Tarleton may have believed, from information he received from spies, that Morgan intended to threaten Ninety Six.[33]

Even more startling than the logistical concerns in Morgan's correspondence is his plainspoken fear for the survival of his force.[34] Two days before the meeting at the Cowpens, Morgan wrote to Greene that he would be unable to fight because of the size of Tarleton's detachment, accurately estimated at between 1,100 and 1,200 men. He knew of Tarleton's whereabouts and believed himself to be the quarry. He informed his commander that he had only 340 volunteers from three states and doubted their reliability in a battle. With the Continentals and Virginians, his force numbered over 900 on that date. Then, as now, a deployed force in defensive positions held the advantage over an attacker.[35] Thus, Morgan must have weighed the reputation of his opponent and the British troops very highly. Certainly, the reverses at Waxhaws and Camden had tempered the judgment of the American leaders, while the patriot victory at King's Mountain was dismissed as an aberration.

Lamenting his inability to control the militia and decrying his numbers, Morgan told his superior that he possessed inadequate strength for "attempts you have hinted at."[36] Greene did not direct Morgan in writing to fight a pitched battle. His clear instructions regarding the British forces were that, should Cornwallis move on

Greene, Morgan should rejoin the main army or strike the flank or rear of the British columns. The only clear implication in the letter was that Morgan should avoid battle, which is precisely what Morgan wanted to do. Perhaps Greene and Morgan had discussed in Charlotte the possibility that Morgan would be the target. Perhaps Morgan lost his nerve. From his subsequent behavior, the former seems more likely.

Tarleton had no such misgivings. Sometimes called "The Green Dragoon" or "Bloody Banny," he had assumed the identity of the English gentry-warrior class. Cecil Woodham-Smith describes that group:

> War was an aristocratic trade, and military glory reserved for nobles and princes. Glittering squadrons of cavalry, long lines of infantry, wheeling obediently on the parade ground, ministered to the lust both for power and for display. Courage was esteemed the essential military quality and held to be a virtue exclusive to aristocrats. Were they not educated to courage, trained, as no common man was trained, by years of practice in dangerous sports? They glorified courage, called it valour, saw war in terms of valour as the supreme adventure.[37]

The Tarletons were not members of this social elite, but they were a family of substance. A great grandfather outfitted and commanded one of Oliver Cromwell's warships. Tarleton's father was a successful Liverpool businessman, Jamaica plantation owner, and slave trader.[38] Banastre Tarleton entered Oxford with his elder brother in 1771, and he remained there until the death of his father in 1773. With an inheritance of £5,000, he left Oxford to study law. This subject appears not to have interested him; after two years of idling in gaming salons, he purchased a cornetship in the 1st Regiment of Dragoon Guards. The post cost his mother £800.[39]

The choice of regiments indicates young Tarleton's character: cavalry represented the concepts of glory, courage, and chivalry that inhabited the aristocratic world to which he aspired—that of the knight in shining armor. Not only that, but the King's Dragoon Guards was the senior line cavalry unit and one of the more prestigious regiments of the army. Tarleton, however, was no mere parade ground dandy. When an opportunity came for service in America, he arranged to be posted to the 16th Light Dragoons. Although cavalry, these were field troops scorned by the status-conscious. They were light, agile men mounted on polo ponies, organized and equipped to maintain constant contact with the enemy, hunt them down, and hold them for the regulars to kill. The 16th was raised in 1759 after a successful experiment three years earlier.[40] The regiment deployed in the fall of 1775.

In America, Tarleton distinguished himself almost immediately. At Princeton, his men captured Lee[41]—the young dragoon personally escorting his prisoner to Lord Cornwallis. Tarleton not only caught Cornwallis' eye, his success also led the patriotic citizenry of Liverpool to elect him captain of their volunteer company. Campaigning in New Jersey gave Tarleton greater notoriety after his horsemen cruelly subdued the rebellious population. With the passing of command from Howe to Clinton in 1778, shakeups in the staff resulted in Tarleton being named brigade major. It was Major Tarleton in command of the 17th Light Dragoons who charged at Monmouth, causing Lee's withdrawal and subsequent disgrace.[42] Grateful for the part the impetuous cavalryman played was the British commander, Cornwallis. Tarleton fully embraced H. Lloyd's offensive doctrine: "No army conquers merely by resisting: you may repel an enemy; but victory is the result of action."[43] Upon the creation in August 1778 of a mixed light regiment of green-clad English, Scottish, and Loyalist volunteers, the officer selected to command it was Tarleton, now promoted to lieutenant colonel at the age of twenty-six. He could attribute his meteoric rise to feats of valor alone; neither wealth nor family connections (he had none) influenced his status. The lesson was clear: courage and resolve were rewarded; indeed, they were a vehicle for social mobility.

As Tarleton hunted the ragtag Americans, his greatest problem was to get to Morgan before the latter could cross the Broad River and rejoin the main American army (see map 4). Tarleton did not consider defeat a possibility, although he expected Cornwallis would meet him, leaving the issue without doubt. He believed his commander was moving, albeit more slowly, to support him. Indeed, he suggested gently that Cornwallis hurry to King's Mountain. He also expected

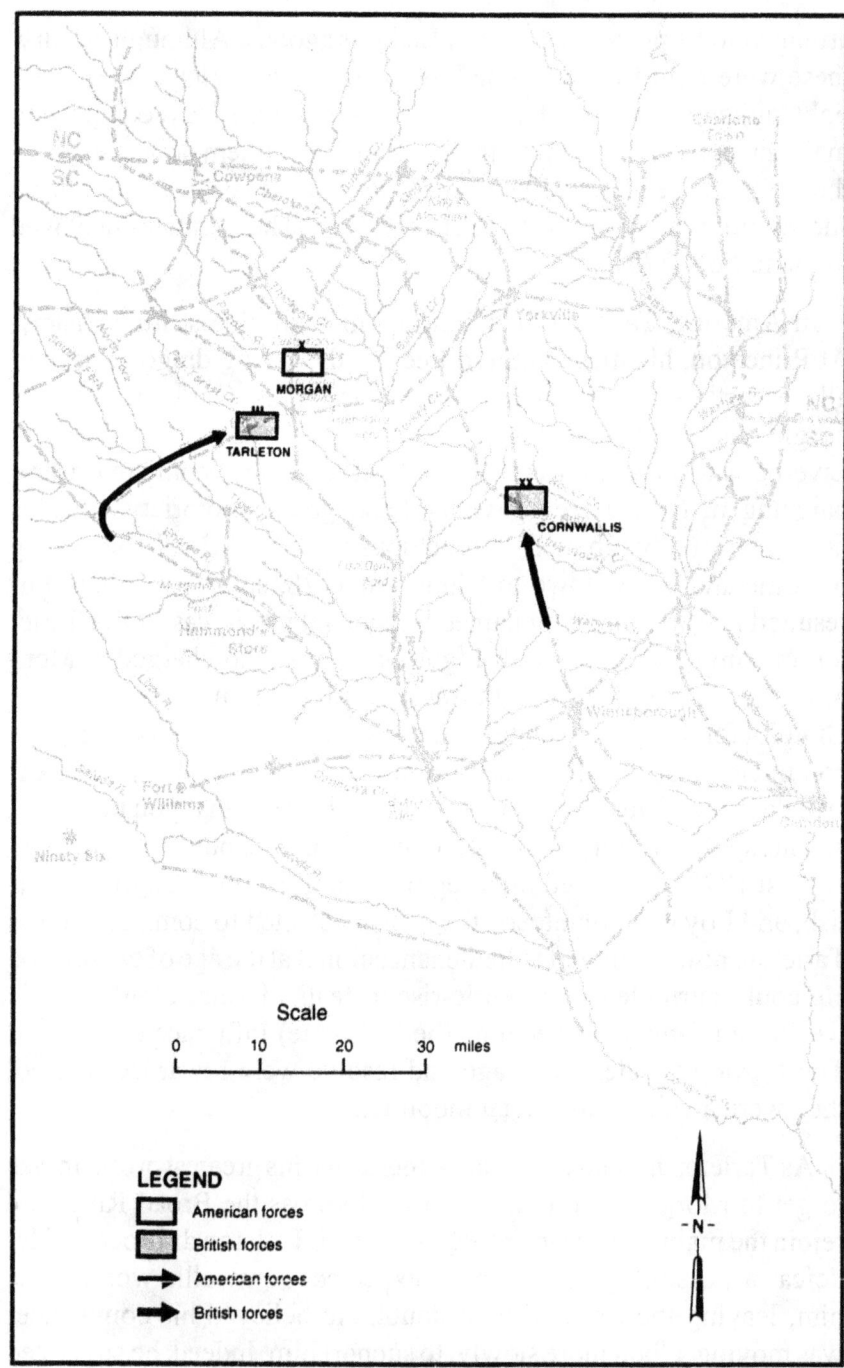

Map 4. Situation, 14 January 1781

the third prong of the army, Leslie's, to be within supporting distance. A report of the presence of American artillery—the consequence of an American ruse in which logs were attached to wagon wheels and paraded in front of Colonel Ridgely's (or Rugely's) Tory garrison on 28 November 1780—concerned him,[44] but Cornwallis assured Tarleton in a letter dated 2 January 1781 that this information was incorrect.[45] Tarleton's instincts told him to pursue as quickly as he could; his commander urged the same.

Tarleton finally found Morgan—or, more accurately, Morgan allowed himself to be found—at Hannah's Cowpens, a location known well to locals and therefore an appropriate rallying point for militia speeding to Morgan's assistance. Within an hour, Cornwallis had lost the most effective and mobile force available to him. Although Morgan had won a decisive tactical victory, he still faced a far superior, if slower, force under Cornwallis. Morgan hurried his small band of veterans back across the Broad River to North Carolina, Greene, and safety (see maps 5, 6, and 7). Still possessing most of his strength and determined to see the campaign through, Cornwallis followed Morgan and Greene north, attempting in vain to destroy the rebel force. The chase sapped British strength, even as Greene gathered supporters from heartened Carolinians. By early spring, Greene's force had swollen to 4,300, while the British army had dwindled to about 2,000. Although Greene sought to avoid combat, he could not resist the opportunity Cornwallis presented him. He turned to meet his hunter[46] at Guilford Court House on 15 March. Cornwallis won the battle but failed to destroy Greene's army. He also failed to rally significant support from colonists in the region.

Cornwallis continued to follow Greene for two weeks, but the campaign had failed. Leaving Lieutenant Colonel Rawdon[47] in command of British troops in South Carolina, Cornwallis marched to Wilmington and then Yorktown. Continued fighting in the Carolinas failed to alter the course set at King's Mountain and the Cowpens. Battles were won and lost by each side, yet none was decisive. The outcome of the war in the south was, in large measure, a consequence of the operational plans of the contesting commanders. Clinton, and in his stead Cornwallis, saw the campaign as a series of opportunities:

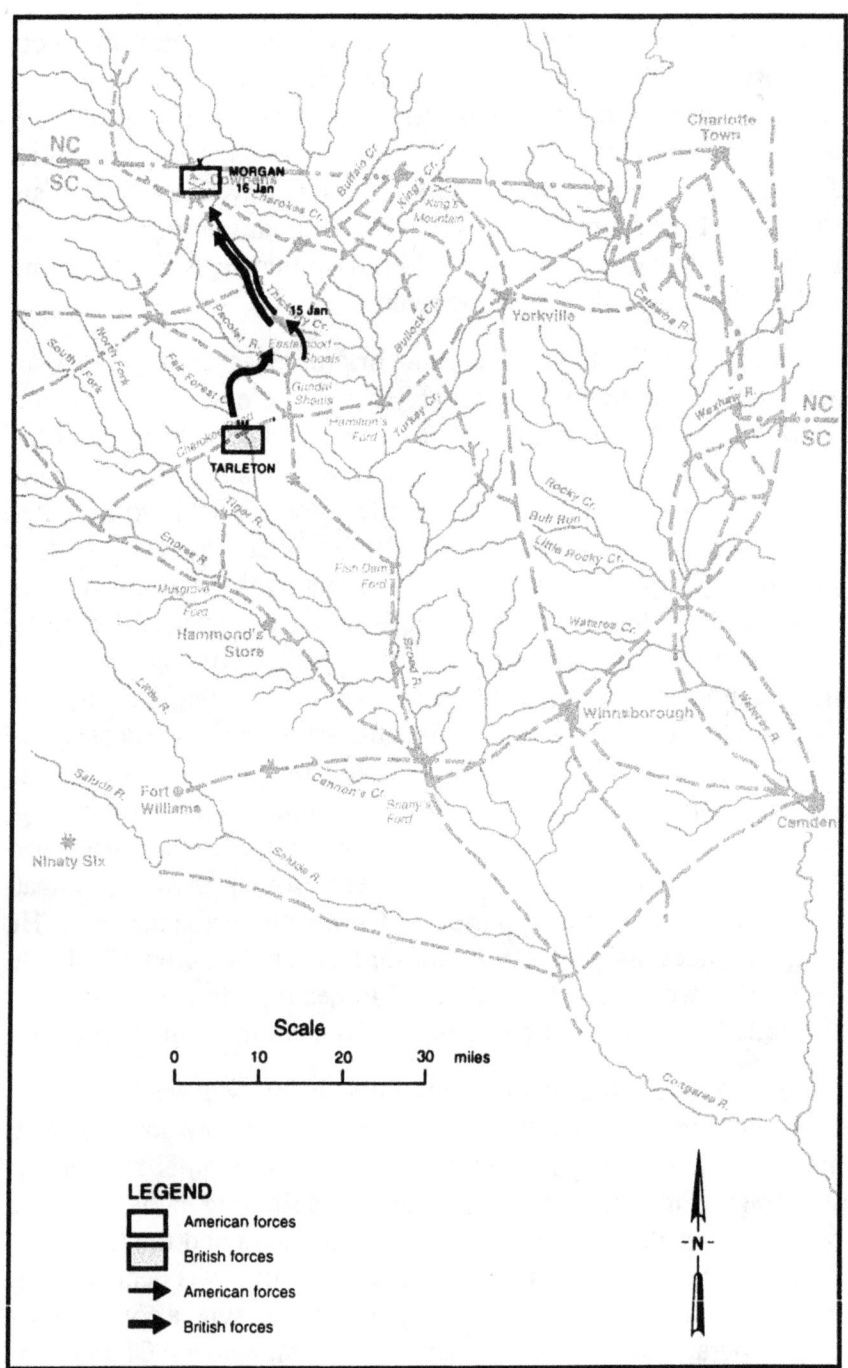

Map 5. Situation, 15 and 16 January 1781

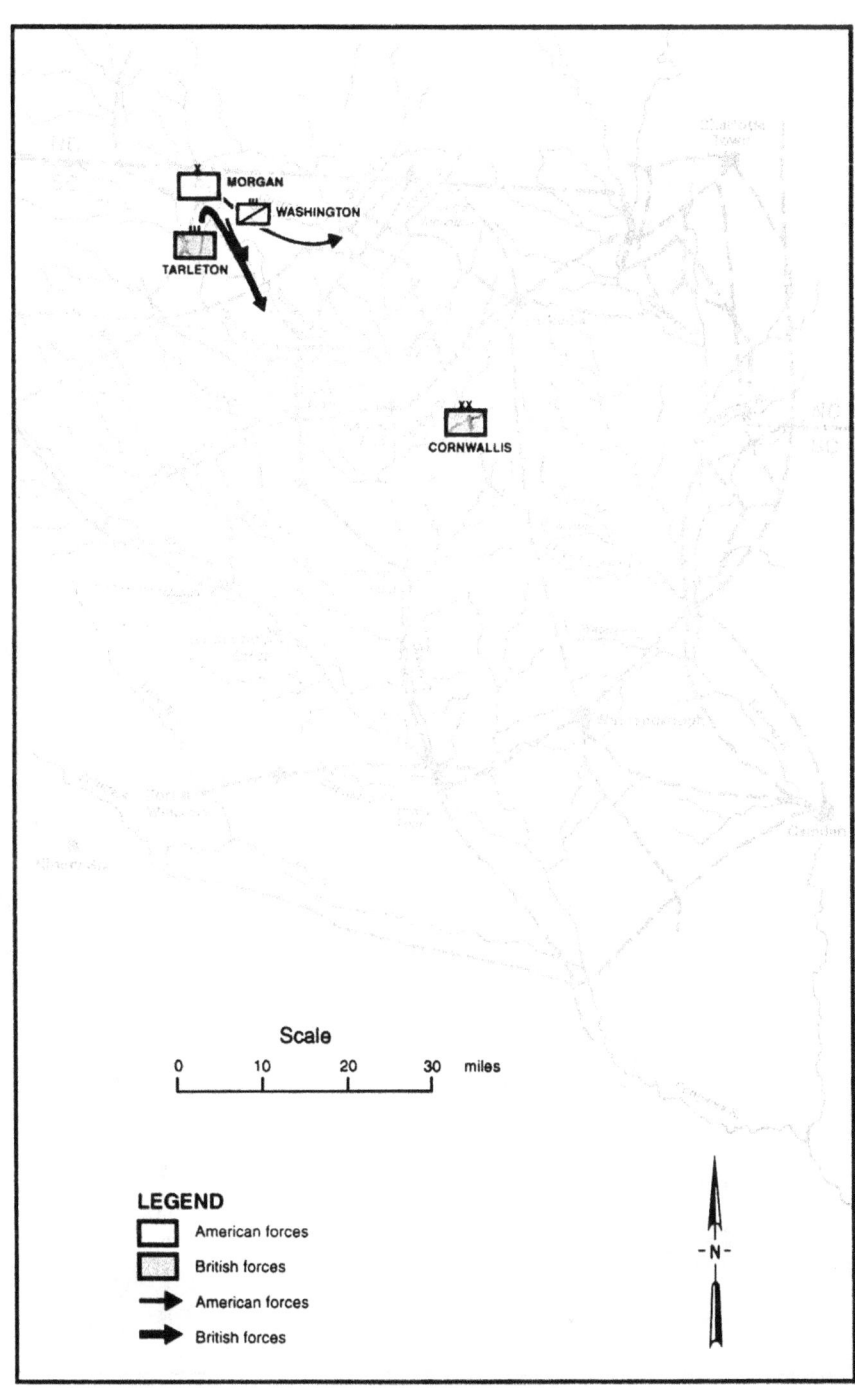

Map 6. Situation, 17 January 1781

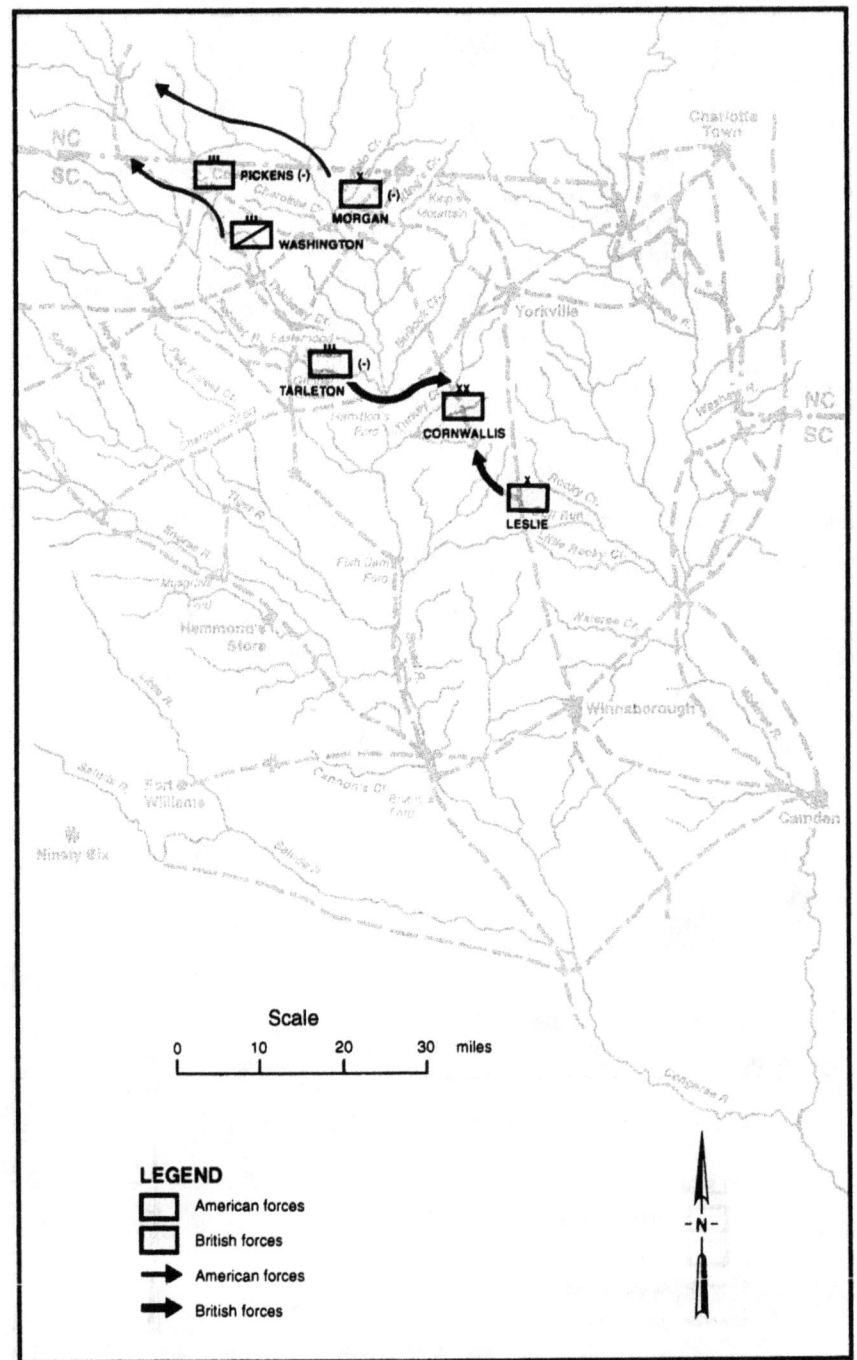

Map 7. Situation, 18 January 1781

success at Savannah could be secured by moving on Charleston; complete control of South Carolina could be gained by threatening North Carolina. In each case, the British commander's objectives became broader as his assets dwindled in a hostile country. In contrast, Greene's objective was to boost the morale of colonists sympathetic to the American cause. This objective did not require open battle. While he assured the survival of his own army, he raised the militia to assist in the whittling down of his opponent's forces. In the eighteenth century, battles occurred only when both commanders determined to stand and fight. In the vast wildernesses of the south, Greene could rest fairly assured that Cornwallis could not corner him. Thus, the American campaign plan, simple and mindful of the situation in the theater of war, permitted tactical commanders (including Greene) to err on the battlefield without altering substantially the course of the war in the south.

NOTES

Chapter 2

1. Weigley, *Army*, 69–73. For a detailed analysis, see also Jac Weller, "Irregular but Effective: Partisan Weapons Tactics in the American Revolution, Southern Theater," *Military Affairs* 21, no. 3 (1957):118–31.

2. For a discussion of South Carolina society, see Robert Stansbury Lambert, *South Carolina Loyalists in the American Revolution* (Columbia: University of South Carolina Press, 1987), 4–9; M. F. Treasy, *Prelude to Yorktown: The Southern Campaign of Nathanael Greene, 1780–1781* (Chapel Hill: University of North Carolina Press, 1963), 3–12.

3. Five wagons were delivered to the regiment in May 1777. See Curtis, *British Army*, 187, 188.

4. See Tarleton-Cornwallis Letters 7–10, Appendix D, 175–77. Citations without titles refer to primary sources reproduced in the appendix of this volume.

5. See Appendix B, for example, the loose organization described in Sexton's memoir, 100.

6. See Clyde R. Ferguson, "Functions of the Partisan-Militia in the South During the American Revolution: An Interpretation," in Higgins, *Revolutionary War*, 239–58.

7. Guyton memoir, 132.

8. For a detailed description of the siege, see Sir Henry Clinton, *The American Rebellion*, ed. William B. Willcox (New York: Archon Books, 1971), 157–72. See also John C. Cavanaugh, "American Military Leadership in the Southern Campaign: Benjamin Lincoln," in Higgins, *Revolutionary War*, 101–31.

9. The engagement is sometimes referred to as "Buford's Defeat." Most historians describe the action as a massacre, as Tarleton apparently ordered or condoned the killing of Americans under a white flag, in an act thereafter described as "Tarleton's Quarter." However, Virginia pension records show that a substantial number of Americans, though wounded, survived the battle and were paroled or discharged. Given the passions aroused by this sort of war, some excesses are likely to have occurred; however, at some point, the killing must have stopped short of massacre.

10. Ira D. Gruber, "British Southern Strategy," in Higgins, *Revolutionary War*, 228. See also Clinton, *Rebellion*, 190, 191.

11. De Kalb remained to command the Continentals in the Southern Army.

12. Paul David Nelson, "Major General Horatio Gates as a Military Leader: The Southern Experience," in Higgins, *Revolutionary War*, 142. Nelson is more critical of Gates in "Horatio Gates in the Southern Department, 1780: Serious Errors and a Costly Defeat," *North Carolina Historical Review* 50 (1973):256–72.

13. In a letter of 6 August 1780, Cornwallis wrote: "It may be doubted by some whether the invasion of North Carolina may be a prudent measure. But I am convinced that it is a necessary one and that, if we do not attack that province, we must give up both South Carolina and Georgia and retire within the walls of Charleston." See Clinton, *Rebellion*, 448.

14. Dederer, *Straw*, 62, n. 9.

15. John S. Pancake, *This Destructive War: The British Campaign in the Carolinas 1780–1781* (University: University of Alabama Press, 1985), 127; Theodore Thayer, *Nathanael Greene: Strategist of the American Revolution* (New York: Twayne, 1960); Elswyth Thane, *The Fighting Quaker: Nathanael Greene* (New York: Hawthorn Books, 1972). For fulsome praise, see the description by Alexander Garden, Greene's aide, in *Anecdotes of the Revolutionary War in America* (Charleston, SC: A. E. Miller, 1822), 76–84.

16. Greene to the president of Congress, Philadelphia, 27 October 1780, cited in George Washington Greene, *The Life of Nathanael Greene*, vol. 3 (New York: Hurd & Houghton, 1871), 35–36.

17. This is also the conclusion of Dennis Michael Conrad, who analyzed Greene's generalship in "Nathanael Greene and the Southern Campaign," Ph.D. diss., Duke University, 1979.

18. The first returns included 2,307 men, of whom 1,482 were fit for duty; only 949 were Continentals. These and ninety cavalry and sixty artillery comprised the army. In a letter Greene wrote to Lafayette, he complained that his "whole force fit for duty that (were) properly clothed and properly equipt (did) not amount to 800 men." Greene to Lafayette, 29 December 1780, cited in Greene, *Life*, vol. 3, 70.

19. Jared Sparks, ed., *Correspondence of the American Revolution*, vol. 3 (Boston: Little, Brown & Company, 1853), 166. Compare Lawrence E. Babits' figures in "Greene's Strategy in the Southern Campaign, 1780–1781," in *Adapting to Conditions War and Society in the Eighteenth Century*, ed. Maarten Ultee (University: University of Alabama Press, 1986), 136–37.

20. See Greene, *Life*, vol. 3, 68–82; Thayer, *Greene*, 293; see Seymour memoir, Appendix B, 102.

21. Babits observes that "throughout the Southern campaign, Greene acted as if he were still the quartermaster general who had brought order to the supply of the Continental Army under Washington," in "Campaign," 148.

22. Since the maneuver produced the desired results, historians more often raise their eyebrows at Greene's boldness; however, they invariably remark on the violation of the principle. See, for example, James Boone Bartholomees, "Fight or Flee: The Combat Performance of the North Carolina Militia in the Cowpens-Guilford Court House Campaign, January to March, 1781," Ph.D. diss., Duke University, 1978; George F. Scheer and Hugh F. Rankin, *Rebels and Redcoats* (New York: The World Publishing Company, 1957), 425, 426. See also Greene-Morgan Letter 2, 212.

23. For a discussion of Greene's operational concept, see Weigley, *War*, 29–36. See also Edwin C. Bearss, *The Battle of the Cowpens* (Washington, DC: Office of Archeology and Historical Preservation, U.S. Department of the Interior, 1967), 1. The original suggestion that Morgan conduct a raid was put forward by North Carolina militia General William Davidson in a letter dated 27 November 1780. See Chalmers Gaston Davidson, *Piedmont Partisan: The Life and Times of Brigadier-General William Lee Davidson* (Davidson, NC: Davidson College Press, 1951), 98.

24. For descriptions of the march, see Appendix B, Captain Kirkwood's diary, 97, 114; Captain William Beatty's diary, 99; Sergeant Major Seymour's journal, 102–4.

25. See Appendix B, Hammond memoir, 96; Seymour memoir, 102; Everhart memoir, 104; Copeland memoir, 105; Dial memoir, 106; Guyton memoir, 108.

26. See Richard M. Ketchum, "Men of the American Revolution XVI: Daniel Morgan," *American Heritage* 27 (1976):97; David Schenck, *North Carolina 1780–1781* (Raleigh, NC: Edwards and Broughton, 1889), 203–4. R. Don Higginbotham, in a biographical sketch of Morgan, writes, "Morgan, falling back toward the border of the Carolinas, made a stand against Tarleton at the Cowpens." See "Daniel Morgan," *American Military Leaders*, ed. Roger J. Spiller (New York: Praeger, 1989), 219. See also Conrad, "Greene," 103. Higginbotham's more detailed explanation in *Daniel Morgan, Revolutionary Rifleman* (Chapel Hill: University of North Carolina Press, 1961), 130–31, portrays a more accurate picture of the events.

27. Cornwallis sent Tarleton the order to move on 1 January 1781. See Tarleton campaign narrative, Appendix B, 112–15.

28. By contrast, Ira D. Gruber portrays Cornwallis as "a confident, gregarious man, filled with energy, and capable of acting decisively even rashly." "Britain's Southern Strategy," in Higgins, *Revolutionary War*, 213.

29. See Cornwallis-Tarleton Letters 7 and 8, Appendix D, 175–76. Tarleton had requested the baggage only on 4 January; see Cornwallis-Tarleton Letter 7, 175–76.

30. See Appendix B, Seymour for a description of the conditions of the troops, 102.

31. See Greene-Morgan Letter 3, Appendix D, 163–64.

32. See Cornwallis-Tarleton Letters 1 and 4, Appendix D, 112–13, 174.

33. See Cornwallis-Tarleton Letters 1 and 4, Appendix D, 112–13, 174.

34. See Greene-Morgan Letter 4, Appendix D, 164–65.

35. Writing from his observations a scant two decades after the battle of the Cowpens, the great military theorist Carl von Clausewitz wrote, "We maintain unequivocally that the form of warfare we call defense not only offers greater probability of victory than attack, but that its victories can attain the same proportions and results," *On War*, ed. and trans. Michael Howard and Peter Paret (Princeton, NJ: Princeton University Press, 1984), 392.

36. See Appendix D, Greene-Morgan Letter 8, 15 January, 169–70.

37. *The Reason Why* (New York: E. P. Dutton, 1960), 1.

38. For more details of Tarleton's background, see Robert D. Bass, *The Green Dragoon* (Columbia, SC: Sandlapper Press, 1972), 11–31.

39. Until the nineteenth century, commissions in the British Army were reserved for those who could afford them, in the belief that the monied classes were schooled for the hardships of military service and were more likely to possess the courage required for it. The cost, £800, may have been a bargain; the same position in the Horse-Guards cost £1,200. The annual pay of a cornet of dragoons was only £255. See Curtis, *British Army*, 158, 159.

40. R. Money Barnes, *A History of the Regiments & Uniforms of the British Army* (London: Seeley Service & Co., 1964), 38, 66. The first known light cavalry in modern Europe were Magyar volunteers. Similar formations were in use in European armies by the end of the seventh century, the English adopting them only with reluctance because of their irregular origins. See David Chandler, *The Art of Warfare in the Age of Marlborough* (New York: Hippocrene Books, 1976), 37–41; John W. Fortescue, *A History of the 17th Lancers* (London: Macmillan, 1895), 5, 6. For comparison, see Christopher Duffy, *The Army of Frederick the Great* (New York: Hippocrene Books, 1974), 98–102.

41. Ironically, as an officer in the British Army, Charles Lee had actually served in the 16th Light Dragoons in Portugal. See Bass, *Dragoon*, 20.

42. Of his decision, Lee said, "If the British cavalry [Tarleton] had vigorously pushed on our right, they might have turned our flank, taken us in reverse, and we had been lost." Bass, *Dragoon*, 45.

43. From H. Lloyd, *Continuation of the History of the Late War in Germany Between the King of Prussia and the Empress of Germany and Her Allies*, Part 2 (London: S. Hooper, 1781), 145. George Hanger, one of Tarleton's protégés, quotes this passage to refute the criticism of Lieutenant Roderick Mackenzie that Tarleton was too precipitate in his attack of Morgan's force. See *An Address to the Army in Reply to the Strictures by Roderick Mackenzie* (London: James Ridgway, 1789), 123.

44. See Kirkwood's diary, Appendix B, 97; See Anderson's diary, Appendix C, 139; Kelley's diary, 142.

45. See Cornwallis-Tarleton Letter 4, Appendix D, 139.

46. See William R. Trotter, "Advantage Found in Retreat," *Military History* 6 (December 1989):38–43; George W. Kyte, "Victory in the South: An Appraisal of General Greene's Strategy in the Carolinas," *North Carolina Historical Review* 37 (July 1960):321–47.

47. Lord Rawdon had been close friends with Tarleton since their days at University College, Oxford, in 1771. See Bass, *Dragoon*, 13.

III. "THIS UNEXPECTED EVENT":
ANNIHILATION AT THE COWPENS[1]

In 216 B.C. on the Italian peninsula at Cannae, the great Carthaginian commander Hannibal, his back to the Aufidus River, met a Roman army almost twice the size of his own under consuls Aemilius and Varro. In a day-long scene of carnage, the Carthaginians hacked and speared to death 70,000 Romans at a cost of 5,700 of their own men.[2] The double envelopment at Cannae has become the classic example of the elusive battle of annihilation, the solution to the dangers of protracted, expensive, and exhausting wars of attrition. The concept of the envelopment so dazzled a chief of the Prussian General Staff that he designed, on a massive scale, an operations plan to recreate it and titled his essay on military history *Cannae*.[3] While Schlieffen's plan, as modified by his successor, failed to achieve the desired result in western Europe in 1914, Generals Paul von Hindenburg and Erich Ludendorff did encircle and destroy a Russian army at Tannenburg the same year.

But for those examples, the only important double envelopment resulting in annihilation occurred in the backwoods of South Carolina at the Cowpens in 1781. The American victor certainly had military experience, but even compared with many of his contemporaries, much less Hannibal, he must be called an amateur. Should Morgan rank with Hannibal as a great captain, or did happenstance lead to an outcome the American commander did not intend? Would either reputation suffer if it were known that each commander seized a rare opportunity as it presented itself?

The Cowpens may be one of the most important battles ever fought on American soil from the standpoint of the tactical lessons one can learn from it. Far from a slugfest, the Cowpens featured both commanders as they maneuvered their troops expertly in an attempt to achieve decisive results (although, obviously, only one succeeded). Moreover, it stands as a superb laboratory for analysis of the psychological factor in war, an opportunity to study the psychological makeup of the British and American commanders and the morale of their troops. In addition, it highlights the differences in discipline and morale between regular soldiers and militia. But, like Cannae (and, for that matter, Tannenburg), the battle had little effect on the war. Never will the Cowpens be more than a fascinating footnote in military history, as its effect was merely to nudge along the thrust of the campaign that had been so decisively affected (as we know in hindsight) by the far less interesting battle at King's Mountain.

At forty-four, Lieutenant Colonel Daniel Morgan was older than many other senior officers in the Continental Army. He had served as a wagoner for Major General Edward Braddock during that officer's ill-fated expedition into western Pennsylvania in 1755. After Morgan raised one of the first rifle companies authorized by Congress, his distinguished behavior in action resulted in his promotion to colonel. Later, he felt unrecognized as others were promoted ahead of him and in a pique resigned his commission.[4] Upon hearing that his old commander from Saratoga had been badly beaten at Camden, however, he hurried south and was surprised to be greeted not only by Gates' replacement but by orders promoting himself to brigadier general.[5]

A better commander could not have been chosen for the foray into South Carolina. Morgan was a commander of proven courage, and he had an uncanny understanding of the psychology of soldiers and a firm grasp of tactical principles. An imposing six feet in height and of great physical strength, he also bore a large scar on his cheek that spoke volumes of his bravery.[6] During his weeks in South Carolina, he followed Greene's directive scrupulously, husbanding his forces and drawing Tarleton ever closer. By the middle of January, he had played out his hand. Tarleton was determined to catch Morgan before the latter could cross the Broad River and before the little American army could swell with militia reinforcements. On the night of 15 January, Tarleton crossed the Pacolet River and surprised some of Morgan's pickets in their camp. With the alarm "brother Ben is coming!" Morgan moved most of his command to Burr's Mill on Thicketty Creek.[7] Greene had expected Morgan to harass the enemy, "to fall upon the flank or into the rear of the enemy" as the situation dictated; Tarleton, however, instead moved to force a decision.

Morgan could flee, demoralizing his troops and exposing them to piecemeal destruction, or he could test his strength against the Green Dragoon in pitched battle.

Morgan chose to fight. Violating the strict letter of his original instructions, he had several advantages that amended the circumstances envisioned in their writing. First, he chose the ground, giving him the advantage of an ambusher. Second, he knew by reputation the methods—and therefore the weaknesses—of his opponent. Third, allowing Tarleton the time to close the gap between the two armies gave the Americans an opportunity to assemble on a battle site of Morgan's choosing, prepare their positions, rest, and eat before the contest of the following day. Tarleton's troops would have none of these advantages. Greene sent Morgan a letter on 13 January that implied Morgan had permission to fight the battle.

Morgan's force was ideally suited to the task. Greene had assigned Morgan remnants of the Continental Line and Virginia state troops under the able Lieutenant Colonel John Eager Howard, as well as Lieutenant Colonel William Washington's 3d Continental Light Dragoons.[8]

Hannah's Cowpens, Morgan's choice for his battle arena, was a typical landmark in western South Carolina, used for grazing herds by local farmers and frontiersmen bringing their cattle to market. Here the militia had rallied several months earlier before joining Ferguson at King's Mountain. Relatively flat open ground sparsely scattered with red oak and pine,[9] the site was ideal for grazing cows or fighting European-style battles. From the direction the British must come (northwest along Mill Gap Road), a single trail opened into a narrow plain that sloped gently but unevenly uphill to the center of the pens. About 200 meters in width where the British would form up, the field widens to about 250 meters at its highest point (about a 990-foot elevation) and, continuing along the trail, tapers slightly as the ground falls toward the banks of the Broad River some eight kilometers beyond.[10] As the British would see it, the field generally sloped downward to the right (or north) flank. In the northeast corner of the field, a ravine divided the northern side, running parallel to and just behind the Continental Line.

On 16 January, Morgan marched his small army to Hannah's Cowpens, arriving there about sundown. The move not only allowed him to select the ground of his choosing,[11] it also placed him farther away from Cornwallis and the danger of encirclement and gave outlying detachments time to gather for the battle. Years later, Morgan gave yet another explanation for his choice of the site:

> I would not have had a swamp in the view of my militia on any consideration; they would have made for it, and nothing could have detained them from it. As to covering my wings, I knew my adversary, and was perfectly sure I should have nothing but downright fighting. As to retreat, it was the very thing I wished to cut off all hope of. I would have thanked Tarleton had he surrounded me with his cavalry. It would have been better than placing my own men in the rear to shoot down those who broke from ranks. When men are forced to fight, they will sell their lives dearly; and I know that the dread of Tarleton's cavalry would give due weight to the protection of the bayonets, and keep my troops from breaking as Buford's regiment did. Had I crossed the river, one half of the militia would immediately have abandoned me.[12]

Although a number of accounts accept this explanation, it seems unlikely. The Continentals had been surrounded at Camden and were destroyed. Furthermore, Morgan's instructions at the time anticipated their removal from harm's way. Furthermore, the Broad River, six miles to the northwest, was too distant to serve as either a barrier to fleeing militia or an anvil for pursuing cavalry. The ground was optimal for Tarleton's cavalry, as the British commander noted, although it sloped gently upward toward the American position.[13] The greatest virtue of the field for the Americans was that several detachments (including that of Washington, who was at Wofford Iron Works reshoeing his horses) could join Morgan without fear of getting lost.[14] This factor may have been decisive in the choice of the site.

Morgan sent a message to Sumter to join him there as quickly as possible. Hearing the call to arms, militia came from miles around.[15] The night gave Morgan time to prepare his men for combat the next day, and the skilled leader made the most of his opportunity. Allowing his troops to prepare physically—cleaning their weapons, eating, and so forth—he walked among them to prepare them emotionally for the horrors of eighteenth-century battle. Major Thomas Young of South Carolina wrote that Morgan showed a keen sense of how to command militia: "He went among the volunteers, helped them fix their swords, joked with them about their sweet-hearts, told them to keep in good spirits, and the day would be ours." Morgan realized that militiamen behaved in battle not as a reaction to years of discipline and drill but based on the enthusiasm of the moment. In his encouragement to the volunteers, Morgan linked their performance in battle to the values all young men hold, telling them, "Just hold up your heads, boys, three fires, and you are free, and when you return to your homes, how the old folks will bless you, and the girls kiss you, for your gallant conduct."[16] He cajoled those whose enlistments had expired to remain for the battle.[17] On the morning of the fight, he rhetorically included them in the decision to meet the dreaded horsemen of Tarleton, asking the South Carolinians, "Shall we fight or fly?"[18] More than jovial banter, Morgan deliberately sought to raise the spirits of soldiers whose behavior in battle varied directly with their morale. Any army suffers emotionally and physically as it withdraws before the enemy; this small American army was ripe for their commander's message.

Before first light, Morgan laid out his plan to meet Tarleton. Some accounts suggest that he addressed the entire force.[19] While "enflam[ing] the courage" of his men certainly sounds like something Morgan would do, that he should address more than 1,000 soldiers (in the dark) seems almost impossible. Indeed, Major Samuel Hammond describes the meeting in which the order was read and claimed that only Colonel Andrew Pickens, Colonel McCall, Major Jackson, and he were present. Probably this order related specifically to the actions of militia troops, as neither Howard nor Washington were in attendance. Major Joseph McJunkin, however, tells us that first Morgan and then Major Jackson (who had been present at the war council) spoke to the militia. Nonetheless, all reminiscences of Morgan's words that night and the following morning verify that they stirred the warlike spirit of the troops. Most likely, Morgan explained his detailed plan to key lieutenants, drew up what officers and soldiers were reasonably available, and exhorted them to be courageous, leaving detailed instructions to battalion officers.

Morgan's plan was beautiful in its simplicity. Counting that Tarleton would behave impetuously as he had in other actions, the Virginian designed his force to behave like a shock absorber. He would deploy his army facing southeast. Eight hundred meters in front of them, Mill Gap Road opened onto the field. Riflemen, accurate to 300 meters, would man the skirmish line from behind the scattered trees to pick off British officers and then retire into the main militia line.[20] As the British continued their advance, the militia would fire three volleys (the "three fires" Young recalled) and retire from the field around the left flank of the Continentals.[21] Morgan hoped that such of Tarleton's force as remained could be defeated by the American regulars and Virginia militia, all under the operational control of Howard.[22] In any case, as withdrawal of the militia was part of the plan, the scheme of maneuver would not be disturbed, and the regulars would not be unnerved (as they had been at Camden) or even disappointed when it occurred. Morgan rightly feared the large contingent of British horse. He gathered up all available horses and called for volunteers to augment Washington's 3d Continental Light Dragoons. Most of the forty-five additional men came from McCall's South Carolina State Troops. This force he held in reserve, behind the gully to the left rear of his line but available for rapid deployment to any endangered sector of the battle.

Exactly what troops deployed that morning, and where, remains uncertain. Fortunately, Morgan and Hammond give us detailed descriptions of the American deployment, supplemented by fragmentary observations by other witnesses.[23] While the accounts of the three officers do not agree in every detail—or agree exactly with other statements regarding the deployment—they can be blended into a coherent picture (see map 8). Clearly the Continental Line (consisting of the remnants of Maryland and Delaware regulars) were the centerpiece of the army. They formed in two ranks, covering about 200 yards.[24] Howard differed with his commander on the location of the

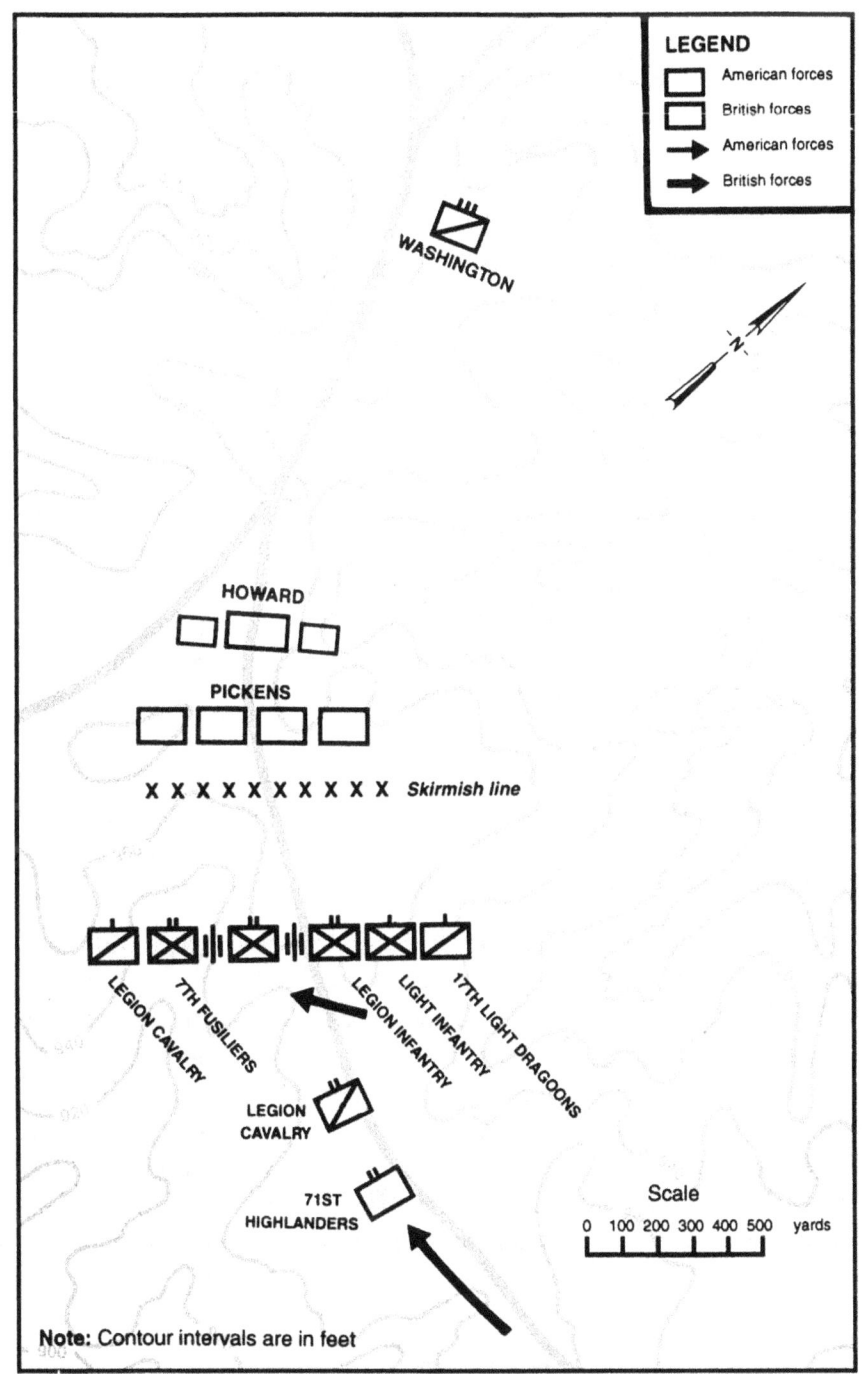

Map 8. Initial dispositions, 0700, 17 January 1781

position of the Virginia militia supplementing the main defense: while Morgan remembered Tate on the right, Howard recalled years later that Tate's company was on the left with that of Triplett. Howard was certainly in a better position to know (as he commanded that portion of the troops), but Morgan's account was written shortly after the battle. Because the Continentals were flanked on both sides by Virginians (Howard tells us Wallace was on the right, Triplett and Tate on the left), Morgan might well have confused the two groups.

Less easy to identify is the position held by the militia commanded by Colonel Pickens. Sergeant Major William Seymour tells us the militia were 200 yards in front of the Continental Line, while McJunkin says 150 yards. However, Morgan reported only that Pickens' volunteers from North Carolina, South Carolina, and Georgia "were situated to guard the flanks."[25] Major Hammond, who reconstructed the order Morgan gave the night before the battle, claims that Pickens deployed to Howard's left flank, while Major Triplett deployed to his right. Young of South Carolina confirms that Pickens' flank was anchored on the left of a ravine. Probably Pickens' men were not directly in front of Howard but centered on his left flank. Wallace's Virginia militia, who could easily have been confused with Triplett's men of the same state, may have seemed (to Hammond who was farther forward with the skirmish line) to have been even with Pickens.

Scattered behind trees about 150 yards in front of Pickens' men were the line of skirmishers. While accounts differ as to who commanded them, Hammond may be accepted as the authority, as his account is so detailed, and he was actually among them. He tells us that the skirmishers were led, from right flank to left, by Majors Cunningham, McDowell, Hammond himself, and Donnolly. It was these men who would fire the first shots of the battle. In front of the skirmish line, perhaps several miles ahead in the wood line, were posted Captain Inman's pickets on horseback to warn the army of the arrival of the British force.[26]

Behind the Continental Line, Morgan posted his reserves. Commanding the 3d Continental Light Dragoons and some of McCall's men, Washington poised for contingencies about 100 yards behind the left flank of the army.[27] Hammond mentions a Main Guard positioned behind Pickens and commanded "as at present by Colonel Washington's cavalry," without identifying it further. No other diarist mentions such a force, and even Hammond's sentence concerning it is vague. Perhaps Hammond was describing the rallying point for the militia after they concluded their portion of the battle. If so, he may be telling us that as the militia streamed to the rear, they would fall under the command of Washington, at least until Pickens could regain control of them.

It was a bitter cold morning, and the soldiers slapped their hands to keep warm as they waited in the dark for the British troops to arrive. No evidence remains of the time the engagement began; not even the sun would signal the onslaught on this overcast day.[28] Only the adrenaline that must have coursed through them could have kept the raw recruits and seasoned veterans of "Tarleton's Quarter" at their psychological peak for the last hour of darkness before the coming challenge.[29]

Tarleton's men had been marching hard through the thick underbrush of Thicketty Creek since 0300. Their commander could sense the presence of his opponent, having taken his camp on the Pacolet River only the previous evening at 2200. His intuition was confirmed by the capture of several of Captain Inman's pickets shortly before dawn. Tarleton, who believed the Americans had marched that night and turned at bay with the swollen river to their backs, was eager to press his attack.[30] As the British broke out of the underbrush, the light company of the Prince of Wales' American Regiment, Legion infantry, and 7th Fusiliers in turn deployed two deep, each rapidly falling in to the left of the unit that preceded it on the march, while the advanced guard of dragoons pushed back the remaining pickets.[31] According to Tarleton, he then directed his line to remove their packs and to file to the right until the flank force (Prince of Wales' Americans) faced its counterpart directly. Lieutenant Roderick Mackenzie portrays a far more hurried onrush without the careful preparation Tarleton describes.[32] While the truth cannot be known, such leisurely alignments in a battle with so much activity, but which lasted only an hour, is difficult to imagine.[33] From an interview with eyewitnesses, Major George Hanger claims Tarleton halted the troops for "near half an hour, and made them throw their knapsacks and blankets to render them lighter for action."[34] However quickly they formed, the British found themselves facing an enemy 300 to 400 yards to their front, deployed and holding their fire.

Accounts of the sequence in the action at the Cowpens differ little and then mostly because of the perspective of the narrator. From the Continental Line, the battle appears to have begun with artillery fire from the two small guns Tarleton had placed in front of his formation.[35] This scenario is reasonable, as the guns had the greatest range of any weapon present, and the British could draw first blood outside the range of the Americans. However, several militiamen claimed first honors for their unit, naming John Savage, who was killed later that morning, as the marksman who brought down "a gayly dressed officer."[36] In his report to Greene, Morgan confirms this general scenario, crediting the first shot to Major Charles McDowall's and Major John Cunningham's skirmishers. Tarleton does not discuss the first shot but states that, after the suppression of fire from raw recruits in the 7th Infantry, his line advanced (see map 9). The skirmishers performed as expected: they aimed carefully at the deployed British, causing at first some return fire from green fusiliers and a reply by the 3-pounders. After sniping from behind cover at officers, they withdrew back into the main militia line commanded by Pickens (see map 10).

Tarleton believed in momentum and, seeing the sharpshooters withdraw, ordered a general advance to smash the Americans. The entire British line moved forward shouting as they went,[37] and the militia braced to meet the shock (see map 11). Recognizing in advance that the performance of the militia was important to the outcome of the day, Morgan had positioned himself among them. To bolster their courage, he shouted over the gunfire, "They gave us the British halloo, boys, give *them* the Indian halloo, by G_," and cheered the men as they fired individually[38] at the oncoming red- and green-coated enemy.[39] The more disciplined return fire from the British appears, from the casualty figures, not to have caused great impact

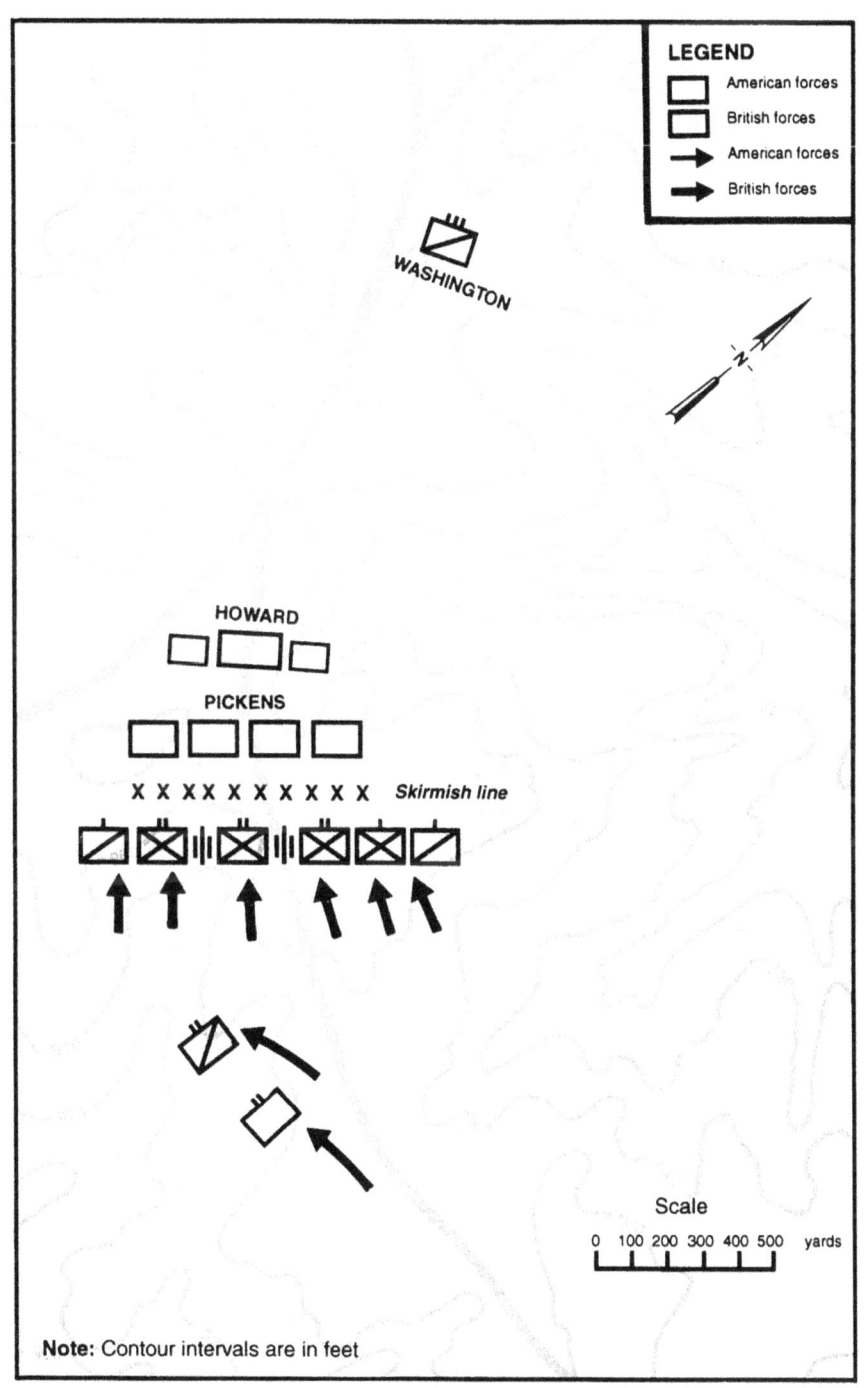

Map 9. British advance, 0710, 17 January 1781

54

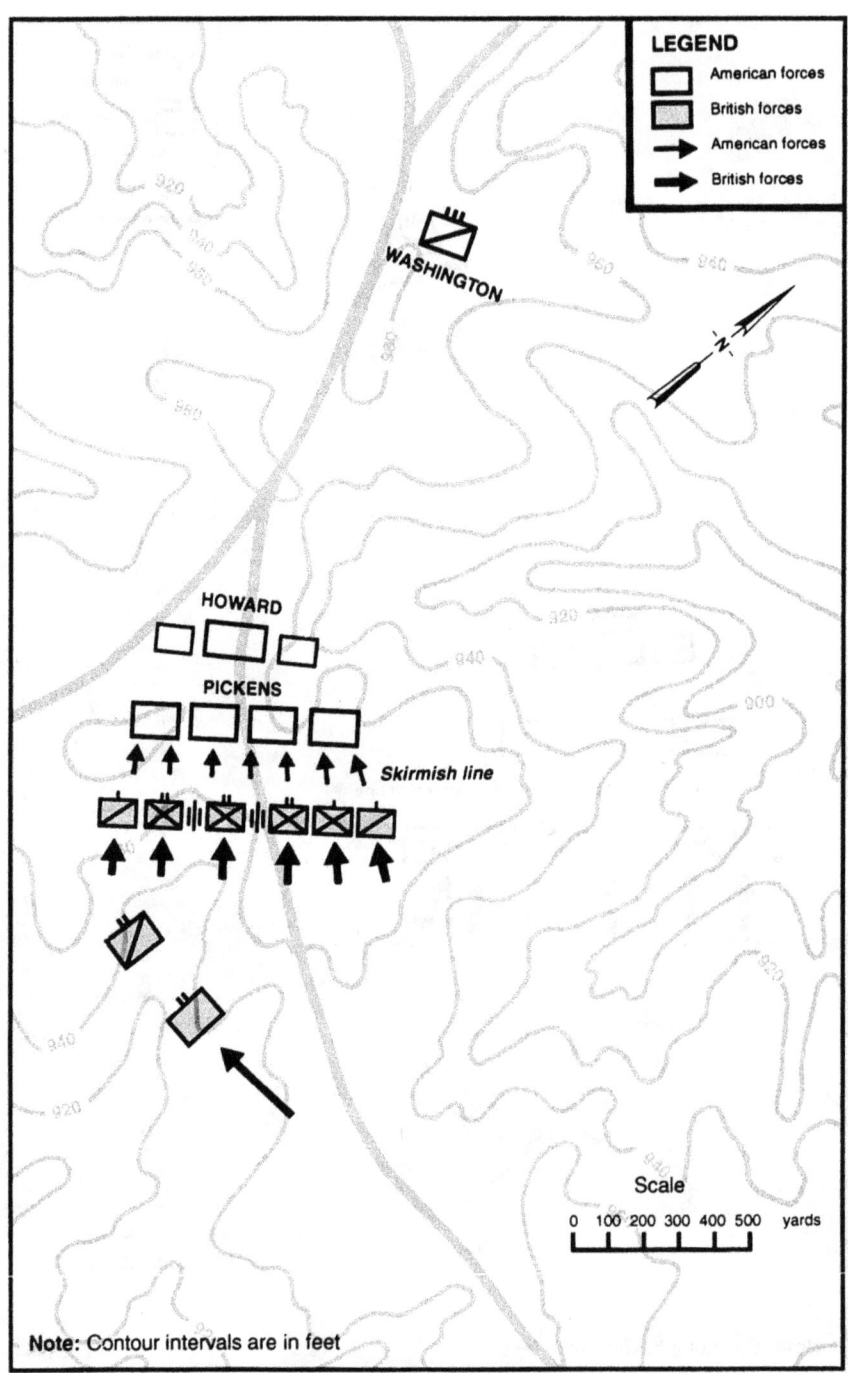

Map 10. Skirmish line withdraws, 0720, 17 January 1781

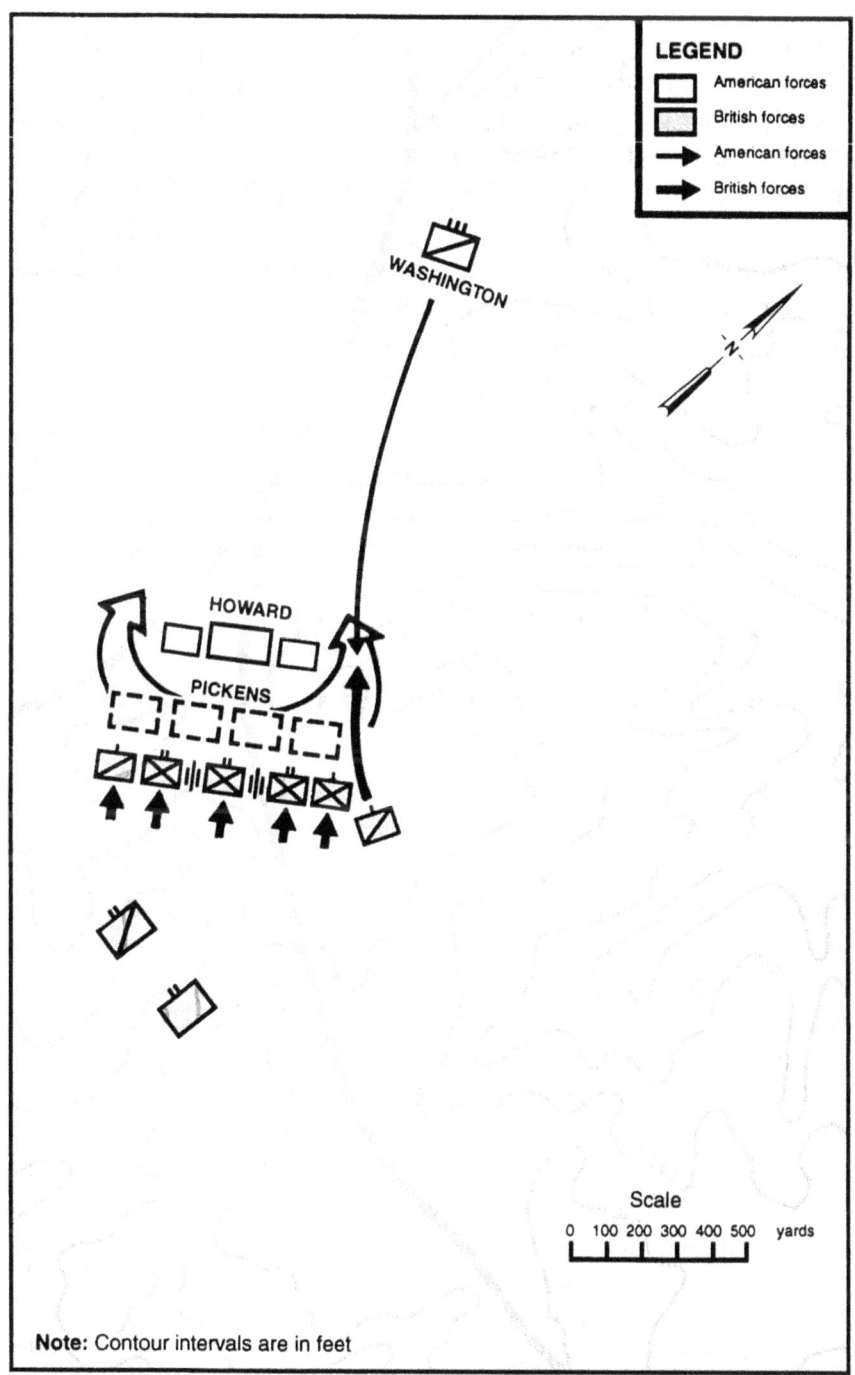

Map 11. British attack and militia withdrawal, 0730, 17 January 1781

among the militia. Perhaps, as Mackenzie argues, the exertions made by the British troops to meet Morgan took their toll that day. Additionally, among the line opposing Pickens were recruits of the 7th Fusiliers, the Legion infantry (many of whom had been impressed from among troops captured at Camden),[40] and a small number of the Prince of Wales' Americans. Thus, the British line, which could be expected to behave like regular troops, might not have produced the same results as a seasoned, well-drilled European unit. In any case, the rebels fired between two and five rounds each and withdrew around the main defenses to their rear.

According to Morgan's scheme, the militia were to withdraw around Howard's left formation and regroup. In fact, they streamed around both flanks but mostly around the left.[41] Tarleton saw an opportunity in this apparently precipitate flight and sent the fifty cavalrymen, placed earlier on the right flank, against the retreating militia in front of them.[42] Apparently, this chase led the British cavalry behind Howard's left flank, to be repulsed only when Washington, waiting 100 yards behind that flank, parried their thrust on his own initiative.

Having vanquished the militia, Tarleton pressed his advantage. Along with the general advance of his line, he ordered up the 71st Highlanders and the reserve cavalry on his left flank and the Legion cavalry on his right (see map 12). He chose the left instinctively but with good reason: the 71st was waiting in reserve behind his left (opposite Howard's right flank), and the Continental Light Cavalry had already demonstrated its ability to protect Howard's other flank. By threatening the American left with cavalry again, Tarleton obviously sought to fix the attention of Washington there, thus making him unavailable where the British commander sought a decision, on Howard's left. Why did the Legion cavalry accompany the 71st? Tarleton ordered them to "incline to the left, and to form a line, which would embrace the whole of the enemy's right flank." He then tells us, however, that the infantry moved on but the cavalry balked.[43] Nonetheless, Tarleton at that moment demonstrated several qualities for which he became well known. His tactical prowess was generally impressive: he manifested that sharp eye for opportunity essential for

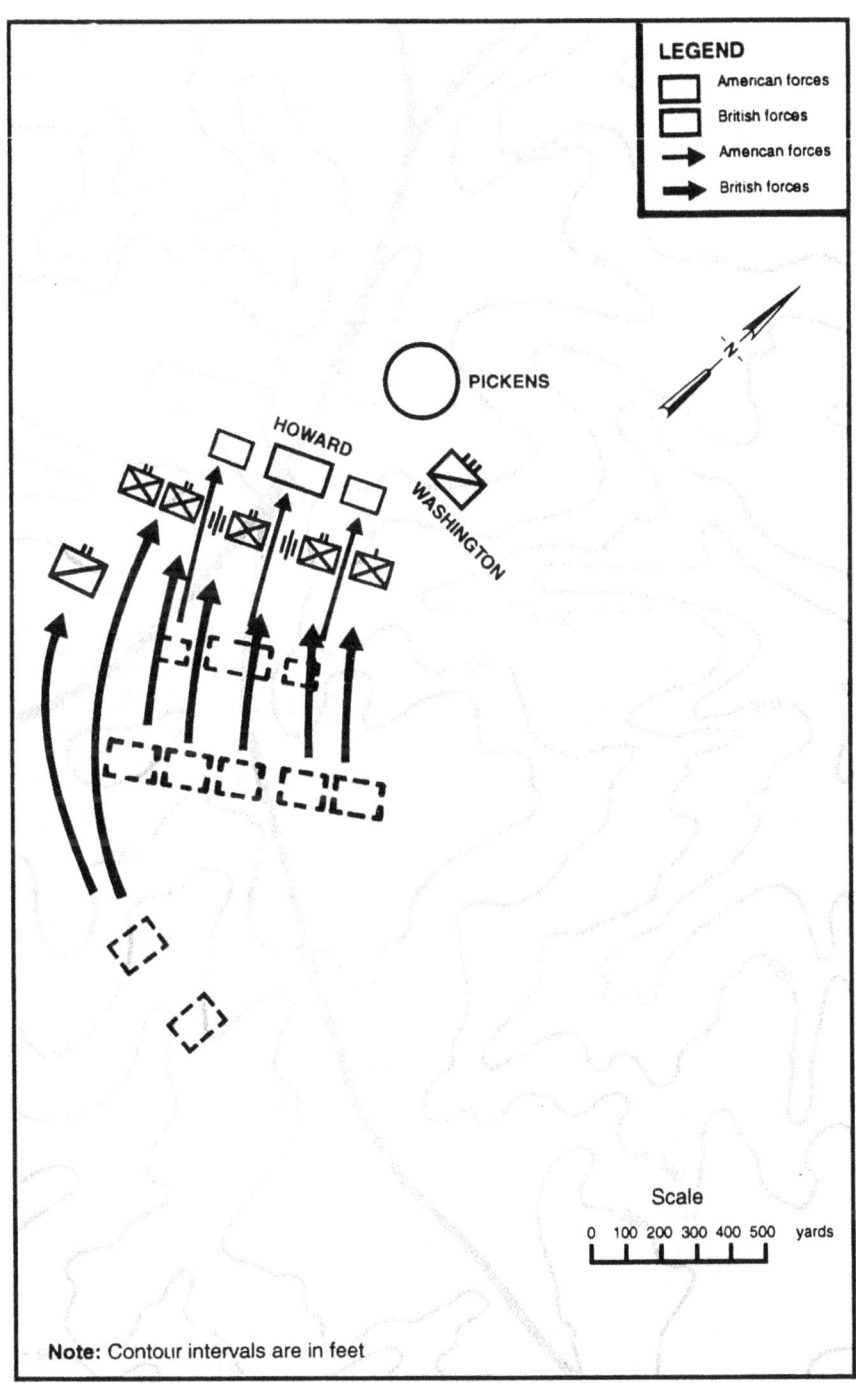

Map 12. Continental Line withdrawal and British attack, 0740, 17 January 1781

the successful tactical leader. But if Lieutenant Mackenzie is correct and the reserves were not yet disentangled from the Thicketty Creek underbrush, the Green Dragoon also showed a blind eye to the limits of his troops' abilities, the same weakness that had resulted in his men's exhaustion on the field that morning.

From his position in the Continental Line, Howard could see the general advance of the British line and the highlanders moving up rapidly on his flank. To prevent this fresh unit from overwhelming him, he sent word to the Virginians on his right to refuse the flank. Had Wallace correctly understood and executed his superior's intent, he would have held his left fast to the Continental Line, acting as a hinge, and swung the remainder of his company rearward 45 degrees like a huge door. Whatever the cause of the misunderstanding, Wallace's men did not execute the maneuver as Howard intended. Rather, they faced about and began marching directly to the rear. Company commanders in the Continental Line misinterpreted Wallace's actions and, believing that they had failed to hear the order for a general withdrawal, followed suit. Only this action prevented a fatal gap from developing in the line between Wallace and the regulars. Morgan observed this development with alarm and rode immediately to Howard, demanding an explanation. Howard, obviously, had none. When Howard pointed out, however, that the regulars were withdrawing in good order, Morgan regained his composure and picked a spot 80 to 100 yards to the rear where he wished the line to re-form.[44]

The unplanned withdrawal of the Continental Line had two consequences immediately important to the outcome of the battle. First, it caused the British to believe the Americans were on the run. Second, and as a consequence of the first, the British lost their balance, as if the resistance were suddenly removed from someone pushing a load. Believing the American regulars to be in full retreat, they lunged forward for the kill, in the process losing the force derived of disciplined drill (see map 13). Suddenly the American line faced about again, their weapons loaded, and delivered a withering volley—Morgan calls it "a fortunate volley"[45]—into the face of the startled British barely thirty meters away.[46] The combination of

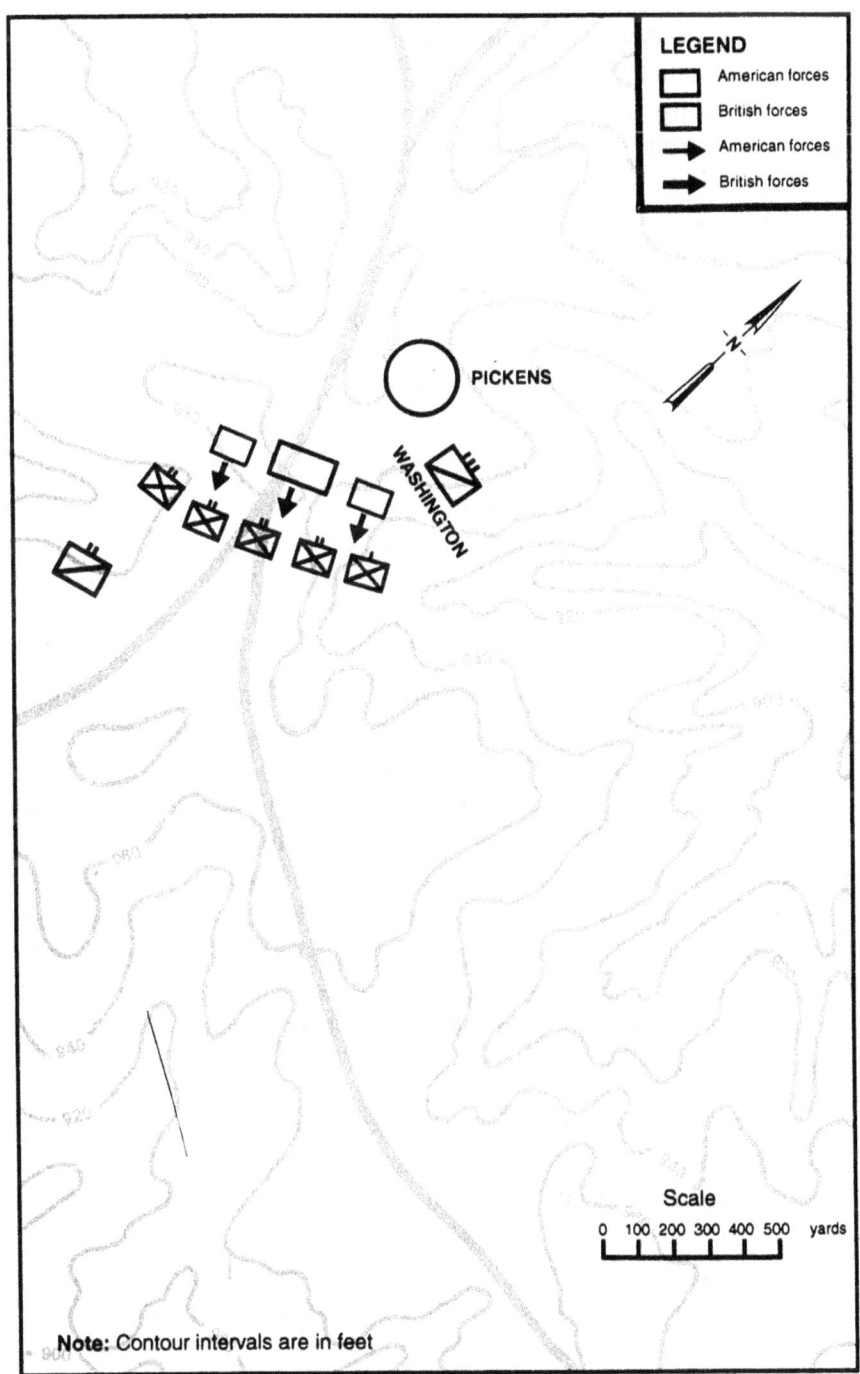

Map 13. Continentals' counterattack, 0745, 17 January 1781

sudden discovery that the battle was now in jeopardy and the agony of being surrounded by large numbers of horribly wounded comrades was devastating to the relatively inexperienced British troops. Regulars, raw recruits, and Tory volunteers reeled back in panic and disarray. Howard recognized the opportunity before him and ordered his men to press home with their bayonets.

At this moment, separate decisions led to the envelopment for which the battle has become famous (see map 14). Washington now parried the fixing attack on the American left flank and moved forward, past Triplett's flank and behind the right flank of the now crumbling British line. Almost simultaneously, Pickens' militia, which had regrouped behind the Continental Line, appeared on the American right, sweeping around behind the other British flank. Was their reappearance part of a contingency plan preconceived by Morgan? If so, he deceived the militia when he promised them freedom after the "three fires." McJunkin says only that Howard ordered a charge, and the militia returned "left and right"; Major Young is no more specific.[47] Hammond, so precise in his details, makes no mention of any such plan. Only Private James Collins tells us that Morgan himself appeared among the militiamen, still recovering from their recent deliverance from a cavalry charge, to exhort them to rejoin the battle.[48] We must conclude that the return of the militia was the consequence of the initiative of a commander—which one, we may never know.[49] Both Pickens and Morgan were close enough to have ordered the maneuver. Either Howard or Washington, already in the operation, could have sent a runner to Pickens with a plea for his support. In any case, surely Pickens would have led the counterattack personally.

Pressed by bayonet-wielding Continentals to their front, Washington's cavalry on their right and rear, and Pickens' militia on their left and rear, the British crumbled quickly. As Tarleton describes the scene, "an unaccountable panic extended itself along the whole line."[50] Unable to flee, pockets of men surrendered. Gunners manning the two 3-pounder cannon resisted longest. Determined to fight to the death, the artillerymen were convinced by Howard to surrender their guns; he then prevented the men from being slaughtered.[51]

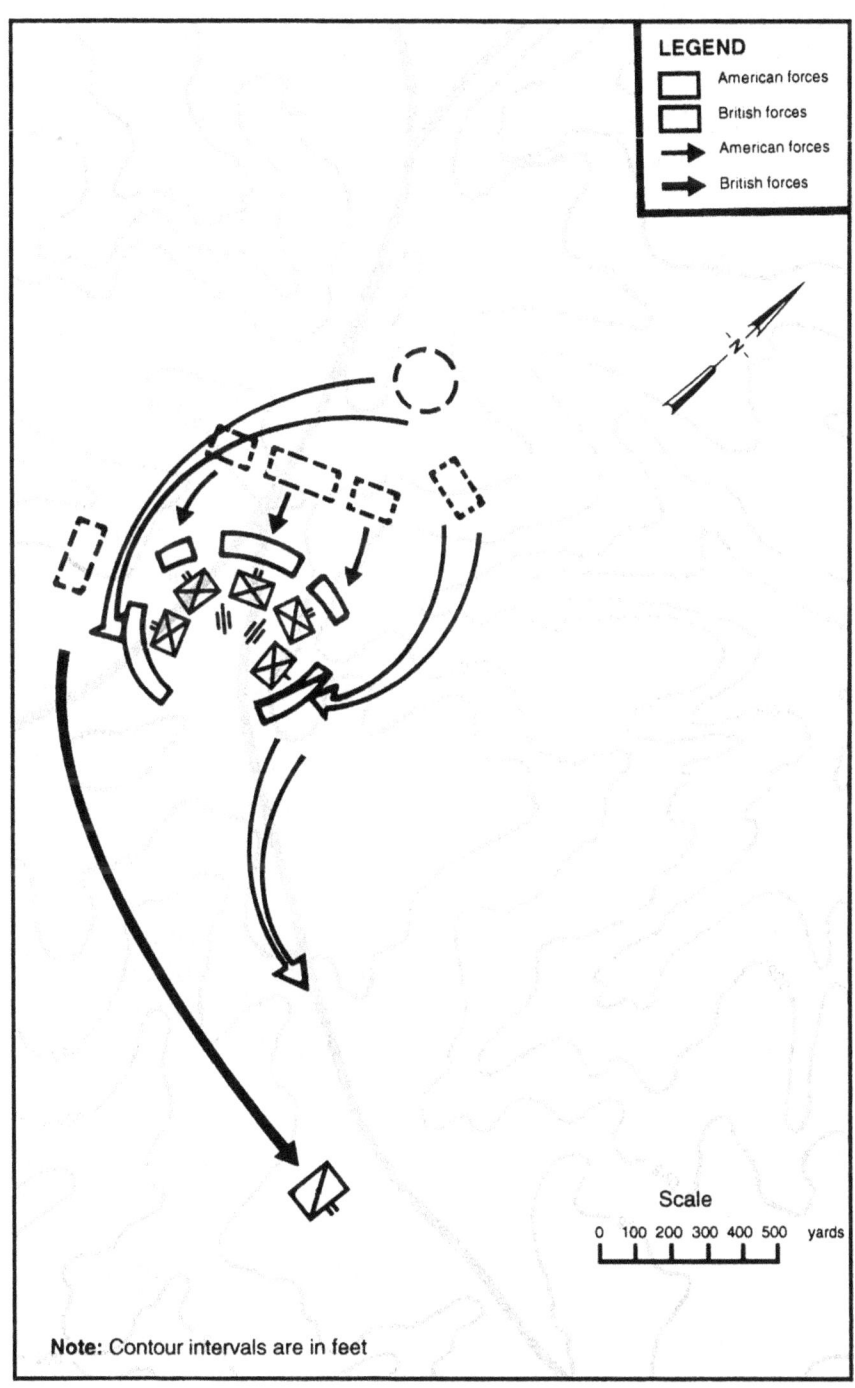

Map 14. Envelopment and destruction, 0750, 17 January 1781

Veterans disputed who received whose sword that hectic morning. Colonel Pickens vaguely recalls that "every officer of that Regiment [the 71st] delivered his sword into my hand."[52] Howard also remembers being given one of those same swords. In any case, the entire infantry of Tarleton's command had become prisoners or were dead.

In a vain effort to retrieve the day, Tarleton attempted to rally his horsemen. Washington had beaten them twice that day; most left the field precipitately. Nonetheless, the Green Dragoon, ever audacious, took fifty loyal troopers—most of them regulars from the 17th Light Dragoons—again into the fray where, once again, they were repulsed. This engagement effectively ended the Battle of the Cowpens.

The battle ended, but its most famous moment remained for the postscript. As Washington and his men chased down Tarleton and his fifty gallant paladins, Tarleton turned at bay several hundred yards away from the scene of triumph and surrender, and Washington and Tarleton crossed swords during the sort of heroic melee expected of cavalrymen. The Virginian may well have been killed were it not for the sure aim of a black soldier who shot one of Washington's assailants.[53] Although Washington's cavalry pursued Tarleton vigorously for twenty-two miles,[54] they were unable to capture him or his little band, but the whole of his baggage was either destroyed or captured.

As the gun smoke cleared, the scene must have seemed horrible. In that small field, ten British officers and more than 100 other ranks lay dead and more than 200 wounded.[55] By comparison, the American toll was mercifully light: 10 to 12 killed and 50 to 60 wounded.[56] There were also more than 500 tired, hungry, and frightened British prisoners, now being disarmed instead of killed (as they had been led to believe). The total loss to the British numbered about 850. Even the victors must have looked unsightly. Not yet nine o'clock, the Americans had overcome the collective effects of fatigue, cold, and the fear that accompanies uncertainty in the face of combat. But it was over; all that remained was collecting the prisoners for transport to safety in Virginia and movement of the army to rejoin Greene.

The small battle on that cold gray morning in January 1781 did not alter the outcome of the war or even the course of the campaign in the south. It did continue the momentum created by the victory over Ferguson's Loyalists at King's Mountain, and it showed the population in the western regions that Tarleton (and, even better, British regulars) could be beaten. The value of the Cowpens as an object of study lies in the tactical arena and the human drama of the participants.

From available evidence, it seems clear that Morgan understood the temperament of his opponent. He lured Tarleton across the Broad River away from Cornwallis. Morgan's army was too small to grapple with the British unaided, so he kept enough distance from Tarleton until he could rally the militia. To maximize the potential of his militia, Morgan deployed his little force to entice Tarleton to attack, while compensating for the potential of Tarleton's cavalry to disrupt his own army. The several counterattacks Washington conducted to parry British attempts to flank him demonstrate his understanding of the proper use of reserves and cavalry. No evidence leads us to conclude that Morgan anticipated or planned the double envelopment. On the other hand, someone had recognized the advantage of reemploying the militia, who must have believed they had done their part already. The only person who could have directed Pickens to counterattack was his commander, Morgan. Even if he did not direct the attack that sealed the fate of the British, Morgan's plan for the battle permitted sufficient flexibility in his men to react to the uncharacteristic collapse of spirit among the redcoated regulars. Daniel Morgan justly deserves the honors accorded him, not for a brilliant Hannibalesque maneuver but for his keen insight into the mind of his opponent and his men and for the construction of a plan that allowed for the unexpected.

NOTES
Chapter 3

1. Extract from Lord Cornwallis' letter to Sir Henry Clinton, 18 January 1781, as cited in Clinton, *Rebellion*, 485.

2. These are Polybius' figures. Polybius, *Histories*, iii, 107. Livy says 45,000 Romans and 2,700 Carthaginians, Livy, *The War with Hannibal*, trans. Aubrey de Sélincourt, ed. Betty Radice (Baltimore, MD, 1968), 149. Historians dispute the actual numbers, but their ratios are about the same in all accounts.

3. Generalfeldmarschall Graf von Schlieffen, *Cannae* (Berlin: E. S. Mittler, 1913). The great German historian Hans Delbrück calls it "a brilliant, unusual victory," *History of the Art of War Within the Framework of Political History*, trans. Walter J. Renfroe, Jr., vol. 1 (Westport, CT: Greenwood Press, 1975), 331. For a thorough discussion of this connection, see Jehuda L. Wallach, *The Dogma of the Battle of Annihilation* (Westport, CT: Greenwood, 1986). Wallach argues that Schlieffen's "obsession with the enemy's annihilation by means of encirclement" and his failure to understand Clausewitz led to the Germans' defeat in World War I.

4. Alexander Garden, Greene's aide de camp, suggests that Morgan's failure to be promoted may have been a consequence of Gates' jealousy at the accolades paid to Morgan's rifle regiment by Burgoyne, *Anecdotes*, 58.

5. William Waller Edwards, "Morgan and his Riflemen," *William and Mary Quarterly*, 1st ser., 23 (October 1914):73–105. After the war, Morgan served in the U. S. Congress. See Bailey, *Heroes*, 9–23. For a fine biography of the American commander, see Higginbotham, *Morgan*.

6. Bartholomees says he was 5 feet 10 inches tall, "Fight or Flee," 102. A most colorful description can be found in Appendix C, in the Neel memoir, 144.

7. See Martin memoir, Appendix B, 104.

8. Washington, of no significant relation to the commander in chief, fought throughout the war with distinction. Transferred to the cavalry after being wounded at Trenton, he fought under Lincoln in South Carolina and skirmished with Tarleton at Ashley Ford and Rantowle's Bridge, Garden, *Anecdotes*, 68.

9. Hammond says red oak and hickory, while Thomas says mostly pine. See memoirs, Appendix C, 131, 145.

10. See also Major Hammond's description of the battle site, Appendix C, 131. Numerous accounts of the battle imply that the Americans deployed with their backs to the Broad River. Nothing could be further from the truth. See Burke

Davis, *The Cowpens-Guilford Courthouse Campaign* (Philadelphia: J. B. Lippencott, 1962), xii; Scheer and Rankin, *Rebels*, 429; Michael D. Mahler, "The 190th Anniversary—The Battle at Cowpens," *Military Review* 51, no.1 (January 1971):57-58.

11. A local patriot, Dennis Tramel, walked the ground with Morgan. See Appendix B, Tramel memoir, 101.

12. William Johnson, *Sketches of the Life and Correspondence of Nathanael Greene*, vol. 1 (Charleston, SC: A. E. Miller, 1822), 376.

13. See Tarleton memoir, Appendix E, 188.

14. For example, see Christopher Hibbert, *Redcoats and Rebels* (New York: W. W. Norton, 1990), 302. See discussion in Bartholomees, "Fight or Flee," 115.

15. See Appendix B, Gresham memoir, 99; and Seymour memoir, 102. Because of Morgan's attention to security, not all of the militia were able to participate, Harden memoir, 105.

16. See Young memoir, Appendix B, 96.

17. See Moore memoir, Appendix B, 110.

18. See McJunkin, Apppendix C, 133.

19. See Howard, Appendix C, 126; and McJunkin, 133.

20. This tactic was customary for light troops and considered very effective in disrupting the continuity of massed formations. In 1757, the celebrated French commander and theorist Marshal Saxe wrote, "a single fire from one of these irregulars perfected in his business, will in general do as much execution, as ten from any other . . . ," Field-Marshal Count Saxe, *Reveries or Memoirs upon the Art of War* (Westport, CT: Greenwood, 1971), 38. By comparison, muskets were accurate only from 80 to 100 meters; however, they could be fired twice as rapidly as rifles. For a discussion of Revolutionary War weaponry, see Davis, *Cowpens*, 13–15; Harold L. Peterson, *The Book of the Continental Soldier* (Harrisburg, PA: Stackpole, 1968), 23–57

21. According to Howard, "they fell into our rear, and part of them fell into the rear of my right flank . . . ," memoir, Appendix C, 126. By implication, then, the flank around which Howard expected them to withdraw was his left. John Baldwin, of McDowell's command, claimed later that they were to withdraw around both flanks. John Thomas remembered the militia plan to move around the right flank. See pension applications, 145.

22. Howard was born in Baltimore County in 1752 and served with the Maryland Line throughout the war. He fought at White Plains, Germantown, and Monmouth before moving south in 1780. After Camden, he was the ranking Continental officer in the south, Bailey, *Heroes*, 38–43.

23. The discussion that follows relies on evidence from Morgan, Howard, Hammond, McJunkin, Young, Anderson, Sergeant Major Seymour, and Private Thomas, all from Appendix C.

24. A Prussian infantry battalion, elbow to elbow, three ranks deep (with the front rank kneeling), occupied a front of 150 yards, Steven Ross, *From Flintlock to Rifle Infantry Tactics, 1740–1866* (Rutherford, NJ: Fairleigh Dickenson University Press, 1979), 25. The Continental Line, however, preferred two lines of men standing about three yards apart, Ernest W. Peterkin, *The Exercise of Arms in the Continental Infantry* (Alexandria Bay, NY: Museum Restoration Service, 1989), 10–11.

25. See Morgan report, Appendix C, 122.

26. See Mackenzie calls these men vedettes, Appendix C, 151. See Young memoir, 148.

27. See Appendix C, Hammond memoir, 135.

28. Numerous chroniclers report that the battle began at sunrise, but none mention the sun. On the other hand, Captain Connally of North Carolina remembered the day being "cold but inclined to be rainey," 176. Even with cloud cover, ambient light would permit visibility at musket range by 0700. Sunrise occurred at 0707 (+/- 2 minutes), per a phone conversation with the U.S. Naval Observatory, 6 March 1992. Thus, morning twilight would have begun about an hour earlier. Clouds benefited the Americans, who would otherwise have had the early morning sun in their eyes. Lieutenant Anderson describes the British forming before sunrise, Appendix C, 139.

29. General Morgan reported that scouts told him about an hour before daylight that the British were within five miles of his position and heading in his direction and that he deployed accordingly. Lieutenant Anderson, Appendix C, memoir 139, confirms the report. The British could not have marched five miles through the Thicketty Creek underbrush in one hour, but both time and distance are estimates here.

30. Here I follow Bartholomees' interpretation of the description, "Fight or Flee," 123. Tarleton received a report that the Broad River ran parallel to Morgan's rear. See Tarleton, Appendix C, 148.

31. The British trimmed their line from three to two ranks in depth, at least in part because their experience in America led them to accept the risk in exchange for increased firepower. The practice was the subject of hot debate in British military circles, E. M. E. Lloyd, *A Review of the History of Infantry* (Westport, CT: Greenwood Press, 1976), 187

32. Compare Tarleton memoir, Appendix C, 148, with Mackenzie memoir, Appendix E, 191.

33. All other evidence being equal, I prefer to follow Mackenzie, who had less to gain by condemning Tarleton than the cavalryman had to lose by being condemned.

34. Sir George Hanger, who served with the cavalry of the British Legion, published a stirring defense of Tarleton in 1789. While Hanger's arguments bring caution to our acceptance of Lieutenant Mackenzie's account, we must keep in mind that Hanger was not present at the Cowpens and, as a legionnaire, would be inclined to loyalty to the man who made his organization famous, Hanger, *Address*, 92–93. Hanger also served with Hessian troops in the war and retired a major general in the Hessian service, Johann Ewald, *Diary of the American War: A Hessian Journal*, trans. and ed. Joseph P. Tusten (New Haven, CT: Yale University Press, 1979), 412.

35. See Anderson memoir, Appendix C, 139; and Dial memoir, Appendix B, 106. These guns were accurate to 800 meters, Davis, *Cowpens*, 16.

36. See McJunkin, Appendix C, 133. Young quotes Lieutenant Colonel Farr of the South Carolina militia as claiming he directed Savage to fire the shot, Appendix C, memoir, 135. See also Bailey, *Heroes*, who may be quoting Young, 191; and Bobby Gilmer Moss, *The Patriots of the Cowpens* (Greenville, SC: Scotia Press, 1985), 96, 256–57.

37. Howard remembered the British line made a great deal of noise to intimidate the Americans, Appendix C, 126. Anderson noted in his diary that "three Huzzas" came from the British line, Appendix C, 139.

38. Morgan's report to Greene states that the militia fired "by regiments." The actual term for volley firing is "by platoons" organized deliberately to keep an incessant fire on the enemy. Probably Pickens' men executed the first volley on command. Given the state of training and organization and the conflicting reports of the number of rounds expended, it is more likely that the militia fired most of their rounds without command. For a discussion of eighteenth-century firing methods, see Ross, *Flintlock*, 25, 26. See also Thomas memoir, Appendix C, 145.

39. See Young memoir, Appendix C, 135.

40. See Chesney memoir, Appendix C, 163; and E. Alfred Jones, ed., *The Journal of Alexander Chesney* (Ohio State University), 90–91.

41. See Baldwin memoir, Appendix C, 154; and Thomas memoir, 145.

42. See McJunkin memoir, Appendix C, 133, on the incident at this moment concerning rifleman Joseph Hughes and the already noted John Savage.

43. See Tarleton memoir, Appendix C, 148.

44. See Morgan, Howard, and Thomas memoirs, Appendix C, 122, 126, 145.

45. See Morgan, Appendix C, 122. Howard remembered it as a "destructive fire," 126–31.

46. See Howard memoir, Appendix C, 126; and Thomas memoir, 145. Lieutenant Anderson claims the range of the British was only ten to fifteen meters, 151.

47. See McJunkin and Young memoirs, Appendix C, 133, 135.

48. See Collins memoir, Appendix C, 145.

49. A 1928 study of the battle suggests that Morgan was in the rear rallying the militia when he saw the Continentals beginning to withdraw. This study cites no authority for the claim, *Historical Statements Concerning the Battle of King's Mountain and the Battle of the Cowpens, South Carolina* (Washington, DC: U.S. Government Printing Office, 1928), 68. Lynn Montross echoes this scenario in "America's Most Imitated Battle," *American Heritage* 7, no. 3 (1956):37. Bailey and Alice Noble Waring claim Pickens acted on his own initiative, *Heroes*, 29; and *The Fighting Elder: Andrew Pickens, 1739–1817* (Columbia: University of South Carolina Press, 1962), 48. Kenneth Roberts describes North Carolina militia lieutenant, Joseph Hughes, as corralling the men as they attempted to scamper away, in *The Battle of the Cowpens: The Great Morale Builder* (Garden City, NY: Doubleday, 1958), 89–90.

50. See Tarleton memoir, Appendix C, 148.

51. Cannon, like regimental colors, were considered to be trophies of war, to be guarded and sought with great zeal. To lose either was a disgrace. See Howard memoir, 126.

52. See Pickens memoir, Appendix C, 125.

53. See Kelley, Appendix C, 142. The soldier's name was Ball. See Garden, *Anecdotes*, 69.

54. See Simmons memoir, Appendix C, 143.

55. Morgan reported these numbers to General Greene shortly after the battle, memoir, Appendix C, 122.

56. See Morgan memoir, Appendix C, 122; and Fortescue, *17th Lancers*, 58. Seymour reports thirty-five killed and wounded; he may have been referring to the Continentals only, memoir, 153. Compare Tarleton's estimates of the casualties, memoir, 160.

IV. THE STAFF RIDE

Unlike many of the popular battlefields that sprawl across the countryside littered with memorials, the site where the battle of the Cowpens was fought can be viewed, almost entirely, from one spot. But for a single memorial to a Charleston militia unit and a marked trail for visitors, the field is free of obstructions. Moreover, the park rangers of the Cowpens National Battlefield have carefully maintained the foliage to match extant accounts of its former appearance. Although the boundaries of the original ground cannot be precisely determined, the estimated widths of the contesting forces suggest that the approximate shape and size of the battlefield correspond to the area maintained today by the rangers.

Today, a gravel walking trail wanders in a lazy oval around the battlefield, extending from the Visitor's Center through what was once the American camp, down the right flank of the American positions, past the spot where the British deployed, and to the farthest point of the clearing where Tarleton's forces debouched from the woods the morning of the battle. As the path continues back to the Visitor's Center, it passes inside the British right flank and on to the left flank of the Continental Line and the reserve position of the 3d Continental Light Dragoons. Periodically spaced along the trail are sketches of the soldiers who fought there, with captions describing the action. In many cases, taped narratives supplement the captions. One can negotiate the trail, stopping at each vantage point, (see vantages at map 15, page 73) in about an hour. This chapter will suggest a more detailed and extensive analysis of the battle that will use the same trail but consume an additional hour.

The path suggested for this staff ride follows the trail but, because of the different focus of this exercise, does not generally use the vantages provided by the park service. To facilitate this staff ride, I have numbered the vantage points where significant action happened on maps and have generally provided anecdotes and points for discussion in a chronological fashion. Beginning at Vantage 2 and proceeding till the study group reaches Vantage 6, I orient the reader to troop dispositions and the planning behind them. From Vantage 6 on, I analyze the battle beginning with the British advance. The trail is marked on the maps attached to this work to indicate the vantages suggested by the text.

Note to the Staff Ride Leader: One method of preparation for staff rides that personally involves the participants is to assign them roles prior to their visit to the battlefield. The appendixes, by providing sketches of the actors in the battle, facilitate such an approach. If sufficient numbers participate, the role of Howard, for example, could be assigned to one person, while someone else could be responsible for the perspective of, say, Sergeant Major Seymour. If the group is smaller, one person might be assigned to master the perspective of the entire Continental Line. Then, at each vantage, participants could act out or discuss their roles in the battle.

Vantage 1

(Morgan's camp)

Situation: From this vantage looking north about three hundred meters is the actual spot of Morgan's camp the night before the battle. On the night of 15 January 1781, Tarleton surprised some of Morgan's pickets on the banks of the Pacolet River. Morgan then moved his little army quickly to Burr's Mill on Thicketty Creek and thence to the well-known gathering place at the Cowpens, closing with his enemy on the evening of 16 January. He immediately sent word to militia leaders in the district to join him there. Before he finalized his plan, Morgan walked over the ground he had chosen to defend, selecting the positions for each component of his army.[1] That night, as he prepared his forces for battle, he concentrated on three key factors: synchronization, logistics, and morale. Major Hammond explains:

> Orders had been issued to the militia, to have twenty-four rounds of balls prepared and ready for use, before they retired to rest. A general order, forming the disposition of the troops, in case of coming to action, had also been prepared, and was read to Colonels Pickens and McCall, Major Jackson and [me], in the course of the evening.[2]

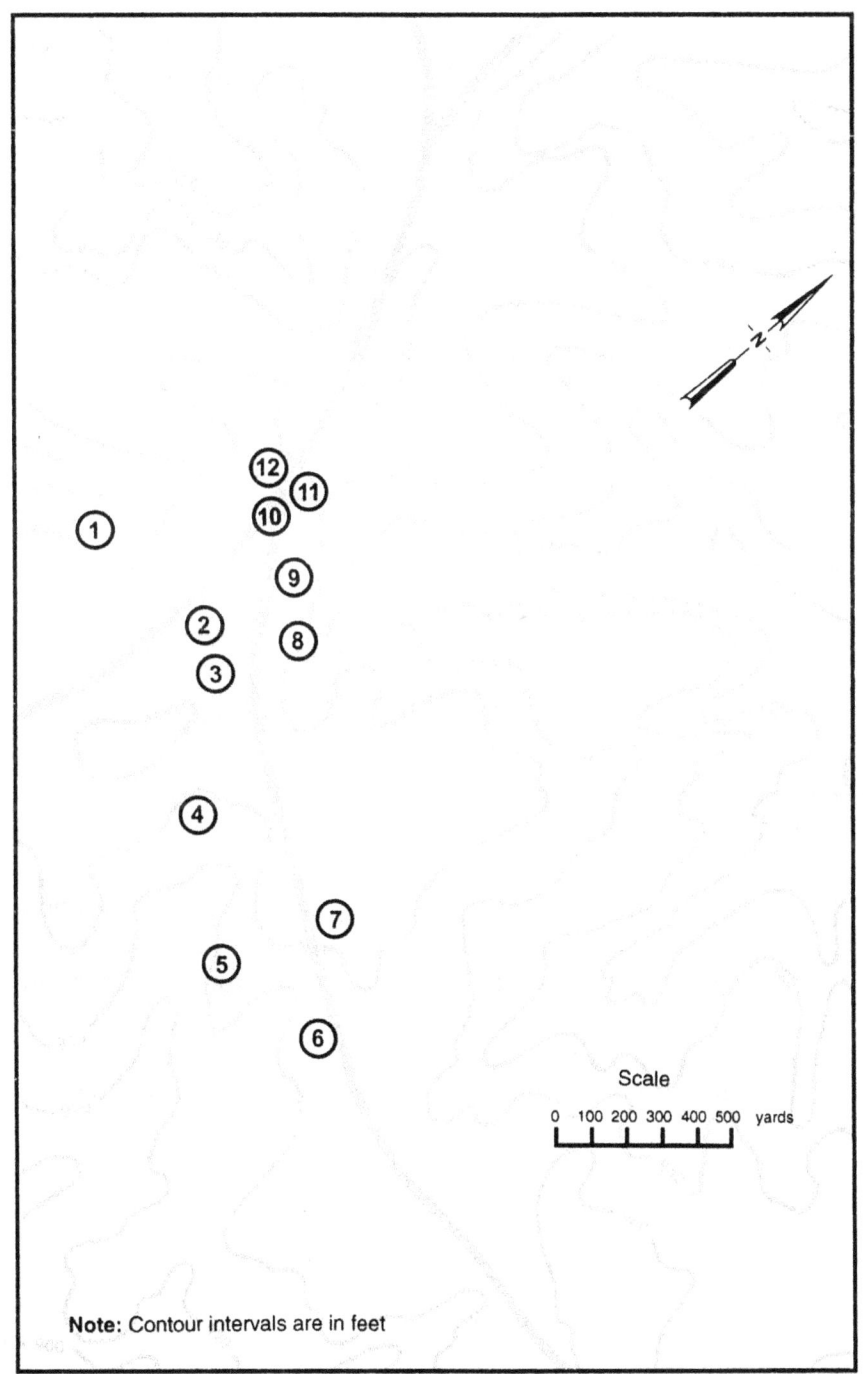

Map 15. Staff ride vantage points 1–12

Ensuring that his soldiers were well-fed and that their arms were prepared for the following day, Morgan went around the campfires speaking with the troops. He appealed to the patriotic sentiments of North Carolina militiamen whose enlistments had expired, begging them to stay.[3] One of his militia officers remembered:

> ... long after I laid down, he was going about among the soldiers encouraging them, and telling them that the old wagoner would crack his whip over Ben. (Tarleton) in the morning, as sure as they lived.
>
> "Just hold up your heads, boys, three fires," he would say, "and you are free, and when you return to your homes, how the old folks will bless you, and the girls kiss you, for your gallant conduct!" I don't believe he slept a wink that night.[4]

Teaching points: Leadership, logistics, planning ahead, commander's intent, and morale.

Vantage 2

(Main line of defense)

Situation: The right flank of the Continental Line rested upon the "head of the ravine on the right" at approximately this spot. From here, in two lines, the Continentals lay across and roughly perpendicular to Mill Gap Road stretching to the northeast. General Morgan placed his best troops in the main line of defense on the reverse slope of a hill with an elevation of 990 feet. Thus, although the British knew where the Americans were, they could not determine the precise deployment of Morgan's main defenses. Additionally, when the British troops advanced upon the Continental Line, as Morgan expected them to do, they would be more likely to fire over the heads of the Continentals, who stood at a slightly lower elevation (about 970 feet).

Teaching Points: Tactics, formations of 1781, surprise, and operational security.

Vantage 3

(Militia line)

Situation: Morgan placed the militia about 150 meters in front of the Continental Line. From their right flank, at approximately this spot, patriots from the Carolinas, Georgia, and Virginia stood in loose order, parallel to the Continental Line. As they had been told the night before, the militia were to fire three volleys and pass around the regulars. Because of their numbers and their loose order, the militia were anchored on the edge of the woods, where the thicker underbrush would prevent the escape of grazing cattle in peacetime or, in this context, a formation being outflanked by British cavalry.

Teaching Points: Operational security, the role of militia, and planning ahead.

Vantage 4

(*Skirmish line*)

Situation: On the trail about 150 meters beyond the marker for the colonial militia (4), stop to discuss the skirmish line, which runs parallel to the militia line and perpendicular to Mill Gap Road (Green River Road). Morgan directed that militia commanders select crack marksmen armed with rifles from among their troops and place them in a skirmish line.[5] These skirmishers, hiding behind trees, were to place aimed fire out to 300 meters, selecting officers as targets. Eighteenth-century officers could be identified at that range by their epaulets and gorgets (small brass chest plates reminiscent of body armor). The tactic of skirmishing common in America among Native Americans and European units trained to fight them was a relatively new concept for Continental forces. Marshal Saxe advocated the use of such skirmishers in the 1750s, and by the time of the American Revolution, infantry units usually had light infantry companies designed to deploy in loose order to disrupt the continuity of the massed formations of the day. These formations, however, rarely carried rifles, which could fire accurately 200 meters beyond the range of muskets.

Teaching Points: Technology and light infantry in the eighteenth century.

Vantage 5

(*British line of battle*)

Situation: The British forces straddled Mill Gap Road, stretching from the left flank at Vantage 5 to the right flank about 300 yards to the northeast. Tarleton deployed his forces in typical European fashion, companies on line. On the extreme left flank stood two troops of British Legion cavalry under Captain Ogilvie. This unit, raised in 1778 from Loyalists in the middle-Atlantic colonies, was commanded by Tarleton himself and brought south in 1779 (the other units under his direction at the Cowpens had only been attached). Of the 250 troopers present at the battle, Tarleton assigned 50 to the left flank, "to protect their own [flank], and threaten the flanks of the enemy."[6] These men had served as the advanced guard for the army.

Forming the infantry line were the 7th Fusiliers, the infantry of the Legion, and several companies of light infantry from the 16th Foot, the 71st Highlanders, and the Prince of Wales American Regiment. Although most of the infantry were British regulars, they could hardly be considered crack troops. The 7th Regiment consisted of recruits, and the largest number in the line, the Legion infantry, were not regulars in any case. Interspersed among the infantry were the only two cannon present at the battle, manned by about twenty gunners of the Royal Artillery. Altogether, these troops numbered about 500 men. To their right were stationed the fifty troopers of the 17th Light Dragoons.

Not present in the British main line were the 1st Battalion, 71st Highlanders, and the bulk of the Legion cavalry, which fell last in the order of march. These British troops were tired and hungry and had been hurrying to meet Morgan for several days. After taking Morgan's recently evacuated camp at Grindal Shoals in the late night, they rested briefly and renewed the hunt just five hours later at 0300 on 17 January.[7] With little rest and no hot meals, the British and Loyalist troops cut their way through marshes and broken ground to reach the Cowpens at daybreak.[8]

Teaching Points: Formations of 1781, linear battlefield, psychological effects of fatigue, task organization, and security.

Vantage 6

(British deployment)

Situation: This vantage stands on Mill Gap Road at approximately the spot where Tarleton's troops emerged from the thick underbrush into the clearing of the Cowpens. After passing Thicketty Creek, Tarleton had ordered up two troops of Legion cavalry under Ogilvie. Shortly thereafter, the troopers captured several scouts under Captain Inman, who was posted to give early warning of the approach of the British. The report of this incident confirmed Tarleton's intelligence that the Americans were ahead and spurred him forward. Ogilvie soon reported gaining contact with an American force formed for battle. Guides described the terrain to Tarleton accurately: open woods with the Broad River six miles off the left flank of the rebel position and curving around their rear. Tarleton (referring to himself in the third person) wrote:

> Lieutenant Colonel Tarleton having attained a position, which he certainly might deem advantageous, on account of the vulnerable situation of the enemy, and the supposed vicinity of the two British corps [Lord Cornwallis' and General Leslie's] on the east and west of the Broad River, did not hesitate to undertake those measures which the instructions of his commanding officer [Lord Cornwallis] imposed, and his own judgment, under the present appearances, equally recommended.

Tarleton ordered Ogilvie to scatter the skirmishers, who obscured his view, and then surveyed the American dispositions personally. Tarleton continued:

> He discovered that the American commander had formed a front line of about one thousand militia, and had composed his second line and reserve of five hundred continental light infantry, one hundred and twenty of Washington's cavalry, and three hundred back woodsmen.[9] This accurate knowledge being obtained, Tarleton desired the British infantry to disencumber themselves of every thing, except their arms and ammunition: The light infantry were then ordered to file to the right till they became equal to the flank of the American front line: The

legion infantry were added to their left; and, under the fire of a 3-pounder, this part of the British troops was instructed to advance within three hundred yards of the enemy. This situation being acquired, the 7th regiment was commanded to form upon the left of the legion infantry, and the other 3-pounder was given to the right division of the 7th: A captain, with fifty dragoons, was placed on each flank of the corps, who formed the British front line, to protect their own, and threaten the flanks of the enemy: the 1st battalion of the 71st was desired to extend a little to the left of the 7th regiment, and to remain one hundred and fifty yards in the rear. This body of infantry, and near two hundred cavalry, composed the reserve. During the execution of these arrangements, the animation of the officers and the alacrity of the soldiers afforded the most promising assurances of success.[10]

Teaching Points: Decisiveness, audacity, flexibility, intelligence estimate, meeting engagement, reconnaissance and reporting, and reserves.

Vantage 7

(*British advance*)

Situation: From Vantage 6, walk northwest along Mill Gap Road (toward the Vistor's Center) about 200 meters. You are now standing in the center of the skirmish line sent forward from Pickens' militia. Two hundred meters to your front is the main militia line. After the British troops dropped their packs and aligned themselves on the enemy to their front, Tarleton gave the order to advance. The attack began with fire from the two light artillery pieces and "three huzzas" from the soldiers.[11] Moving forward at a steady walk, the British received fire from sharpshooters behind the trees. The sharpshooters picked off several officers, then withdrew back into the main militia line. One memoir writer recalled:

> A column marches up in front of Brandon's men led by a gayly dressed officer on horseback. The word passes along the line, "Who can bring him down? John Savage looked Col. Farr full in the face and read yes in his eye. He darted a few paces in front, laid his rifle against a sapling, a blue gas streamed above his head, the sharp crack of a rifle broke the solemn stillness of the occasion and a horse without rider wheeled from in front of the advancing column. In a few minutes the fire is general.[12]

Unswerving, the British troops continued their advance. Morgan admiringly reported that the militia "gave them a heavy and galling fire." Nonetheless, given the rate of fire, the rate of advance, and the maximum effective range of the eighteenth-century musket, steady British troops armed with sixteen-inch bayonets were an intimidating force to backwoodsmen armed with slow-firing rifles or a mixed assortment of personal firearms. After firing three volleys, the militia withdrew around the flanks of the Continental Line in accordance with Morgan's directive. Far from a panicked retreat, their orderly movement evoked the admiration of the sergeant major of the Delaware Regiment, who noted, "They retreated, but in very good order, not seeming to be the least bit confused."[13] Throughout the action, the British advanced at a steady pace. The British believed they had occasioned the withdrawal. Lieutenant Mackenzie reported haughtily: "The military valour of British troops . . . was not to be resisted by an American militia. They gave way on all quarters, and were pursued to their continentals."[14]

Teaching Points: Withdrawal under pressure, skirmishers, discipline, close combat, and assessment of battlefield information.

Vantage 8

(Dragoons' pursuit of the militia)

Situation: Walk another 300 meters toward the Visitor's Center. This spot is the center of the line of the initial position of the Continental Line, the left flank of which extended about 100 meters to the northeast. Having fired the three volleys Morgan asked it to, the militia promptly withdrew, "retreating agreeably to their orders."[15] Seeing the withdrawal of the militia, the fifty troopers of the 17th Light Dragoons fell upon them in pursuit, cutting and slashing at the back of the Americans. One frightened militiaman recounted his fear at that moment: "'Now,' I thought, 'my hide is in the loft.'"[16] Available to meet this situation was Washington, charged by Morgan to wait "at such a distance in [the rear of the Continental Line] as not to be subjected to the line of fire directed at them, and to be so near as to be able to charge [the British] should [the line] be broken."[17]

Not specifically targeted at the British dragoons, Washington was nonetheless ideally positioned, according to the McJunkin memoir:

> Two dragoons assault a large rifleman, Joseph Hughes by name. His gun was empty, but with it he parries their blows and dodges round a tree, but they still persist. At the moment the assault on Hughes began John Savage was priming his rifle. Just as they pass the tree to strike Hughes he levels his gun and one of the dragoons tumbles from his horse pierced with a bullet. The next moment the rifle carried by Hughes, now literally backed over, slips out of his hands and inflicts such a blow upon the other dragoon that he quits the contest and retires hanging by the mane of his horse.

Soon, however, the militia are relieved from the British dragoons by a charge of the American light horse. The British cavalry are borne from the field.[18]

The same militiaman whose "hide" was "in the loft" was delivered from the saber of a British dragoon and later described admiringly the effect of Washington's counterattack:

> Col. Washington's cavalry was among them, like a whirlwind, and the poor fellows began to kneel from their horses, without being able to remount. The shock was so sudden and violent, they could not stand it, and immediately betook themselves to flight.[19]

According to Cornet James Simmons of the 3d Continental Dragoons, the American horsemen "after a smart Action . . . instantly defeated [the dragoons] leaving in the course of ten minutes 18 of their brave 17th Dragoons dead on the spot . . ."[20]

Teaching Points: Initiative, mission-type orders, commander's intent, shock action, and counterattack.

Vantage 9

(Colonel Howard's misunderstood order)

Situation: One hundred meters behind the militia array stood the Continental Line, with the attached Virginians under Wallace on the right flank and those of Triplett and Tate on the left. It is unlikely that the Americans, Continental Line or militia, stood in parade-perfect order.[21] Stretched at open order in two ranks, the line would have been about 200 meters long. The main line of defense, the Continental Line of Howard, was well prepared. They were fed, rested, and their arms and equipment ready. They had seen the militia perform as expected, "Well Disputing the ground that Was between them and us," and in good spirits.[22] The withdrawal of the militia, however, not only triggered the pursuit of the 17th Light Dragoons but also caused the British, accustomed to success against Americans in open battle, to sense that the tide had turned their way. Tarleton directed the infantry to continue their advance and for the Legion cavalry to attack around the 71st, who were attempting to go around the American flank. According to Tarleton, the British pushed forward and exchanged fire with the Continental Line:

> As the contest between British infantry in the front line and the continentals seemed equally balanced, neither retreating, Lieutenant-colonel Tarleton thought the advance of the 71st into line, and a movement of cavalry in reserve to threaten the enemy's right flank, would put a victorious period into the action. The 71st were desired to pass the 7th before they gave their fire, and were directed not to entangle their right flank with the left of the other battalion. The cavalry was ordered to incline to the left, and to form a line, which would embrace the whole of the enemy's right flank. Upon the advance of the 71st, all the infantry moved on: the continentals and back woodsmen [Virginians] gave ground: The British rushed forwards.[23]

While Tarleton saw the reaction of the Continentals to the threat from the 71st as another sign of the rebel force giving way, the reality behind the American lines was far different. Howard, seeing the British attempt to move around his right, ordered Wallace's company of Virginians to "refuse the flank," that is, to swing back about 45 degrees thus making the flank more distant from the British column and therefore harder to gain. What method he chose to convey the order, he does not tell us, but Wallace misunderstood it. Rather than refusing the flank, the Virginians withdrew straight to their rear. As Howard recalled:

> The officers along the line, seeing this, and supposing that orders had been given for a retreat, faced their men about, and moved off. Morgan, who had mostly been with the militia, quickly rode up to me and expressed apprehensions of the event; but I soon removed his fears by pointing to the line, and observing that the men were not beaten who

retreated in that order. He then ordered me to keep with the men, until we came to the rising ground near Washington's horse; and he rode forward to fix on the most proper place for us to halt and face about. In a minute we had perfect line.[24]

Meanwhile, the Legion cavalry attack Tarleton had ordered never developed.[25]

Teaching Points: Confusion, effects of morale, maneuver, location of the commander, fratricide, withdrawal under pressure, synchronization, improvisation, and battlefield communications.

Vantage 10

(The Continental Line fires)

Situation: Move 100 meters along Mill Gap Road to the northeast. The Continental Line moved here with its center of mass at this spot and its dispositions parallel to their primary position.

When Howard's Continentals reached the spot Morgan had marked, he ordered the men to face about and fire into the ranks of the attacking British, now less than fifty meters to their front. The surprise was complete; the British, who believed the Continentals had lost their nerve at the sight of the bayonets, had broken ranks with the intent to deliver the killing blow. Howard recorded the British surprise: "Our men commenced destructive fire, which they [the enemy] little expected, and a few rounds occasioned great disorder in their ranks."[26] Anderson recorded the action:

> The Enemy thinking We Were broke set up a great Shout Charged us With their bayonets but in no Order. We let them Come Within ten Or fifteen yards of us then give them a full Volley and at the Same time Charged home. They not expecting any Such thing put them in Such Confusion that We Were in amongst them With the Bayonets Which Caused them to give ground and at last to take to the flight.[27]

Tarleton admitted that his troops were thrown into confusion by the sudden and unexpected fire from the Continentals: "An unexpected fire at this instant from the Americans, who came about as they were retreating, stopped the British, and threw them into confusion. Exertions to make them advance were useless."[28]

Teaching Points: Psychological impact, effect of firepower, and surprise.

Vantage 11

(Encirclement)

Situation: Looking back down Mill Gap Road at this point in the battle, you would see the American line advancing immediately to your front, with militia returning to the action around Howard's right flank and Washington around Howard's left to embrace the British in a double envelopment. Out of harm's way to your right front would be 250 Legion cavalry. Morgan, now confronted with this sudden and unanticipated reversal of fortune, rapidly assessed the situation and directed movement of the troops in reserve to envelop the demoralized British. The Continental Line pushed the British with bayonets from the front, as the reserves sealed off their withdrawal. Accounts differ, however, as to the precise mechanism by which the militia and dragoons were set in motion around the flanks. Howard claims that Washington charged of his own volition. Young recalled Colonel Brandon riding up to Washington to initiate the charge—implying that an order had come from Morgan or a request from Pickens. Collins remembered that Morgan rode in front of the militia and cried, "Form, form, my brave fellows! give them one more fire and the day is ours. Old Morgan was never beaten."[29] Morgan, in his report to General Greene, sheds no light on the issue. The envelopment could have been the brain child of Pickens or Washington; however, Morgan, free with mention of the valor and virtue of his subordinates in his dispatch recording the battle, makes no mention of either of them in this context. Such coordinated movement of militia and Continental dragoons is difficult between peers in the best of circumstances and nearly impossible in the heat of battle between officers unaccustuomed to working together. Thus, Morgan is the most likely source for the order.

Finally, the combination of lack of sleep and food, the toll among the officers (Mackenzie believed two-thirds of the British officers were casualties), the surprise of the American counterattack, and the isolation of the British from a route of withdrawal caused the British infantry to begin surrendering. Said McJunkin: "One battalion throws down their arms and the men fall to the earth. Another commences flight, but Washington darts before them with his cavalry and they too ground their arms."[30] As the 71st Highlanders, 7th Fusiliers, and Legion infantry laid down their arms, the gunners of the Royal Artillery fought on. During the final British assault, the two guns must have been left slightly to the rear. As the British infantry withdrew before the American bayonets, they left the guns behind. These the artillerymen defended with great valor, according to Hammond:

> My attention was now drawn to an altercation of some of the men with an artillery man, who appeared to make it a point of honour not to surrender his match. The men provoked by his obstinacy, would have bayonetted him on the spot, had I not interfered, and desired them to spare the life of so brave a man. He then surrendered his match.

Teaching Points: Bravery, improvisation, maneuver, psychological impact, stress of combat, initiative, and coordinated attack.

Vantage 12

(*Complete victory*)

Situation: Without moving from Vantage 11, look back to Vantage 5 where the British deployed. Those British troops not caught in the encirclement to your immediate front escaped along Mill Gap Road and disappeared from the battlefield at that point. Tarleton, seeing the desperate circumstances of his infantry, made two attempts to reverse the tide of battle. First, he directed the uncommitted Legion cavalry "to form about four hundred yards to the right of the enemy, in order to check them, whilst he endeavoured to rally the infantry to protect the guns." When these attempts failed, he rode to the Legion cavalry and exhorted them to charge, hoping, as Tarleton recalled, that

> the weight of such an attack might yet retrieve the day, the enemy being much broken by their late rapid advance; but all attempts to restore order, recollection, or courage, proved fruitless. About two hundred dragoons forsook their leader, and left the field of battle.

Undaunted, Tarleton took the remaining fifty horsemen and charged the American cavalry without effect.[31] Seeing the day was lost, Tarleton withdrew with his small band. Lieutenant Colonel Washington followed in pursuit, according to Kelley:

> COL. Washington & two or three men pursued Tarleton 18 or 15 miles & he [Kelley] understood that during this chase Washington would have been killed by one of the British but that one of Washington's men shot the fellow['s] arm off and Washington made a hack at Tarleton & disabled Tarleton[']s fingers & glanced his head with his sword and took a good many prisoners.[32]

A Lieutenant Frazier of the 71st had been left in charge of the baggage. Upon hearing of the outcome of the battle (probably from panicked Legionary cavalry), he destroyed what could not be evacuated and took the wagons to Winnsboro. Young, serving with McCall's horsemen, made for the British trains, about twelve miles to the east, and captured two British soldiers, two servants, and some stores. Some members of his party continued the pursuit resulting in the capture of at least one of the enemy.[33]

Teaching Points: Bravery, initiative, pursuit, and exploitation of success.

NOTES

Chapter 4

1. See Tramel deposition, Appendix B, 101.

2. See Major Hammond's account for the reconstruction of the operations order issued on 16 January 1781, Appendix C, memoir, 96.

3. See Moore memoir, Appendix B, 110.

4. See Young memoir, Appendix B, 96.

5. These men were led (from right flank to left) by Major John Cunningham (Georgia volunteers), Major Charles McDowell (North Carolina militia), Major Samuel Hammond (South Carolina militia), and Captain Donnolly (Georgia volunteers).

6. See Tarleton memoir, Appendix C, 148.

7. According to Mackenzie, the march began at 0200, letter, Appendix C, 151.

8. Mackenzie describes the march as being "rapid," Appendix C, 151–54. Tarleton agrees substantially, but claims the march was "exceedingly slow" because of darkness, terrain, and advanced and flank-guard activities, Tarleton memoir, Appendix C, 148. Each participant obviously wishes to support his assessment of blame. Given the distance involved and the terrain and light conditions, the march was clearly forced.

9. Compare Morgan and Mackenzie for American strength, memoirs, Appendix C, 122, 151.

10. See Tarleton memoir, Appendix C, 148–51.

11. See Anderson memoir, Appendix C, 139.

12. See McJunkin memoir, Appendix C, 141; see also Young memoir, 135.

13. See Seymour memoir, Appendix C, 141.

14. See Mackenzie memoir, Appendix C, 161.

15. See Morgan's report of the battle, Appendix C, 122–25. Not all accounts agree to the same number of rounds being fired. With rifle and musket rates of fire differing and the militia firing without command, the number of rounds expended by the men would have varied from one to five.

16. See Collins memoir, Appendix C, 145.

17. See Morgan's report, Appendix C, 122–25. Washington initially positioned his force behind the left wing of the Continental Line. When the British artillery opened fire, Washington displaced farther to the left (not, as Young says, to the right) in obedience to the spirit of Morgan's instructions, Young memoir, 135.

18. See McJunkin memoir, Appendix C, 133.

19. See Collins memoir, Appendix C, 145.

20. See Cornet James Simmons memoir, Appendix C, 143.

21. See chapter 3 for a discussion of conflicting evidence of the positions of Howard's units.

22. See Anderson memoir, Appendix C, 139. Seymour reported on the state of morale among the Continentals, memoir, 141.

23. See Tarleton memoir, Appendix C, 148.

24. See Howard memoir, Appendix C, 126.

25. Tarleton gives no explanation for the Legion cavalry's failure to comply with orders. Mackenzie says the Legion cavalry "stood aloof," Appendix C, 151–54. But a vague remark by Alexander Chesney, a local Loyalist, suggests one answer: "the prisoners on seeing their own Regt opposed to them in the rear would not proceed against it and broke . . ." See Chesney, Appendix C, memoir, 154–55. If by prisoners Chesney means British Legion troopers who had been captured at Camden, "then their own Regt" refers to Pickens' militia.

26. See Howard memoir, Appendix C, 126. Morgan reported that the Continentals "formed, and advanced on the enemy, and gave them a fortunate volley . . ." This sequence is unlikely as eighteenth-century soldiers fired their muskets from the halt. See Morgan memoir, Appendix C, 122.

27. See Anderson memoir, Appendix C, 139, 41.

28. See Tarleton account, Appendix C, 148–51.

29. See Howard memoir, Appendix C, 126–31; Young memoir, 135; and Collins memoir, 145.

30. See McJunkin memoir, Appendix C, 133.

31. See Tarleton account, Appendix C, 148–51; and Mackenzie letter, 151–54.

32. See Kelley deposition, Appendix C, 142. Tarleton makes no mention of the incident.

33. See Young memoir, Appendix C, 135.

APPENDIX A

Order of Battle

British Force

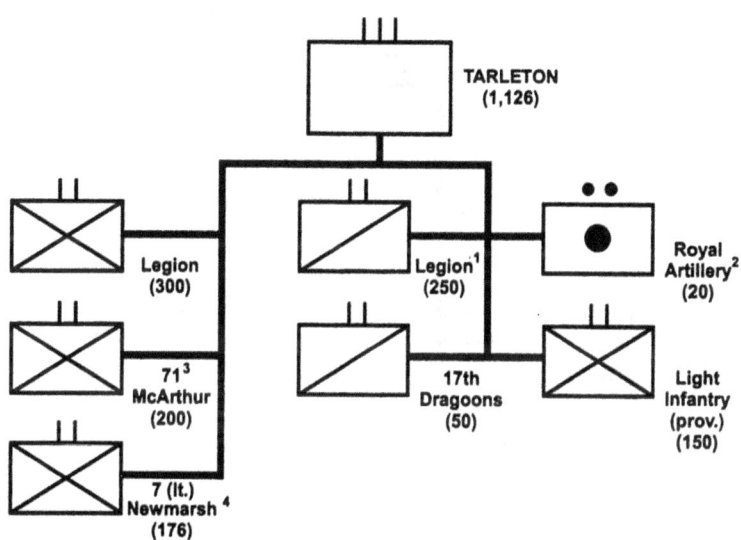

---

1. Mackenzie estimated the total British cavalry force at 350 troopers. Cornwallis' troop returns of 15 January 1781 show 451 in the Legion (Walter Clark, *State Records of North Carolina*, vol. 17 (Goldsboro, NC: Nash Brothers, 1896), 1009.

2. Adrien Carauna lists the crew for the guns at twelve but they could be operated by as few as three gunners, *Grasshoppers and Butterflies: The Light 3-Pounders of Patterson and Townshend* (Bloomfield, Ontario, 1979), 11. The number is an estimate; Lawrence Babits states the number is thirty-six, *Cowpens Battlefield a Walking Tour* (Johnson City, TN: Overmountain Press, 1993), 15.

3. Cornwallis' troop returns for 15 January 1781 show 249 men in the 1st battalion and 69 in the light company, as cited in Clark, *State Record*, vol. 17, 1009. Tarleton says 200, Appendix B, memoir, 112–15.

4. The regimental rolls listed 167 rank and file enlisted and 9 officers, W. Wheaton, *Historical Record of the Seventh Royal Regiment of Fusiliers* (Leeds, 1875), 76; Clark, *State Records*, vol. 17, 1009).

Continental Line (American Forces)

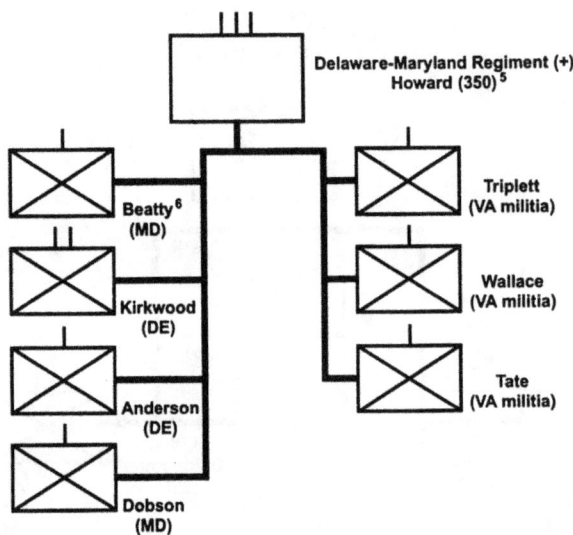

---

5. Mackenzie says the Continental Line was 250, letter, Appendix C, 148–51. Tarleton says 500, memoir, 148–51. Howard recalls "about 350 men" but does not specify whether that number included the militia in his line. I am assuming his number included all those who fell under his operational control for the battle, as depicted here. Babits shows almost 600 in his order of battle, *Cowpens*, 55.

6. Beatty is not listed in Moss, *Patriots*, but his extensive and convincing diary argues otherwise, Beatty memoir, Appendix B, 99.

Militia (American Forces)

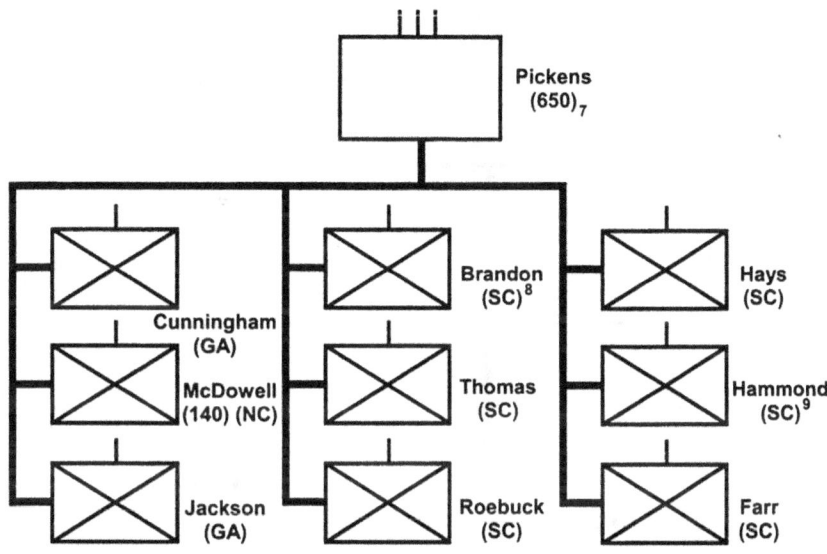

---

7. Colonel Pickens did not actually command all militia forces. They did, however, serve in his line at the battle.

8. Brandon was born in Pennsylvania in 1741 and moved to South Carolina in 1755. He joined Colonel Thomas' Spartan Regiment in 1776, rising to the rank of major, Bailey, *Heroes*, 141–53.

9. Of McCall's command.

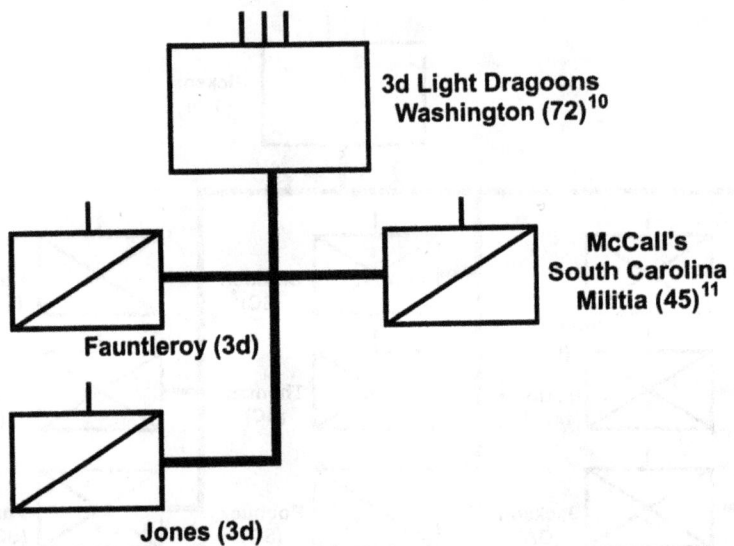

---

10. From Josiah Martin, who counted them on 16 January, memoir, Appendix B, 109.

11. From McJunkin memoir, Appendix C, 133.

APPENDIX B

Documents Pertaining to the Campaign Leading to the Cowpens, 1 November 1780 to 17 January 1781

Contents

	Page
1. Major Samuel Hammond, South Carolina Militia	96
2. Major Thomas Young, South Carolina Militia	96
3. Captain Robert Kirkwood, Delaware Regiment, Continental Army	97
4. Captain William Beatty, Maryland Regiment, Continental Army	99
5. Captain George Gresham, Georgia Militia	99
6. Captain Samuel Sexton, South Carolina Militia	100
7. Captain Dennis Tramel, South Carolina Militia	101
8. Lieutenant Nathaniel Dickison, North Carolina Militia	101
9. Sergeant Major William Seymour, Delaware Regiment,	102
10. First Sergeant Benjamin Martin, Virginia Militia	104
11. Sergeant Lawrence Everhart, 3d Light Dragoons, Continental Army	104
12. Sergeant James Harden, South Carolina Militia	105
13. Private Benjamin Copeland, South Carolina Militia	105
14. Private Jeremiah Dial, South Carolina Militia	106
15. Private Andrew Ferguson, South Carolina Militia	107
16. Private Jeremiah Files, South Carolina Militia	107
17. Private Aaron Guyton, South Carolina Militia	108
18. Private Josiah Martin, North Carolina Militia	109
19. Private Samuel Moore, North Carolina Militia	110
20. Private William Neel, Virginia Militia	110
21. Private Samuel Park, South Carolina Militia	111
22. Lieutenant Colonel Banastre Tarleton, Commander, British Forces	112
23. Lieutenant Roderick Mackenzie, 71st Highland Infantry Regiment	114

1. Major Samuel Hammond of Virginia was elected a lieutenant in 1775 and served in a number of actions with a militia company until 1778. After moving to South Carolina in 1779, he was commissioned a captain and fought numerous actions against Tories, including King's Mountain. At the Cowpens, he commanded McCall's unit in the militia line. After the war, he represented Georgia in the U. S. Congress and served as secretary of state for South Carolina. The following excerpt from a Revolutionary War pension application describes Hammond's war experiences.[1]

> [Hammond] ... continued until Clarks affair on Long Cane near 96 was not in that engagement being out of command at the time was left behind on their retreat, followed with & joined Col William Washington & Col McCall to whose command he was attached & joined Gen Morgan next day was in several light skirmishes with the Enemy previous to the battle of the Cowpens & was with the General there. Commanded on the left of the front line as Major of McCalls Regiment it is here necessary to observe that Col McCall had been promoted to the command of a Regiment of Cavalry authorized to be enrolled for six months & applicant appointed to the Majority Neither had yet been Commissioned, & very [?] few arrived with swords & pistols—the Refugee Militia attached to their respective commands enrolled in the Regiment and were promised by the Governor to be provided with clothing & arms as soon as they could be procured—not a day was lost in recruiting nor was the full number made up before the Battle—the few 25—to 30 that were equipped as Horsemen were placed under Col MCall and attached to Col Washington Command. Those who were not so equipped were armed with rifles & placed under the applicant—After the action the service was so pressing & the movements of the Army so rapid that no accounting could be attended to & after Cowpens the applicant was kept constantly on detachment upon the Enemy's lines, so that he could not recruit in the Army as he had previously done. The evening of the day of the Battle of the 17 he was detached by order of Genl. Morgan to look into Cornwallis' Camp on the Broad River, to report his movement & communicate with Genl. Pickins or himself daily until further orders. This service was performed regularly until the british took up camp at Ramsour's Mills.

2. Major Thomas Young was an officer of the South Carolina militia who had fought at King's Mountain. He describes Morgan's preparations for the battle of the Cowpens, and especially his rallying speech to the militia in this account:[2]

We ... returned to Morgan's encampment at Grindall Shoals, on the Packolette, and there we remained, eating beef and scouting through the neighborhood until we heard of Tarlton's approach. Having received intelligence that Col. Tarlton designed to cross the Packolette at Easternood Shoals above us, Gen. Morgan broke up his encampment early on the morning of the 16th, and retreated up the mountain road by Hancock's Ville, taking the left hand road not far above, in a direction toward the head of Thickety Creek. We arrived at the field of the Cowpens about sun-down, and were then told that there we would meet the enemy. The news was received with great joy by the army. We were very anxious for battle, and many a hearty curse had been vented against Gen. Morgan during that day's march, for retreating, as we thought, to avoid a fight. Night came upon us, yet much remained to be done. It was all important to strengthen the cavalry. Gen. Morgan knew well the power of Tarlton's legion, and he was too wily an officer not to prepare himself as well as circumstances would admit. Two companies of volunteers were called for. One was raised by Major Jolly of Union District, and the other, I think, by Major McCall. I attached myself to Major Jolly's company. We drew swords that night, and were informed we had authority to press any horse not belonging to a dragoon or an officer, into our service for the day.

It was upon this occasion I was more perfectly convinced of Gen. Morgan's qualifications to command militia, than I had ever before been. He went among the volunteers, helped them fix their swords, joked with them about their sweet-hearts, told them to keep in good spirits, and the day would be ours. And long after I had laid down, he was going about among the soldiers encouraging them, and telling them that the old wagoner would crack his whip over Ben. (Tarleton) in the morning, as sure as they lived.

"Just hold up your heads, boys, three fires," he would say, "and you are free, and when you return to your homes, how the old folks will bless you, and the girls kiss you, for your gallant conduct!" I don't believe he slept a wink that night!

3. Captain Robert Kirkwood was commissioned in 1776 and served throughout the war with the Delaware Continentals. This journal reflects the movement of his regiment during the months before and after the Cowpens battle. Kirkwood remained in the army after the American Revolution and was killed in action near Fort Recovery in 1791.[3]

Nov. 4. This day Genl Morgan's Infantry with Col. Washingtons Horse, marched Down to Ridgely's Mill, within 13 miles of Cambden; reconnoitre the Enemy.

9th. Returned again to camp. (100 miles)

22nd.This Day the Maryland Division arrived at Camp.

27. This Day the troops under Command of Genl. Gates marched to Charlotte, where they built Hutts.

28th. This Day had orders to hold our selves in readiness a moments warning to March. Accordingly left our tents standing with all our sick behind and marched to twelve mile Creek, which at this place Divides No. & So. Carolina; & from thence to the Hanging Rock, the Infantry remained at this place until Col. Washington went down to Col. Ridgely's, and with the Deception of a pine knot took the garrisons Consisting of one Col. one Majr. and 107 privates:—from thence returned to Camp, December the second. (100 miles)

Decmbr.

6th. This Day Maj. Genl. Greene took command of the Southern Army in room of Maj. Genl. Gates.

17th. March'd to Charotte (13 miles)

21st. March'd to Biggon Ferry on Catawba River. (13 miles)

22nd. Crossed the Ferry and March'd. (5 miles)

23rd. March'd (16 miles)

24th. March'd (13 miles)

25th. March'd to Pacolet. (8 miles)

Jan. 1st.

11th. March'd. (10 miles)

16th. March'd to the Cowpens. (12 miles)

17th.Defeated Tarlton.

18th.March'd for the Catawba River and arrived the 23rd. (100 miles)

Feb.

1st.March'd to Col. Locke. (30 miles)

2nd. Marched and crossed the Yadkin River. (12 miles)

4th. March'd this night. (13 miles)

5th. March'd this day. (16 miles)

4. Captain William Beatty, in this journal extract, describes the march of Morgan's forces from Charlotte to the Cowpens. The author joined the Continental Army in 1776 and served almost continuously until his death at Hobkirk's Hill, 25 April 1781. At the Cowpens, he commanded a company of the Maryland Line.[4]

> Genl Greene had Superseded Genl Gates in his command of the Southern Army a Day or two before. When I join'd the troops were Hutting which they Compleated a few days after. Decr 16th two Companies of Lt Infantry being ordered out I got Comd of the Compy form'd by the late 7th Regt.
>
> Wednesday Decr 20th 80 the Army march'd from Charlotte 10 miles to Ford's farm; the 21st to Richardson's Creek 18 Miles from Fords; the 22nd to Brown's Creek 19 Miles from Richardson's; the 23rd to Cedar Creek 16 Miles from Brown's; the 24th Pass'd by Anson C. House to Haly's Ferry, 18 Miles from Cedar Creek. The 25 was Taken up in Crossing the Ferry; the 26th we reach'd Hick's Creek 15 Miles below Haly's Ferry in South Carolina. This being the place the Genl intended to take post at, we began to build small Huts, the 27th. January 5th 1781 A Soldier was shot for Desertion.
>
> Jan. 10th A very heavy rain fell which Rais'd the River Pee-Dee and small Creeks so much that the troops were obliged to draw corn in lieu of Meal on the Eleventh.
>
> Friday 12th In the night I went hunting; 13th I wrote to F__ & P__ Wednesday 24th. The Army in consequence of A Victory obtain'd by B. Genl Morgan, on the 17th Instant over a superior force of the Enemy, Comd by Colo Tarleton, near the cowpens fired a Few de joy[5] I wrote to C__ & G. Thursday Jany 25th 81 Genl Stephens Militia left us; their times being expired.

5. Captain George Gresham enlisted in 1777 and served in mounted Georgia militia units. In 1781 he commanded a troop of mounted militia that fought at the Cowpens.[6]

> ... some reinforcement was then collected, with which in January 1781, a party of Tores [sic] was surprised in the fork of saluda and Broad Rivers. Information came to us that General Morgan was within a few miles, pursued by the enemy. We started immediately to join him and in our way, having fallen in with part of the British advance we had a skirmish and made some prisoners. We reached the General the

evening preceding the battle of the Cowpens and were placed under the command of Colonel Washington. Early the next morning the enemy attacked our lines but they were soon broken and retreated in every direction leaving their dead, wounded, artillery, baggage and many prisoners. We continued with the army two days and were then ordered away to disperse some tories who were assembling near Inoree River.

6. Captain Samuel Sexton was born in 1762. A volunteer elected captain of his company and veteran of several battles, he describes here the circumstances that led to his joining the patriot cause:[7]

> I was seized, while just a boy, by a party of tories, and so severely beaten that my life was despaired of, when Major Jonathan Davis, who lived in the neighborhood found me, and took me to his house, provided a surgeon, and rendered me every assistance at his own expense. After remaining at his house about nine weeks, and after I had partially recovered a band of tories come to the house, and again seized me, strapped me, and again beat me: At the suggestion of Major Davis I made my escape, and joined the American army at the Cowpens, the day before the battle of the 17th of January, 1780 or 1781 was fought at that place. On my route to the Cowpens I succeeded in inducing twenty-five men to join me, and was chosen their captain. We heard of a contemplated attack from the tores [sic], and lay in ambush until they came up and defeated them. We proceded [?] and offered our services to the army at the Cowpens, were received and I and my Company were put under the command of Colonel Hays, who was under General Pickens under General or Colonel Morgan of the Regular or Continental Army. I was in the battle of Cowpens, at the head of and in command of my company, under Col. Hays. I remember Colonel Washington, who commanded a body of horse, and a Captain Lee, of his command these are all the officers, except Colonel Morgan belonging to the Regular army whom I now recollect nor do I recollect any of the militia, except Col Hayes regiment. After the battle I was ordered, together with three or four other companies, of Colonel Hays command, to Hillsborough. . . . I never received any commission as a captain,[8] but was chosen by my company, was so referred to [?] in the service, and was engaged in the battle of the Cowpens, and the Hanging Rock, at the head of my company, and was by all officers recognized, as Captain.

7. Captain Dennis Tramel was a North Carolina volunteer who saw service at Augusta. After moving to South Carolina, he joined Colo-

nel John Thomas and fought at King's Mountain. He also commanded a company in a number of battles. In this narrative, Tramel describes Morgan's selection of the ground for the battle.[9]

> Applicant there joined the Regiment to which he had formerly belonged, which was at that time under the command of Col Roebuck. In the mean time Genl. Pickens had raised his troops, and Genl Morgan from the East was sent on to the South and genl Pickens joined him. Applicant was also attached to the Army under the command of Genl. Morgan and Genl. Pickens. Genl. Morgan had the principal command. The British army composed of British and Tories under the command of Col. Tarlton was there encamped upon the South side of the Pacolet River near Grindols shoals. The Army under the command of Genl. Morgan retreated to a place called the Cowpens between the branch of horse creek and Suck creek where the engagement took place between the two armies. That place being in two and a half miles of the residence of said applicant and he being well acquainted with the local Situation of the ground Genl Morgan called upon said applicant to assist in selecting the *Battle Ground*; said applicant with the company under his command together with Genl. Morgan and his life-guard and Aide d camp went out and selected the ground upon which the Battle was fought. After the battle ground was chosen this applicant well remembers the expression of Genl. Morgan which was as follows; to wit. addressing himself to applicant said he Captain here is Morgan's grave or victory. Early in the morning of the day following the engagement commenced, it being the 17th day of January 1781. Soon after the battle was over Genl. Morgan moved off with the prisoners leaving this applicant with his company to bury the dead of both parties, and to keep off the scouting parties of Tories; to wit. Will Cunningham and Col Young who commanded scouting parties of tories, who would commit depredations and flee to the Indian Nation and other remote places - with the tories under their command. Our wounded was taken to the house of Doctr Robert Nelson who waited and attended upon them, he being within five miles of the battle ground. Applicant continued in the Neighborhood with his company for the protection of the wounded...

8. Lieutenant Nathaniel Dickison was elected first lieutenant of his company of North Carolina militia. He served in that capacity in the militia line at the Cowpens.[10]

> The declarant entered the service of the U. S. as a substitute in the name and stead of one Frederick Hall in the year 1780 under Capt Jos.

Cloud in Stokes County North Carolina, his Col name was Tipton who commanded the 3rd Regiment of Militia. He thinks he recollects Col Morgan & that they joined him not very far from the Cow Pens ... Joined Co. Morgan in a bout eight miles of the Cowpens a bout the 15th of Jan. 1781. we lay there till the 16th and marched to the Cowpens & on the 17th we fought what is called the battle of the Cowpens where declarant was wounded in his left groin by a musket ball. He being so badly wound that to this day he is cripple from the same. He was out this tour three months & owing to his severe wound he was sent home & never after entered the service.

9. Sergeant Major William Seymour served in the Delaware Regiment in the southern campaign and at the battle of the Cowpens. The following is excerpted from his journal.[11]

> On the 6th December, 1780, General Greene arrived at Charlotte and took command of all the Southern Army in the room of General Gates.
>
> On the seventh inst. were brought into camp twelve deserters from the First Regiment Light Dragoons, who were making their way home to Virginia.
>
> 12th December, 1780, the Tory prisoners who were confined in the prevost were sent to Charlotte, there to have their trial.
>
> Col. Washington, with the Light Horse, marched from here on the 13th of this instant towards Hanging Rock.
>
> We lay on this ground from the 22nd November till the 17th December, and marched to Charlotte, fifteen miles. Same day General Smallwood set out on his march for Maryland. At this time the troops were in the most shocking condition for the want of clothing, especially shoes, and we having kept open campaign all winter the troops were taking sick very fast. Here the manly fortitude of the troops of the Maryland Line was very great, being obliged to march and do duty barefoot, being all the winter the chief part of them wanting coats and shoes, which they bore with the greatest patience imaginable, for which their praise should never be forgotten; and indeed in all the hardships which they had undergone they never seemed to frown.
>
> General Greene with his troops marched from Charlotte on the 20th December, directing his route towards Chiraw Hills, in order to forage and there spend the remainder of the winter.

On the 21st ult. the troops under General Morgan marched from Charlotte, being joined by two companies more of light infantry detached from the Maryland Line, directing our march towards the Pacolet River. First day's march from Charlotte we came to Catabo [Catawba] River. Next day we crossed the river at Bizer's ferry. Next day we marched to Cane Creek; next, being the 24th, we were alarmed about two o'clock in the morning by some men on horseback coming to our advance picquet, at which the sentinels challenging and no answer being made, upon which the sentinels fired and afterwards the whole guard, when immediately the whole turned out and continued under arms til daybreak. This day we crossed the Broad River, and the next day, being the 25th, we encamped at Pacolet River.

On the 27th the General received intelligence that Colonel Tarleton was advancing in order to surprise us; upon which there were strong picquets erected all round the encampment, putting ourselves in the best posture of defence. The rolls were ordered to be called every two hours, and reports given by those that were absent. We arrived here in five days since we set out on our march from Charlotte, fifty-eight miles, it being very difficult marching in crossing deep swamps and very steep hills, which rendered our march very unpleasant. The inhabitants along this way live very poor, their plantations uncultivated, and living in mean dwellings. They seem chiefly to be offspring of the ancient Irish, being very affable and courteous to strangers.

On the 31st December Colonel Washington was detached to Fort William in order to surprise some Tories that lay there; and meeting with a party of them near said place, upon which ensued a smart engagement, the latter having one hundred and sixty men killed, and thirty-three made prisoners.

On the first of January, 1781, there was one of the Tories tried and found guilty of desertion to the enemy and piloting the Indians on our army, they making great havoc among them, upon which he was hanged on a tree the same day till he was dead.

On the 4th there was one of Col. Washington's Horse tried and found guilty of desertion to the enemy, when agreeable to his sentence he was shot the same day.

We lay on this ground from the twenty-fifth December, 1780, till the fourteenth January, 1781, and then proceeded on our march farther up the river towards the iron works in order to frustrate the designs of the enemy who were coming round us, Colonel Tarleton on one side and Lord Cornwallis on the other. We encamped on the Cowpen plains on the evening of the sixteenth January, forty-two miles, being joined by some Georgia volunteers and South [Carolina] militia, to the number of between two and three hundred.

10. First Sergeant Benjamin Martin served four enlistments with Virginia troops in the Revolutionary War. In August 1780, he became first sergeant of Captain Triplett's company, which was commanded by Captain Combs at the Cowpens.[12]

> Colonel Daniel Morgan was promoted to Brigadier General the augusta and lockbridg [sic] Militia was formed into a Battallion [sic] Captain Triplett was promoted Major and John Combs was made Captain in his place—General Greene detached general Morgan, with the Maryland troops under Colonel Howard the Virginia militia under Major Francis Triplett and Colonel William Washingtons light horse General Morgan marched down on Pecklet [Pacolet] River and took camp on a hill near the River and continued to send out detachments and defeat the Torys and about the middle of January we were informed that Collonel [sic] Tarlton was coming on us with a Superior force we Retreated to a place we called the Cowpens and took up camp all in order for Battle. The Brittish [sic] attacked us only in the morning. I was in the lead all the time of the actions. I [covered?] Captain Combs he was killed. Captain Dobson and Lieutenant [James] Ewing was on the left of the Maryland troops neare me - the Brittish were completely defeated we marched on with the prisoners to Salsberry [sic]. . . .

11. Sergeant Lawrence Everhart served in Fauntleroy's Company of the 3d Dragoons. This description is extracted from his application for veterans benefits, apparently dictated by Everhart, dated 7 April 1834.[13]

> From Rugeley's we marched to Ninety Six & joined Morgan - Here we met with [?] and had several many [?]: our corps not [?] sustaining many losses, the enemy considerable damage - from this place we retired to Pacelet river near the mountain. Here Washington set out for Hammons Store where there was a nest of Tories, leaving me in charge of the baggage, & he took almost fifty or sixty prisoners, killing some—He returned in two days. From Pacolet we moved to Cowpens about Christmas or New Years day of 1781. Here we were day & night reconnoitering, until the memorable day of January 1781. For the details of that engagement, the petitioner refers to the documents hereto annexed towit [sic] the letter of Col Wm Washington in his own hand writing dated Sandy Hill Mar 11 1803 and the affidavit of James Simons bearing date Nov 8 1803 who was a lieutenant in the action of Cowpens. Petitioners horse being shot he was captured early in the

morning by Quarter Master Wade of the British Army with whom he had some previous acquaintance & by him taken to Col Tarlton: our army at this point of time being perhaps three miles in the rear—Dismounting from his horse, that officer asked the petitioner after some previous conversation if he expected Mr. Washington & Mr. Morgan would fight him that day. Yes if they can keep together only two hundred men was the reply. Then he said it would be another Gates' defeat. I hope to God it will be another Tarlton's defeat said this petitioner. I am Col. Tarlton, Sir. And I am Sergeant Everhart. My wounds were bleeding at this time but soon afterwards were dressed by the surgeon. I received from the enemy great kindness. After the battle, Col. Washington sent two dragoons with me about three miles from the ground to take care of me: Dr. Pindell = formerly of Hagerstown Maryland surgeon of our corps dressed my wounds, remained here until the latter part of February & went thence to Catawba river where I remained a few days.

12. Sergeant James Harden served in the militia beginning in 1777; after April 1780, he belonged to the company of Captain Jeremiah Dixon. This excerpt offers an example of the use Morgan made of the militia. In particular, this account indicates that not all available troops rallied to the fight on the morning of 17 January.[14]

When Colonel Washington and General Morgan in the latter part of December 1780 or early in January 1781 were detached by General Green against the British stations in and around Ninety Six Capt. Dixon with his volunteers, long thoroughly acquainted with the surrounding Country, were called on to bring in Supplies for the American Army. which service we continued to dicscharge until about the battle of the Cowpens, immediately after which General Morgan & Colnl. Washington retreated into North Carolina with the trophies of their victory. At the time of the battle we were out on the duty aforesaid, searching for British and Tory Scouts, within hearing of the Gunns.

13. Private Benjamin Copeland served under Lincoln at the siege of Charleston and volunteered his services with Washington during the raids against Tories in the fall of 1780. "Our Regiment" refers to the 3d Light Dragoons.[15]

... about the last of December 1780 our Regiment of about 70 men with Col Washington at our head & about were detached and marched forty miles the first day & on the next day surprised a body of Tories at Ninety Six [Hammond's Store?] & about 150 we took prisoners and

> & killed & wounded about forty without any loss on our side. About middle January 1781 we fought the Battle of Cowpens near Pacolet River under the command of Genl Morgan—in this battle we had about 10 or 12 men killed & 50 or 60 wounded we took prisoners & killed & wounded altogether about 700 men besides two pieces of artillery & several baggage waggons & dragoon horses besides several small arms—Our Regiment pursued Tarletons Regiment for several miles when a majorety [sic] of them finally escaped we then marched directly for Dan River.

14. Private Jeremiah Dial was born in Ireland and emigrated to Newberry District, South Carolina, in 1771. During the Revolution, he took the place of his father—who had been drafted in 1779—and fought in a number of actions against the Tories. At the Cowpens, Dial served as a mounted volunteer with Washington.[16]

> ... when Col Washington came into South Carolina with a number of light horse troops this applicant was with several others under the command of Maj Hampton and attached to Washington company to pilot him through some parts of South Carolina in the pursuit of the tories, as this applicant and the others taken with him, were well acquainted with the Country - This was in the beginning of the winter of 1780. This applicant went with Washington to Hammond's Store where they overtook and put to flight a large number of tories, some of whom the killed and wounded—This store was in Newberry County Washington then sent one of his Lieutenants or captains with a small party of men to take Williamson's fort on Little river in Newberry County not more than eight or ten miles from Hammond's Store. This applicant was one of the party sent [. . .] and rejoined Washington who then went back towards the border of Carolina to join Genl Morgan—This applicant states that as well as he recollects Washington found Morgan a few days before the battle of the Cowpens and as well as he remembers when Washington's company in which he was joined Morgan he was retreating before Col Tarlton and his forces—at all events Tarlton was in pursuit of him—When Morgan and Col or Gineral [sic] Pickens who commanded the Malitia [?] at the place called the Cow Pens they stoped [sic] to fight the British under Tarlton—This battle was fought on the 17th day of January 1781. This applicant particularly recollects this battle because it was the greatest he ever was in—This applicant states that Tarleton commenced this battle early in the morning by firing his field peeces [sic] at Morgans army but he does not remember how long the battle lasted— Washington's Cavalry with whom this applicant fought during the engagement were stationed

in the rear of Morgan's forces and when the British broke through the left wing of the Malitia [sic] Washington's cavalry made an attack upon them and defeated them with considerable loss . . .

15. Private Andrew Ferguson was one of a number of free blacks who fought in the Revolutionary War. Born in Virginia of free black parents, Ferguson was drafted at age fifteen in 1780 and fought in a number of important engagements, including Brandywine, King's Mountain, Cowpens, Guilford Courthouse (where he was severely wounded), Ninety Six, and Eutaw Springs.[17]

> I am a colored man. . . . Two weeks previous to my being drafted I was in company with my father (Andrew Pegleg as he was called) was taken prisoner by the British under John and James Buzbie. We ran away from them becaues the [sic] whiped [sic] us with the cat o. nine Tails and fell in with the American soldiers under Green. Gen. Green told us that if the British ever [sic] got us again They would kill us and he had better draft us and go up around out of a little now (?) black lickets (?) and he told us we should go with him and must fight the British. I was just then under the immediate command of Captain William Harris and Colonel William McCormick and stayed under the command of this company during most of the time I was out . . . after the Battle he marched us down into South Carolina to the River Pacolet not far from the Cow Pens as he said to join Green but I did not see Green there. While we were at the river Pacolet–the British under Col Tarlton came upon us and Col Morgan marched us up towards the Cow Pens but before we got there we made a Stand and whiped [sic] the British completely this took place I think some time in the month of January 1781.

16. Private Jeremiah Files enlisted with Colonel Pickens on Christmas Eve 1780 and served in his father's company at the Cowpens.[18]

> . . . that on Christmas Eve in the year 1780 he enrolled himself as a volunteer under Col Andrew Pickens and at the time of his enrollment resided in Abbyville District in the State of South Carolina and marched from thence as a volunteer with Col Pickins to Grenville [sic] Shoals on Packlet [sic] River and there joined Gen Morgan about the first of January in the year 1781 and then placed under the command of Capt. McKall [sic] in the Battallion of Major White in the Regiment of Col Andrew Pickens of the South Carolina Militia. My father John Files, Lieut & Hugh Baskin ensign in said Company—and from Grenville Shoals we marched under Gen Morgan to the Cowpens and was in the Battle fought there against Tarlton's Legion on the Wednes-

day morning of the 17th of January 1781—& recollects a continental officer—called Col Howard & Col Wm Washington of the Light Horse. This Deponent was wounded by Tarleton's Dragoons on the head—on the left Arm and on the right Hand each wound was made with a sword & the wounds are now visible the wounds Greatly Disabled this Deponent—& stuned [sic] him for some time. & one Capt Alexander of Rowan Co North Carolina was the first man came to his relief & informed him of our victory—& from thence he was carried in a Horse Bier three days with Gen Morgans Army and arrived at the Town of Gilbert in North Carolina and there Left the Army and was taken to Gen Charles McDowells at the Quaker Meadows on the Catawba River and there with one Michael Cane an American and Sixteen wounded British soldiers were placed under a surgeon by the name of Rudolph (a Dutchman) & there remained sixteen days & from thence Left the British soldiers and removed six miles to Martin Deadwiler's on Tyger River and remained there 18 Days—& aplicant [sic] returned home & remained unable to do duty until the first of June in said year. . . .

17. Private Aaron Guyton was a recruit from the Ninety Six District. Just seventeen when he enlisted with Captain Nathaniel Jeffries in 1779, he saw action in several skirmishes with Tories before arriving at the Cowpens. This remarkable passage addresses Colonel Washington's raid campaign, describes vividly the organization of the militia, and comments on the internecine warfare in South Carolina following the departure of Morgan's army.[19]

I was under Col Brandon who had a few *Brave Men* who stood true for the cause of Liberty in the back part of the State who composed our little Army I was out the most of this time Some times we had 75 Some Times 150 men, and some times we had 4 or 5 Cols with from 50 to 150 men. Each of them had Command of a Regt at home & some times not more than 5 of his men with him. The Cols were Brandon, Hayes, Roebuck, White,—in December 1780 Genl Morgan & Col Washington of the Cavalry came out and took Camp near Pacolet River was soon joined with what few Malitia [sic] was in our part I think the 1st or 2nd day he came I joined him. And hearing of 2 or 300 Torys in a body on Bush River Morgan detached Washingtons Horse [meaning his cavalry] & the Militia to dislodge them the distance was about 40 miles. We came on their camp & killed & wounded numbers of them took many prisoners, and returned to Morgans camp. In a few days Morgan hearing of a detachment under Col Tarleton coming on him and dreading to engage him so near Lord Cornwallis' Army, retreated two days up the Country to a place called the *Cow Pens*. at this time we had no Officer in our Company & only two or three or four men. And the morning before the Battle 17 Jany 1781 we joined Capt John Thompsons Compy. We defeated, killed & took all except Tarleton & his light Horse prisoners —Tarleton let Cornwallis know how things was who instantly pursued Morgan. A part of us and some Georgia refugees followd in the rear of Wallis' Army almost to the Catawba River and we picked up a good many of the straglers [*sic*] in the rear of Cornwallis -. . .

Morgan & his Army having retreated from our State it was now almost Fire & Faggot Between Whig & Tory, who were contending for the ascendancy it continued so till the 15th or 20th of May. I was almost constantly out.

18. Private Josiah Martin volunteered in 1780 to serve in the company of Captain John Barber. This narrative describes the movements and actions of his unit prior to the battle of the Cowpens.[20]

He belonged to a company of volunteers, about 15 or 20 in number generally & commanded by Capt Barber. . . . Its movements was directed against the Tories of Lincoln & the adjoining county of Rutherford. One of its first expeditions was, in early corn planting time 1780, to the house of one Ambrose Mills in Rutherford County on White oak creek of Broad river, who was supposed to be raising a regiment of tories. Barber's company Stayed at Mills' a week or more, lived upon his meat & corn, & ranged in the neighborhood. Mills promised to be neutral, & the company returned home. They learned that Mills, not regarding his promise raised a regiment of tories, received the commission of Colonel from the British, & was taken by the Whiggs in battle at Kings Mountain & hung. . . . Afterwards Barber being advanced to the rank of Major raised a company which applicant joined & marched with it to Morgans camps on the Pacolet river near Grendal's Shoals where we elected Thos. White our captain. We remained in Camps [*sic*] with Morgan until the rains raised the waters when the Militia were allowed to cross the Packalet for the purpose of procuring provisions. Two days afterwards Col Howard came along by our fires & asked where Major Barber was. We asked what was the matter. He said nothing much, but brother Ben was coming. We immediately recrossed the Packalet to Morgan's camp. Early in the morning the regulars commenced march, the militia being on horseback started about 12 O'clock & overtook the regulars the evening before the battle of the Cowpens. Col. Washington was there with his company of Cavalry which amounted to 72 as counted by the applicant the day before the battle. The other officers who commanded in the battle besides those already names, he recollects Col Pickens Militia & Maj McDowell. The battle was fought early in the morning in the open woods. At the termination of the battle our Capt. Thos. White was missing, but was there the next day when we returned from the pursuit. We then followed after Morgan who had gone on with the prisoners. After overtaking them Morgan & regulars left us, & we with Col Washington conducted the prisoners to Burk town. . . .

19. Private Samuel Moore served in the North Carolina militia under Major Joseph McDowell and Captain Whiteside during several campaigns of the Revolution, including the Cowpens. This account includes a description of the impassioned plea General Morgan made to the men in Moore's unit to persuade them to remain with the army after the expiration of their enlistment.[21]

> . . . his [Moore's] twelve months had expir'd a short time, say two months[22] before the battle at the Cowpens—Morgan was expecting a reinforcement of fresh troops, who had not yet arrived, and insisted that Capt. Whiteside and others, whose time had expired, should not leave him, in his exposed condition, to contend with a handfull of men against a powerful and Victorious enemy. This appeal, which could not be heard with indifference, was not without its effect, and captain Whiteside and his men remained until after the Battle—and the expected Supply of troops not *yet* having arrived, this Declarant was not discharged but sent with the prisoners to Salisbury as above stated [earlier in his deposition]. Amongst these prisoners there was one John Hailey an Englishman who now lives a near neighbor to this Declarant in White County Tennessee, but to whom he was not then personally known; and for *that reasons*, although the said Hailey's son has married the stepdaughter of this Declarant, he cannot avail himself of his testimony.

20. Private William Neel was a Virginian who served several years in militia units until he volunteered to go south with Captain Patrick Buchanan.[23]

> In the year 1780 (as he thinks) he went as a volunteer from Staunton in Augusta County Virginia with a company under the command of Capt. Patrick Buchanan with two other companies commanded by Tate & Gilmore to [?] the state of North Carolina and Joined Genl Morgan at Six Mile Creek (after passing by Hillsborough, Salisbury &) this place was called head quarters where Genls Smallwood & Morgan

were encamped with their troops. At this place to wit six mile creek the army remained encamped for some time Colo. Washington commanded the horse Colo Howard the regular infantry and captains Wallace, Brooks & Driggers [?] belonged to the regular forces. Under Genl Morgan he went to the Packolett's River South Carolina and was at the battle of the Cowpens or Tarlton's defeat when ... there were near 500 prisoners taken. At this battle the South Carolina mounted militia under Colo Brannon [sic] proved very defective in the commencement of the action but were subsequently rallied and assisted to complete the victory. After the battle the troops suffered greatly in their return to Salisbury N. Carolina with the prisoners from the high waters cold rains [?] and want of provisions at Broad River; Catawba there were several lives lost from high waters.

21. Private Samuel Park served in 1780 and 1781 in the South Carolina militia. This excerpt describes the actions of militia forces prior to the battle of the Cowpens.[24]

> ... he entered the service of the United States as a Volunteer under *Captain James Dugan* in the autumn of *1780* month of October and served in the Militia under the following named officers *Ginl. Andrew Pickens* (The Militia Genl) Col. Joseph Hays. Major Garret Smith. Capt James Dugan & Thomas Stark 1st Lieut. He entered the Service in District ninety Six South Carolina (since Newberry County) he commenced his march from this place to Youngs where a body of torys had rendezvoused. Genl Pickens Col Hays and Col Washington with his horse troops met near Pacolet Shoals Joined each other and proceeded to Youngs to disperse the Torys aforesaid. From Youngs we who were under the command of Genl. Pickens continued to scour the country in quest of the Tories for the space of two or three months when we joined Genl Morgan on toward Shoals on Pacolet river and marched directly on toward the Cowpens which was distant about sixty miles. arrived at the cowpens about dusk in the evening and the next morning about sunrise was attacked by the troops under the command of Col. Tarleton and after a bloody battle in which our troops proved victorious. Col. Tarleton marched from the Cowpens in the direction of Winnsborough where he Joined Lord Cornwallis. Genl Morgan and Genl. Pickens marched in the directgion [sic] of Guilford Court House. He recollects Genl Morgan. Col Washington with his corps of Draggoons the general circumstances of the service are previously [in a deposition of 14 April 1834] stated. There was a continental regiment under the command of Col Howard at the Cowpens and also John Thomas a militia Col. and Capt Farris (or Harris).

22. In his third-person account of the campaign, Lieutenant Colonel Banastre Tarleton, commander of British forces at the Cowpens, describes the planning and movement of his forces prior to the battle.[25]

> General Leslie, with one thousand five hundred and thirty men, was greatly advanced on his march toward the army, when the operations of the Americans to the westward of the Broad river laid immediate claim to the attention of the British. General Morgan, with the continental light infantry, Colonel Washington's cavalry, and large detachments of militia, was reported to be advancing to Ninty Six. Although the fortifications were in tolerable condition at that place, and sufficiently strong to resist an assault, yet the preservation of the country in its neighborhood was considered as great an object for the garrison and the loyalists of the district, that Earl Cornwallis dispatched an aid-de-camp on the 1st of January [1781] to order Lieutenant-colonel Tarleton over Broad river, with his corps of cavalry and infantry, of five hundred and fifty men, the first battalion of the 71st, consisting of two hundred, and two three-pounders, to counteract the designs of General Morgan, by protecting the country, and compelling him to repass the Broad river. Tarleton received a letter the next day from his lordship, communicating an earnest wish, that the American commander, if within his reach, should be "pushed to the utmost[''']; and requiring, likewise, his opinion, whether any move of the main army would be advantageous to the service.[26] On the receipt of this letter, he directed course to the westward, and employed every engine to obtain intelligence of the enemy. He had not proceeded above twenty miles from Brierley's ferry, before he had undoubted proofs, that the report which occasioned the order for the light . . . troops to march was erroneous. The secure state of Ninty Six, and the distance of General Morgan, immediately prompted Tarleton to halt the troops under his command, as well as to allow time for the junction of the baggage of the different corps, which had been left on the ground when they first decamped, as to give information to Earl Cornwallis of the situation and force of Morgan, and to propose operations which required his sanction and concurrence.
>
> As Lieutenant-colonel Tarleton had been entrusted with the outline of the future campaign, he thought it encumbent on him to lay before his Lordship, by letter,[27] the probable accounts of Morgan's force and designs; the necessity of waiting for the baggage of the light troops in their present situation, as any future delay might prove a great inconvenience to the army; and the plan of operation which struck him as equally necessary and advantageous for the King's service. He repre-

sented the course to be taken, which fortunately corresponded to the scheme of the campaign: He mentioned the mode of proceeding to be employed against General Morgan; He proposed the same time, for the army and light troops to commence their march: He explained the point to be attained by the main body: And he declared, that it should be his endeavour to push the enemy into that quarter.

Earl Cornwallis approving the suggested operations, the light troops only waited for their baggage to proceed.[28] Two hundred men of the 7th regiment, who were chiefly recruits, and designed for the garrison at Ninty Six, and fifty dragoons of the 17th regiment, brought the waggons from Brierley's to camp. On their arrival, Lieutenant-colonel Tarleton crossed Indian, and afterwards Dunken creek, though both were considerably swelled by a late fall of rain: He hourly received accounts of the increase of Morgan's corps, which induced him to request Earl Cornwallis, who was moving on the east of Broad river, to give him permission to retain the 7th regiment, that the enemy might be sooner pressed over Broad river, or some favourable situation obtained, whence great advantage might be derived from additional numbers: Having received leave to carry forwards the 7th regiment, he continued his course on the 12th to the westward, in order to discover the most practicable fords for the passage of the Ennoree and Tyger, and that the infantry might avoid the inconveniences thay had undergone in crossing the other waters. An useful expedient was concealed under this apparent necessity. In proportion to the approach of the light troops to the sources of the rivers, and the progress of the main army to King's mountain, General Morgan's danger would increase, if he remained to the westward of the Broad river. The Ennoree and Tyger were passed on the 14th, above the Cherokee road, and Tarleton obtained information in the evening that General Morgan guarded all the fords upon the Pacolet. About the same time Earl Cornwallis advertised Tarleton,[29] that the main army had reached Bull's run, and that General Leslie had surmounted the difficulties which had hitherto retarded his march. At this crisis Lieutenant-colonel Tarleton assured Earl Cornwallis that he would endeavour to pass the Pacolet, purposely to force General Morgan to retreat towards the Broad river, and requested his lordship to proceed up the eastern bank without delay, because such a movement might perhaps admit of co-operation, and would undoubtedly stop the retreat of the Americans.

On the 15th circumstantial intelligence was procured by Lieutenant-colonel Tarleton of the different guards stationed on the Pacolet. A march was commenced in the evening toward the iron works, which are situated high upon the river; but in the morning the course was altered, and the light troops secured a passage within six miles of the enemy's camp. As soon as the corps were assembled beyond the Pacolet, Lieutenant-colonel Tarleton thought it advisable to advance towards some log houses, formerly constructed by Major Ferguson, which lay midway between the British and Americans, and were reported to be unoccupied by General Morgan. The necessity and utility of such a proceeding appeared so strong, that some dragoons and mounted infantry were sent with all possible expedition to secure them, lest a similar opinion should strike the American commander, which might be productive of great inconvenience. Tarleton intended to take post, with his whole corps, behind the log houses, and wait for the motions of the enemy; but a patrole discovering that the Americans were decamped, the British light troops were directed to occupy their position, because it yielded a good post, and afforded plenty of provisions, which they had left behind them, half crooked [sic], in every part of their encampment.

> Patroles and spies were immediately dispatched to observe the Americans: The dragoons were directed to follow the enemy till dark, and the other emissaries to continue their inquiries till morning, if some material incident did not occur: Early in the night the patroles reported that General Morgan had struck into byways, tending towards Thickelle [Thicketty] creek: A party of determined loyalists made an American colonel prisoner, who had casually left the line of march, and conducted him to the British camp: The examination of the militia colonel, and other accounts soon afterwards received, evinced the propriety of hanging upon General Morgan's rear, to impede the junction of reinforcements, said to be approaching, and likewise to prevent his passing Broad river without the knowledge of the light troops, who could perplex his design, and call in the assistance of the main army if necessity required. Other reports at midnight of a corps of mountaineers being upon the march from Greene river, proved the exigency of moving to watch the enemy closely, in order to take advantage of any favorable opportunity that might offer.

23. Lieutenant Roderick Mackenzie, an officer of the 71st Highlanders and witness to the battle, published these letters. Obviously hostile to Tarleton, his letters react directly to Tarleton's account of the campaign.[30]

Letter IX

My Dear Sir,

I now proceed to examine the account which our author has given to the world of his defeat at the Cowpens, but previous to this investigation it will be necessary to inquire, what degree of credit is due to his description of the advance to the field of battle. The traits of self-importance which it contains are too apparent to escape the notice of any reader; in his relation of circumstances antecedent to this disaster, he says, pages 211, and 212, that [he explained the entire campaign to Lord Cornwallis]. How rapid was the advance of this gentleman to the summit of military knowledge!

Lieutenant Colonel Tarleton landed in America in the year 1777, with the rank of Cornet of Dragoons, and in the beginning of 1781, we find him the primus mobile, the master spring which puts the whole machinery of the army in motion. It is a received maxim to listen with caution to the hero of his own story, but we are naturally prepossessed in favor of those who speak modestly of themselves, and honourably of others; my present object, however, is to consider how far our author has followed the line which he declares himself to have prescribed.

He says, page 220, [that the distance from Wynnesborough to King's Mountain was only sixty-five miles, and laments that Cornwallis had not moved there].

The imputed censures in the above passage demand a dispassionate investigation. Let us admit, that the possession of King's Mountain was a point preconstructed between Earl Cornwallis and Lieutenant Colonel Tarleton; it shall also be granted, that the attainment of that eminence by the main body, was a measure well calculated to cut off Morgan's retreat; neither is it meant to be denied that Lieutenant Colonel Tarleton used means to overtake the American detachment which do him no discredit: but granting all that, it is contended, that the rapidity of his movements did not afford Earl Cornwallis time to arrive at the point above-mentioned; and it shall be demonstrated, that an allowance of additional time for that arrival, was entirely in the power of our author; and farther, that it would have been attended with many conspicuous advantages.

His mode of reasoning, in the present instance, is invidious in the extreme, with respect to the General [Cornwallis], and equally contemptuous of the judgment of every officer in his army: it is a bold stroke of imposition even upon the common sense of mankind; because it will be readily granted, by every person, that a march of sixty-five miles may easily be made out in the course of ten days, he, therefore, eagerly takes advantage of that obvious fact, to support his uniform drift, of attempting to render the General reprehensible. And as his Lordship commenced his march on the 7th or 8th, if difficulties and obstacles, which our author artfully conceals, had not intervened, he might certainly have arrived at the place of destination by the 17th. But let us take a candid and impartial view of this matter, and it will clearly appear, that this censurer of his General's conduct had no right to expect the arrival of the army at King's Mountain, by the time which he specifies.

We have his own testimony, pages 219 and 248, of his having received due information that the army on the 14th [of January] had not got farther than Bull Run. This is then the point, both with respect to time and distance, from which we are to estimate the movements of the main body, as well as of the detachment; and hence we are to fix the criterion from which we are to derive our judgment of the subsequent conduct of both commanders.

The distance of Bull Run, where the General was on the 14th, from King's Mountain, is forty-five miles. Our author's position at the same period of time, was not more remote from the spot of his precipitate engagement [the battle of the Cowpens] with the enemy than thirty miles. This engagement took place on the morning of the 17th, before one hour of daylight had passed. Instead therefore of an allowance of ten days, for a march of sixty-five miles, we now find, in fact, that the General had only two days to perform a march of forty-five miles; and it is but bare justice to point out the many obstacles which the army, on this occasion, had to surmount. Both the ground through which his Lordship had to pass, and the weather, opposed all possibility of a quick progress. Every step of his march was obstructed by creeks and rivulets, all of which were swelled to a prodigious height, and many rendered quite unfordable, in consequence of a heavy fall of rain for several weeks; to these difficulties were also added, the encumbrance of a train of artillery, military stores, baggage, and all the other necessary appointments of an army. On the other hand, our author had only to lead on about a thousand light troops, in the best condition, and as little encumbered as possible; with these, as I assuredly can attest, by swimming horses and felling trees for bridges, means were impractical for his Lordship's army, he came up with the enemy much sooner than expected.

I have now laid before you a simple and fair statement of the advance, as well of the army as of the detachment, previous to the unfortunate action at Cowpens, and furnished you with a clue by which you may unravel the windings and doublings of our author, in anxious quest of materials for censure of a General irreprehensible in every part of his conduct, during the whole of this march.

Our author's words, page 220, [condemn Lord Cornwallis for failure to keep his forces within supporting distance of each other; Mackenzie cites Ferguson's defeat as a recent example[31]].

The real province of an historian is to relate facts; by this principle he should abide; whenever he deviates from it, and indulges in fanciful conjecture concerning probable contingencies, if not totally divested of partiality, he is certain of misleading his readers. That our author was not aware of the force of this remark, is sufficiently evinced. His Lordship's attention to the situation of the enemy, of the country, and of his own detachments, has been, with respect to Ferguson, already pointed out. He neither advised the advance of that unfortunate partisan into the back settlement, nor was even apprised of it; having therefore, no concern in the measure, he could not, in any justice, be responsible for its consequences, and it is the height of illiberality to throw reproach upon him on that account.

Of all men, Lieutenant Colonel Tarleton should be the last to censure Lord Cornwallis for not destroying General Morgan's force; as it will appear that the provision made for that service was perfectly sufficient; and though it can by no means be admitted that his Lordship should have manoeuvred so as to get General Greene into his power after the defeat at Cowpens; it may, however, be affirmed, that if the troops lost on that occasion had escaped the misfortune which befel [sic] them, and had been combined with the British force at the battle of Guilford, the victory must have been much more decisive; and General Greene would probably have brought off as few of his army, as his predecessor in command, General Gates, did at Camden.

I will hazard an additional reflection: Had Earl Cornwallis not been deprived of his light troops, the blockade at York Town had never taken place; and the enemies of our country, in consequence of the signal successes which attended a Rodney and a Heathfield, would have sued for that peace, the terms of which they afterwards prescribed.

As the effect of the defeat at Cowpens was of so serious a nature, it becomes necessary to state the purpose for which Lieutenant Colonel Tarleton was detached; to enquire how far the force placed under his command was adequate to the service it was sent to perform; to examine whether proper use was made of the advantages which occurred on the morning of the 17th of January, both before and during the action, and to trace to its very source, a fountain that overflowed with blood, and swept along its torrent destruction to the interests of Great Britain.

I am, etc.

NOTES
Appendix B

1. Revolutionary War Pension Applications, 31 October 1832 - S2187-M804/1176, hereafter referred to as RWPA. A number of soldiers from the battle applied for pensions years later and described the event to prove they had participated. Typed copies of all pension applications in this study can be found at the Cowpens National Battlefield, courtesy of Professor Lawernce E. Babits of East Carolina University (Moss, *Patriots*, 128; Bailey, *Heroes*, 116–31).

2. Major Thomas Young, "Memoir of Major Thomas Young, A Patriot of South Carolina," *The Orion* 3 (October-November 1843), n. p. The Cowpens was fought on Young's seventeenth birthday (Bailey, *Heroes*, 250–66).

3. Robert Kirkwood, *The Journal and Order Book of Captain Robert Kirkwood of the Delaware Regiment of the Continental Line*, ed. Rev. Joseph Brown Turner (Wilmington: Historical Society of Delaware, 1910), 5–6. The journal entries reproduced here can be found on pages 12–13.

4. William Beatty, "Journal of Captain William Beatty 1776–1781, of the Maryland Line," *Maryland Historical Magazine*, no.3 (1908):118–19. The original manuscript of this journal is held in the files of the Maryland Historical Society and is published in *The Historical Magazine and Notes and Queries Concerning the Antiquities, History and Biography of America*, vol. 1 (Morrisania, NY: Henry B. Dawson, 1867).

5. Beatty means a *Feu de joi*, in which celebrants discharge their weapons in the air to express elation.

6. RWPA, 20 October 1837, W2933, M804/1129, Moss, *Patriots*, 118.

7. RWPA, 17 September 1833, R9400, M804/2154, Moss, *Patriots*, 259.

8. In an earlier deposition of 15 May 1828, Sexton claimed he held a commission in the "State line" from about a year after he formed his company.

9. RWPA, 10 December 1780, R10672, M804/2408, Moss, *Patriots*, 290–91.

10. RWPA, 23 June 1835, S3289, M804/814, Moss, *Patriots*, 80.

11. Seymour, William. *A Journal of the Southern Campaign* (Wilmington: Historical Society of Delaware, 1896), 10–15.

12. RWPA, R6965, Moss, *Patriots*, 181.

13. RWPA, 7 April 1834, S25068, M804/944. See also "Sketch of the Life of Lawrence Everheart," in Thomas Balch, *Papers Relating Chiefly to the Mary-

land Line During the Revolution (Philadelphia: T. K. and P. G. Printers, 1857), 42–52.

14. RWPA, 21 August 1832, R4592, M804/1186, Moss, *Patriots*, 131.

15. RWPA, 2 September 1834, S21122, File M804/650, Moss, *Patriots*, 63–64.

16. RWPA, 15 August 1832, W914, M804/808, Moss, *Patriots*, 79–80.

17. RWPA, 16 August 1838, S32243, M804/966, Moss, *Patriots*, 98.

18. RWPA, 3 February 1834, S13026, M804/973, Moss, *Patriots*, 100.

19. RWPA, W21237, M804/1149, Moss, *Patriots*, 122–23.

20. RWPA, 1 October 1832, W1047, M804/1641, Moss, *Patriots*, 182–83.

21. RWPA, 11 October 1832, W2656, M804/1759, Moss, *Patriots*, 209.

22. Two months is too long; Morgan was only in South Carolina thirty-two days when the battle occurred.

23. RWPA, 29 October 1832, S15945, M804/1804, Moss, *Patriots*, 217–18.

24. RWPA, 26 August 1834, S32428, M804/1869, Moss, *Patriots*, 228–29.

25. Banastre Tarleton, *A History of the Campaigns of 1780 and 1781 in the Southern Provinces of North America* (Dublin: T. Cadell, 1787), 216–20. I have replaced Tarleton's method of documentation with a modern format.

26. All letters referred to in this passage are reproduced in Appendix D, Tarleton-Cornwallis correspondence. See Letter 4, 174.

27. See Letter 7, Appendix D, 175–76.

28. See Letter 9, Appendix D, 177.

29. See Appendix D, Letters 13 and 14, 178.

30. Roderick Mackenzie, *Strictures on Lt. Col Tarleton's History of the Campaign of 1780 and 1781, in the Southern Provinces of North America* (London, 1787), 79–90. I have summarized Mackenzie's lengthy quotations from Tarleton's work.

31. Major Patrick Ferguson, sent by Cornwallis on a raiding expedition, was defeated at King's Mountain on 7 October 1780, just three months before the engagement at the Cowpens.

APPENDIX C

Documents Pertaining to the Battle of The Cowpens, 17 January 1781

Contents

	Page

1. Brigadier General Daniel Morgan, Commander of Continental Forces at the Cowpens 122

2. Colonel Andrew Pickens, Commander of the South Carolina Militia at the Cowpens 125

3. Lieutenant Colonel John Eager Howard, Commander of the Continental Line of Morgan's Force 126

4. Major Samuel Hammond, South Carolina Militia 131

5. Major Joseph Mcjunkin, South Carolina Militia 133

6. Major Thomas Young, South Carolina Militia 135

7. Captain Henry Connally, North Carolina Militia 138

8. Lieutenant Thomas Anderson, Delaware Regiment, Continental Army 139

9. Sergeant Major William Seymour, Delaware Regiment, Continental Army 141

10. James Kelley, 3d Light Dragoons, Continental Army...................... 142

11. Cornet James Simmons, 3d Light Dragoons, Continental Army 143

12. Private John Baldwin, North Carolina Militia 144

13. Private William Neel, Virginia Militia 144

14. Private John Thomas, Virginia Militia 145

15. Private James Collins, South Carolina Militia 145

16. Private Henry Wells, Delaware Regiment, Continental Army 147

17. Lieutenant Colonel Banastre Tarleton, Commander of British Forces at the Cowpens 148

18. Lieutenant Roderick Mackenzie, 71st Highland Infantry Regiment 151

19. Alexander Chesney, Loyalist Guide 154

1. Brigadier General Daniel Morgan sent this letter to his superior, General Nathanael Greene, as his after-action report of the battle. Note that Morgan only sent his report two days after the battle.[1]

Camp on Cain Creek on Pedee
Camp near Cain Creek, Jan 19th, 1781

Dear Sir: The troops I have the honor to command have gained a complete victory over the detachment from the British Army commanded by Lieut.-Col. Tarleton. The action happened in the 17th inst., about sunrise, at the Cowpens. It, perhaps, would be well to remark, for the honor of the American arms, that although the progress of this corps was marked with burning and devastation, and although they waged the most cruel warfare, not a man was killed, wounded, or even insulted, after he surrendered. Had not the Britons during this contest received so many lessons of humanity, I should flatter myself that this might teach them a little. But I fear they are incorrigible.

To give you a just idea of our operations, it will be necessary to inform you that, on the 14th inst., having received certain intelligence that Lord Cornwallis and Lieut. Col. Tarleton were both in motion, and that their movements clearly indicated the intention of dislodging me, I abandoned my encampment at Grindall's Ford on the Pacolet, and on the 16th, in the evening, took possession of a post about seven miles from the Cherokee Ford, on the Broad river. My former position subjected me at once to the operations of Cornwallis and Tarleton, and in case of a defeat my retreat might easily have been cut off. My situation at Cowpens enabled me to improve any advantage that I might gain and to provide better for my security should I be unfortunate. These reasons induced me to take this post, at the risk of its wearing the face of a retreat.

I received regular intelligence of the enemy's movements from the time they were first in motion. On the evening of the 16th inst., they took possession of the ground I had removed from in the morning, distant from the scene of action about twelve miles. An hour before daylight one of my scouts returned and informed me that Lieut. Col. Tarleton had advanced within five miles of our camp. On this information, I hastened to form as good a disposition as circumstances would admit, and from the alacrity of the troops, we were soon prepared to receive them. The light infantry, commanded by Lieut. Col. Howard, and the Virginia militia under the command of Major Triplett, were formed on a rising ground, and extended a line in front. The third regiment of dragoons, under Lieut. Col. Washington, were posted at such a distance in their rear, as not to be subjected to the line of fire directed at them, and to be so near as to be able to charge them should they be broken. The volunteers from North Carolina, South Carolina, and Georgia, under the command of the brave and valuable Col. Pickens, were situated to guard the flanks. Maj. McDowall, of the North Carolina volunteers, was posted on the right flank in front of the line, one hundred and fifty yards; and Maj. Cunningham, of the Georgia volunteers, on the left, at the same distance in front. Colonels Brannon and Thomas, of the South Carolinans, were posted on the right of Maj. McDowall, and Cols. Hay and McCall, of the same corps, on the left of Maj. Cunningham. Capts. Tate and Buchanan, with the Augusta [Virginia] riflemen, to support the right of the line.

The enemy drew up in single line of battle, four hundred yards in front of our advanced corps. The first battalion of the 71st regiment was opposed to our right, the 7th regiment to our left, the infantry of the legion to our centre, the light companies on our flanks. In front moved two pieces of artillery. Lieut. Col. Tarleton, with his cavalry, was posted in the rear of the line.

The disposition of battle being thus formed, small parties of riflemen were detached to skirmish with the enemy, upon which their whole line moved on with the greatest impetuosity, shouting as they advanced. McDowall and Cunningham gave them a heavy and galling fire, and retreated to the regiments intended for their support. The whole of Col. Pickens' command then kept up a fire by regiments, retreating agreeably to their orders. When the enemy advanced on our line, they received a well-directed and incessant fire. But their numbers being superior to ours, they gained our flanks, which obliged us to change our position. We retired in good order about fifty paces, formed, and advanced on the enemy, and gave them a fortunate volley, which threw them into disorder. Lieut. Col. Howard observing this, gave orders for the line to charge bayonets, which was done with such address that they fled with the utmost precipitation leaving their fieldpieces in our possession. We pushed our advantage so effectually, that they never had an opportunity of rallying, had their intentions been ever so good.

Lieut. Col. Washington, having been informed that the Tarleton was cutting down our riflemen on the left, pushed forward, and charged them with such firmness, that instead of attempting to recover the fate of the day, which one would have expected from an officer of his splendid character, broke and fled.

The enemy's whole force were now bent solely in providing for their safety in flight—the list of their killed, wounded, and prisoners, will inform you with what effect. Tarleton, with the small remains of his cavalry, and a few scattered infantry he had mounted on his wagon-horses, made their escape. He was pursued twenty-four miles, but owing to our having taken a wrong trail at first, we could never overtake him.

As I was obliged to move off of the field of action in the morning, to secure the prisoners, I cannot be so accurate as to the killed and wounded of the enemy as I could wish. From the reports of an officer whom I sent to view the ground, there were one hundred non-commissioned officers and privates, and ten commissioned officers killed, and two hundred rank and file wounded. We now have in our possession five hundred and two non-commissioned officers and privates prisoners, independent of the wounded, and the militia are taking up stragglers continually. Twenty-nine commissioned officers have fell into our hands. Their rank, &c., you will see by an enclosed list. The officers I have paroled: the privates I am conveying by the safest route to Salisbury.

Two standards, two fieldpieces, thirty-five wagons, a travelling forge, and all their music are ours. Their baggage, which was immense, they have in a great measure destroyed.

Our loss is inconsiderable, which the enclosed return will evince. I have not been able to ascertain Col. Pickens loss, but know it to be very small.

From our force being composed of such a variety of corps, a wrong judgment may be formed of our numbers. We fought only eight hundred men, two-thirds of which were militia. The British, with their baggage-guard, were not less than one thousand one hundred and fifty, and these veteran troops. Their own officers confess that they fought one thousand and thirty-seven.

Such was the inferiority of our numbers that our success must be attributed, under God, to the justice of our cause and the bravery of our troops. My wishes would induce me to mention the name of every sentinel in the corps I have the honor to command. In justice to the brave and good conduct of the officers, I have taken the liberty to enclose you a list of their names from a conviction that you will be pleased to introduce such characters to the world.

Maj. Giles, my aid, and Capt. Brookes, as brigade-major, deserve and have my thanks for their assistance and behavior on this occasion.

The Baron de Gleabuch, who accompanies Major Giles with these dispatches, served with me as a volunteer, and behaved in such a manner as to merit your attention.

>I am sir, your obedient servant,
>Daniel Morgan

Our loss was very inconsiderable, not having more than twelve killed and about sixty wounded. The enemy had ten commissioned officers and upwards of one hundred rank and file killed, two hundred rank and file wounded, and twenty-seven officers and more than five hundred privates which fell into our hands, with two pieces of artillery, two standards, eight hundred stand of arms, one travelling-forge, thirty-five wagons, ten negroes, and upwards of one hundred dragoon horses.

Although our success was complete, we fought only eight hundred men, and were opposed by upwards of one thousand British troops.

2. Colonel Andrew Pickens was born in 1739 in Pennsylvania and emigrated with his family to South Carolina as a boy. When war erupted in 1775, Pickens declared for the rebel cause and was present at the fighting in 1776 at Ninety Six fort. He commanded the South Carolina militia at the Cowpens. He was an extremely popular officer with local troops, having recently won a skirmish against British, Tories, and Indians at Kettle Creek. He sat at the Constitutional Convention and was elected to Congress in 1794. This brief description of the Cowpens is extracted from a letter Pickens wrote in 1811 to Henry Lee, who was compiling a history of the campaign in the south.[2]

>Pendleton District 28th Aug. 1811

Dr. Sir,

Your favor of the 3rd alto I have recd, & in answer to some of your interrogatories, I can answer pretty correctly; others being of a more delicate nature ought not to be too highly coloured—

[The next four pages describe Pickens' childhood and his service in the war until the Cowpens campaign. Unfortunately, he assumed that Lee knew the story of the battle, thus depriving generations of his eyewitness account, except for this brief remark.]—You know the particulars of the battle of the Cowpens—That part of the 71st which was there surrendered to me & I believe every officer of that Regiment delivered his sword into my hand—I see in a publication, the life of the late Genl Jackson of Georgia, by a Judge Carlton of Savannah,[3] that Major McCarthur [sic] of the 71st Regiment delivered his sword to him—I think Jackson never told him so—Major McCarthur surrendered to me, some distance from the battlefield & delivered his sword to me—Jackson acted with me at that time as Brigade Major—I sent back to Genl Morgan, by Major Jackson, Major McCarthur, with the sword—When I met Coln Washington with his cavalry in pursuit of Tarleton, I ordered Jackson who was brave & active, to return as quickly as possible with as many mounted militia as he could get—We pursued with Coln Washington 22 miles & made prisoners of several of Tarleton's rear [guard] but could not bring him to action. We did not get back to the battle ground till the next morning & overtook Genl Morgan with the prisoners, in the night at Gilbert's Town [near Rutherfordton, North Carolina] — Next day Genl Morgan ordered me to take charge of the prisoners & take the upper rout, while he with the Infrantry [sic] under Coln (John) Howard[4] & Coln Washington's cavalry took the lower rout, to draw Lord Cornwallis after him—We all got safe over the Catawba River & joined again at Sherral's ford (on the Catawba) after a grueling march of four days with the prisoners — Most of the other scenes of the war at that time & in that quarter are known to you therefore it would be superfluous to dwell upon them. . . .

3. Lieutenant Colonel John Eager Howard commanded the Continentals in Morgan's army. General Greene's aide, Alexander Garden, described Howard admiringly as having every requisite for the perfection of the military character—patience, judgment, intrepidity, and decision.[5] Howard wrote these two excerpts some time after the battle, to correct inaccurate reports of it and answer questions about it.

A[6]

Morgan was careful to address the officers and men, to inspire confidence in them. As to what Morgan has since said, "I would not have had a swamp in the view of the militia"—I do not think it deserves any consideration. They were words used in conversation, without any definite meaning. I am positive that Triplett and Tate were on my left. Major M'Dowell was of North Carolina. I do not think there was such an eminence; there was a slight rise in the ground; nor was Washington's horse posted behind it, but on the summit; for I had a full view of him as we retreated from our first position.

Seeing my right flank was exposed to the enemy, I attempted to change the front of Wallace's company, (Virginia regulars;) in doing it, some confusion ensued, and first a part, and then the whole of the company commenced a retreat. The officers along the line seeing this, and supposing that orders had been given for a retreat, faced their men about, and moved off. Morgan, who had mostly been with the militia, quickly rode up to me and expressed apprehensions of the event; but I soon removed his fears by pointing to the line, and observing that the men were not beaten who retreated in that order. He then ordered me to keep with the men, until we came to the rising ground near Washington's horse; and he rode forward to fix on the most proper place for us to halt and face about. In a minute we had a perfect line.

The enemy were now very near us. Our men commenced a very destructive fire, which they little expected, and a few rounds occasioned great disorder in their ranks. While in this confusion, I ordered a charge with the bayonet, which order was obeyed with great alacrity. As the line approached, I observed their artillery a short distance in front, and called to Captain Ewing, who was near me, to take it. Captain Anderson (now General Anderson, of Montgomery county, Maryland) hearing the order, also pushed for the same object, and both being emulous for the prize, kept pace until near the first piece, when Anderson, by placing the end of his espontoon forward into the ground, made a long leap which brought him upon the gun, and gave him the honour of the prize.

My attention was now drawn to an altercation of some of the men with an artillery man, who appeared to make it a point of honour not to surrender his match. The men, provoked by his obstinacy, would have bayonetted him on the spot, had I not interfered, and desired them to spare the life of so brave a man. He then surrendered his match.

In the pursuit, I was led towards the right, in among the 71st, who were broken into squads, and as I called to them to surrender, they laid down their arms, and the officers delivered up their swords. Captain Duncanson, of the 71st grenadiers, gave me his sword, and stood by me. Upon getting on my horse, I found him pulling at my saddle, and he nearly unhorsed me. I expressed my displeasure, and asked him what he was about. The explanation was, that they had orders to give no quarter, and they did not expect any; and as my men were coming up, he was afraid they would use him ill. I admitted his excuse, and put him into the care of a sergeant. I had messages from him for some years afterwards, expressing his obligation for my having saved his life.

Their artillery was *not thrown into the rear*, but was advanced a little at the head of the line, and was taken as I have mentioned. Washington did not *encounter the artillery*. He moved to the left from our rear, to attack Tarleton's horse, and never lost sight of them until they abandoned the ground. Major M'Arthur very freely entered into conversation, and said that he was an officer before Tarleton was born; that the best troops in the service were put under *"that boy" to be sacrificed; that he had flattered himself the event would have been different, if his advice had been taken, which was to charge with all the horse, at the moment we were retreating.*

B[7]

The 1st question you propose is

When my regiment fell back at the battle of the Cowpens, was it by my order for the purpose of extricating my flanks or was it occasioned by the fire of the enemy?

A. It was not occasioned by the fire of the enemy. The militia were formed in front of me, and the moment the british militia [the Legion] formed their line they shouted and made a great noise to intimidate, and rushed with bayonets upon the militia who had not time, especially the riflemen[8] to fire a second time. The militia fell into our rear, and part of them fell into the rear of my right flank where they afterwards renewed the action. The british advanced until my regiment commence firing. I soon observed, as I had but about 350 men and the british about 800, that their line extended much further than mine particularly on my right [word "flank" crossed out], where they were pressing forward to gain my flank.—To protect that flank, I ordered the company on my right to change its front so as to oppose the enemy on that flank. Whether my orders were not well understood or whether it proceeded from any other cause, in attempting this movement some disorder ensued in this company which rather fell back than faced as I wished them. The rest of the line expecting that a retreat was ordered, faced about and retreated but in perfect order. At this moment Genl. Morgan rode to me and ordered me to retreat to Washington's horse about 100 yards, and there form.—This retreat was accidental but was very fortunate as we thereby were extricated from the enemy. As soon as the word was given to halt and face about the line was perfectly formed in a moment. The enemy pressed upon us in rather disorder, expecting the fate of the day was decided. They were by this time within 30 yards of us with two field pieces; my men with uncommon coolness gave them an unexpected and deadly fire. Observing that this fire occasioned some disorder in them I ordered a charge which was executed so promptly that they never recovered. When I came up to the two pieces of artillery which we took, I saw some of my men going to bayonet the man who had the match. He refused to surrender it, and I believe he would have suffered himself to have been bayoneted, if I had not rescued him rather than give up his match.

I can account for the retreat but I suppose it would not be necessary to introduce the matter into your history, and as it may involve the character of an officer I wish it to be forgotten; however, I will state the fact and you may make what use you please of it—This company on my right were Virginians, commanded by Capt. Wallace who some time previous had formed a connexion with a vile woman of the camp, and the infatuation was so great that on guard or any other duty he had this woman with him and seemed miserable when she was absent. He seemed to have lost all sense of the character of an officer. He was in this state of mind at the time of the action. As well as I can recollect Morgan afterwards reprimanded him severely & forced him to break off the connexion. As soon as we joined the army he was ordered to join his regiment and at Guilford was killed. It was generally said by the officers that he distinguished himself in that action as if determined to retrieve his character.

Question 2nd. Was the fire which I gave, after this circumstance & before I charged bayonet, before or after the charge bade by Colo. Washington, & was his charge mainly on the british cavalry, or had he reached the infantry before they were thrown into disorder?

An. The militia all rode to the ground and their horses were tied in the woods in the rear of my left flank. about the time of our retreat, a large body of british cavalry passes round my left flank and pursued the flying militia to their horses. Washington observing this charged them. As well as I can recollect this charge was made at the same moment that I charged the infantry, for as soon as we got among the enemy & were making prisoners I observed the enemy's cavalry retreating the way the[y] had advanced, by our left flank, and Washington in pursuit of them and he followed them some distance—You will observe by this statement that Washington's charge had no connexion with mine as his movement was to the rear in a quite different direction.

I will take this opportunity of mentioning a fact which you may notice or not. Washington had given positive orders to his men to fire a pistol. In the pursuit he had got a head of his men, perhaps 30 yards. Three of the british officers observing this wheeled about and made a charge at him. The officer on his right was raising his arm to cut at him when a sargent [sic] came up and made a stroke at this officer which disabled his arm.—The officer on the left ["was preparing" is crossed out] at the same moment was preparing to make a stroke at him when a boy, a waiter, who had not the strength to wield a sword, drew his pistol and shot and wounded this officer, which disabled him. The third person, who Washington thinks was Tarleton, made a thrust at him which he parryed. This person then retreated 10 or 12 steps and wheeled about and fired a pistol which wounded Washington's horse.

In Tarleton's account of this action it is stated that a party of Americans had pushed down the road some distance and had taken the baggage and that a part of Tarletons horse charged them & retook the baggage. We had a German a volunteer who had been in the Hussars in Europe. He called himself the Baron Glaubeck but turned out to be an imposter—He met with some five or six militia men well mounted had pushed down the road and got a head of Tarletons horse and had taken the baggage which he was obliged to leave and the baggage was destroyed by this body of Tarleton's horse. [Howard's marginal note here says: "Tarleton says that 14 officers & 40 men charged Washington's horse and drove them back to the . . . This is not correct. This affair checked Washington's pursuit, but he did not fall back."]

Question 3rd At Guilford did Colo Gunby command the same regiment which was at the Cowpens & was you with him or on the flanks with Washington or Lee?

Answer. The Maryland line consisted of 7 regiments about half full when we marched into Carolina. After the actions of the 16th and 18th of August 1780 what men we had left were formed into two regiments and the supernumerary officers sent home.—The Maryland troops with me at the Cowpens were picked out of the two regiments. I had also a company of Virginians under Capt Wallace, as before stated, and two companies of Virginia Militia or volunteers, one commanded by Capt Tripolet [sic] from Fauguhar, the other by a capt Tate from Rockbridge or one of the western Counties. Tate joined us again afterwards and was with Lee at Guilford, where he was wounded and I believe died of his wounds.

When we joined Genl. Greene's army at Guilford before the retreat into Virginia, my light infantry were augmented, but before the action at Guilford we were ordered to join our respective regiments, and then I acted as Lt. Colo. under Gunby.

In the book I have mentioned there is a correct plan of the ground and different positions of the troops in the action at Guilford. If I thought you had this book I would refer to it and could describe the situation in a few words.

There was a new regiment (Regiment Extraordinary) sent out from Maryland which had been raised by the state, and it was thought that the officers had been more favored than the officers of the old regiments. It joined us a few days before the action and there were such jealousies among the officers that Genl Greene sent all the new officers home, and made a new arrangement of the two regiments. This was at the time my light infantry joined their regiments. The most of the new men were thrown into the second regiment which was very deficient of officers.

4. Major Samuel Hammond commanded the left flank of the militia line at the Cowpens. A native of Virginia, Hammond moved with his father's family to South Carolina in 1779. As he had military experience, he was commissioned and fought in a number of skirmishes prior to joining Morgan. His account is important as the only recreation of Morgan's operations order for the Cowpens. After the battle, Hammond remained in South Carolina under the command of Colonel Pickens.[9]

On the evening of the 16th of January 1781, General Morgan encamped near a place called the Cowpens. The author of these remarks, being then out with a detachment, did not join the camp until 8 o'clock in the evening, when he was informed by the general, that he intended to give the enemy battle the next morning, if he should press hard upon him. The ground on which the troops were placed, was a small ridge, crossing the road at nearly right angles. A similar ridge, nearly parallel with this, lay between three hundred and five hundred yards in his rear. The valley between was made by a gentle slope; it was, of course, brought within range of the eye; passing from one to the other ridge, the land was thickly covered with red oak and hickory with little if any underbrush. The valleys extending to the right of the general's camp, terminated in a small glade or savanna.

Orders had been issued to the militia, to have twenty-four rounds of balls prepared and ready for use, before they retired to rest. A general order, forming the disposition of the troops, in case of coming to action, had also been prepared, and was read to Colonels Pickens and McCall, Major Jackson and the author of these notes, in the course of the evening. No copy was ever afforded to either of these authors, before the battle, and the author of these notes has never since seen them, but in the course of the same evening he made the following notes upon them, then fresh in his memory, and which was shown to Major Jackson and Colonel McCall, and approved by them as correct as far as they went. To show those concerned what would be their stations, the author drew out a rough sketch of the position set forth in the general order, and after the action, the rough sketch of the enemy's position was added. No perfect or accurate sketch of the enemy's position was ever drawn: this was only taken by the eye, not with mathematical instruments; and yet no opportunity has been afforded of correcting it. Nevertheless, this gives you a still better idea of the affair, than could be obtained without it.

The order commenced in substance thus:

As the enemy seems resolved to force us into action, the numbers and spirit of this little band of patriot soldiers seems to justify the general in the belief that they may be met with confidence, defeated and driven back. To prepare for which, the following order will be observed:

The front line will be composed of that part of Colonel McCall's regiment of South-Carolina State troops, who have not yet been equipped as dragoons, under the command of Major Hammond; the Georgia volunteers, commanded by Lieutenant-Colonel Cunningham, and the North Carolina volunteers, under the command of Major McDowal. Colonel Cunningham will take post on the right, Major McDowal on the left of the line, southwest of the road, upon the rising ground beyond the valley in front, three hundred to three hundred and fifty yards in rear of this cantonment or camp, with the left resting upon the road. Major Hammond will take post on the left of the road, in line with Colonel Cunningham; supported on the left by Captain Donoly, of the Georgia refugees.

The second line will be composed of the continental regiment of Maryland troops, commanded by Lieutenant-Colonel Howard; on the left of the second line, falling back one hundred yards in its rear, a continuation of the second line, or third line, will be formed, advancing its left wing towards the enemy, so as to bring it nearly parallel with the left of the continental troops, upon the second line. The Virginia militia, commanded by Major Triplet, with the South-Carolina militia, commanded by Captain Beaty, will form to the right of the second line; the left nearly opposite to the right of the second line, one hundred yards in its rear; the right extending towards the enemy, so as to be opposite to or parallel with the second line. The main guard will hold its present position, and be commanded as at present by Colonel Washington's cavalry, with such of Colonel McCall's regiment of new raised South-Carolina State troops, as have been equipped for dragoons, will be a reserve, and form in the rear of Colonel Pickens, beyond the ridge, one or two hundred yards, and nearly opposite the main guard, north of the road.

This is not meant as a correct report of the general order, but as nearly so as the memory, influenced by such events, could be expected to retain. The sketch annexed will give you a further illustration of the important event.

5. Major Joseph McJunkin wrote this, advertised as a memoir, although it seems more to be a fanciful history of the campaign. Major McJunkin served as an officer in Pickens' militia. A Pennsylvanian by birth, he moved with his family to South Carolina in 1755.[10]

When Morgan was apprised of Tarleton's approach he fell back a day's march from his position on the Pacolet. He perhaps doubted the propriety of giving battle at all. His force was considerably inferior to that arrayed against him. The officers and men comprising the entire body of his militia were almost wholly unknown to him except by report. He could not know what confidence to place in their skill and courage. A retrograde movement was necessary to enable him to call in scattered detachments. On the night of Jan. 16 the last of these joined him some time after dark. He now had his entire force and the question must be decided, "Shall we fight or fly?" The South Carolina Militia demanded a fight. Their general could, from past experience and common fame, command their courage in their present position, but let them cross Broad River and he would not answer for their conduct. Here the final decision is to risk battle. The Cols. Brandon and Roebuck, with some others, had the special charge of watching Tarleton's movements from the time he reached the Valley of the Pacolet. They sat on their horses as he approached and passed that stream and counted his men and sent their report to headquarters. They watched his camp on the night of the 16th until he began his march to give battle. Morgan appears to have had the most exact information of everything necessary.

On the morning of the 17th he had his men called up. He addressed them in a strain well adapted to enflame their courage. Major Jackson of Georgia also spoke to the militia. The lines formed and the plan of battle disclosed. Three lines of infantry were drawn across the plain. First the regulars and some companies of Virginia militia are posted to where the final issue is expected. In front of these the main body of militia under Gen. Pickens are drawn up at the distance of 150 yards.

Still in front of these at a distance of 150 yards a corps of picked riflemen is scattered in loose order along the whole front.

The guns of the vedettes [a screen of mounted troops], led by Capt. Inman, announce the approach of the foe, and soon the red coats stream before the eyes of the militia. A column marches up in front of Brandon's men led by a gayly dressed officer on horseback. The word passes along the line, "Who can bring him down?" John Savage looked Col. Farr full in the face and read yes in his eye. He darted a few paces in front, laid his rifle against a sapling, a blue gas streamed above his head, the sharp crack of a rifle broke the solemn stillness of the occasion and a horse without a rider wheeled from the front of the advancing column. In a few moments the fire is general. The sharpshooters fall behind Pickens and presently his line yields. Then there is a charge of the dragoons even past the line of regulars after the retreating militia. Numbers are cut down.

Two dragoons assault a large rifleman, Joseph Hughes by name. His gun was empty, but with it he parries their blows and dodges round a tree, but they still persist. At the moment the assault on Hughes began John Savage was priming his rifle. Just as they pass the tree to strike Hughes he levels his gun and one of the dragoons tumbles from his horse pierced with a bullet. The next moment the rifle carried by Hughes, now literally backed over, slips out of his hands and inflicts such a blow upon the other dragoon that he quits the contest and retires hanging by the mane of his horse.

Soon, however, the militia are relieved from the British dragoons by a charge of the American light horse. The British cavalry are borne from the field. Meanwhile the British infantry and the regulars under Col. Howard are hotly engaged; the fight becomes desperate. Howard orders a charge, the militia comes back, and fall in right and left. The British line is broken, some begin to call for quarters, the voice of Howard is heard amid the rush of men and clangor of steel: "Throw down your arms and you shall have good quarters."

One battalion throws down their arms and the men fall to the earth. Another commences flight, but Washington darts before them with his cavalry and they too ground their arms. In the conclusion of this foray you might have seen Major Jackson of Georgia rush among the broken ranks of the 71st Regiment and attempting to seize their standard, while they are vainly trying to form by it; you might have seen Col. Howard interposing for the relief of his friend when entangled among his foes. At the end of the strife you might have seen the same young man, Major McArthur,[11] the commandant of the British infantry, to Gen. Morgan and receiving the General's thanks for the gallantry displayed on the occasion. You might have seen some five or six hundred tall, brawny, well clad soldiers, the flower of the British Army, guarded by a set of militia clad in hunting shirts "blacked, smoked and greasy."

The plain was strewn with the dead and dying. The scattered fragments of the British Army were hurrying from the scene of carnage. Washington hastily collected his cavalry and dashed off in pursuit of Tarleton. He was preceded, however, by a party that started with a view of taking possession of the baggage wagons of the enemy. The victory was complete.

The militia engaged in this battle belonged to three States, the two Carolinas and Georgia. Two companies from Virginia were present, but were in line with the Maryland Regiment under Howard. The North Carolina militia were led by Major McDowell. The Georgia militia were under the immediate command of Majors Cunningham and Jackson; the Captains were Samuel Hammond, George Walton, and Joshua Inman. Major Jackson also acted as Brigade Major to all the militia present. The South Carolina militia were directed by Gen. Pickens. The Colonels were John Thomas, Thomas Brandon, Glenn Anderson, and McCall; the Lieutenant Colonels, William Farr and Benjamin Roebuck; the Majors, Henry White and Joseph McJunkin; Captains, John Alexander, Collins, Elder, Crawford, with Lieuts. Thomas Moore and Hugh Means . . .

On the night before the battle forty-five militia soldiers were enrolled as dragoons and placed under the command of Col. McCall and annexed to Washington's cavalry.[12] These officers and men, in the respective commands, were far from being tyros in the art of war. They were marksmen and had generally been in the war from the commencement. In regard to the conduct of Major McJunkin on this testimony of those who acted under him and with him is to this effect: That he exhibited undaunted courage in action and contributed largely in bringing the militia in order to the final onset by which the battle so honorably terminated.

6. Major Thomas Young, an officer of the South Carolina Militia who had fought at King's Mountain, here describes his observations of the Battle of the Cowpens.[13] He appears to have served in McCall's cavalry.

> Our pickets were stationed three miles in advance. Samuel Clowney was one of the picket guards, and I often heard him afterwards laugh at his narrow escape. Three of Washington's dragoons were out

on a scout, when they came almost in contact with the advanced guard of the British army; they wheeled, and were pursued almost into camp. Two got in safely; one poor fellow, whose horse fell down, was taken prisoner. It was about day that the pickets were driven in.

The morning of the 17th of January, 1781, was bitterly cold. We were formed in order of battle, and the men were slapping their hands together to keep warm—an exertion not long necessary.

The battle field was almost a plain with a ravine on both hands, and very little under growth in front or near us. The regulars, under the command of Col. Howard, a very brave man, were formed in two ranks, their right flank resting upon the head of the ravine on the right. The militia were formed on the left of the regulars, under the command of Col. Pickens, their left flank resting near the head of the ravine on the left. The cavalry formed in rear of the centre, or rather in rear of the left wing of the regulars. About sun-rise, the British line advanced at a sort of trot, with a loud halloo. It was the most beautiful line I ever saw. When they shouted, I heard Morgan say, "They gave us the British halloo, boys, give *them* the Indian halloo, by G__"; and he galloped along the lines, cheering the men, and telling them not to fire until we could see the whites of their eyes. Every officer was crying don't fire! for it was a hard matter for us to keep from it.

I should have said the British line advanced under cover of their artillery; for it opened so fiercely upon the centre, that Col. Washington moved his cavalry from the centre towards the right wing.

The militia fired first. It was for a time, pop—pop—pop—and then a whole volley; but when the regulars fired, it seemed like one sheet of flame from right to left. Oh! it was beautiful! I have heard old Col. Fair [Lieutenant Colonel William Farr] say often, that he believed John Savage fired the first gun in this battle. He was riding to and fro, along the lines, when he saw Savage fix his eye upon a British officer; he stepped out of the ranks, raised his gun—fired, and he saw the officer fall.

After the first fire, the militia retreated, and the cavalry covered their retreat. They were again formed and renewed the attack, and we retired to the rear. They fought for some time, and retreated again—and then formed a second line. In this I can hardly be mistaken, for I recollect well that the cavalry was twice, during the action, between our army and the enemy. I have understood that one of the retreats was ordered by mistake by one of Morgan's officers. How true this is I cannot say.

After the second forming, the fight became general and unintermitting. In the hottest of it, I saw Col. Brandon coming at full speed to the rear, and waving his sword to Col. Washington. In a moment the command to charge was given, and I soon found that the British cavalry had charged the American right. We made a most furious charge, and cutting through the British cavalry, wheeled and charged them in the rear. In this charge, I exchanged my tackey for the finest horse I ever rode; it was the quickest swap I ever made in my life!

At this moment the bugle sounded. We about half formed and making a sort of circuit at full speed, came up in the rear of the British line, shouting and charging like madmen. At this moment Col. Howard gave the word "charge bayonets!" and the day was ours. The British broke, and throwing down their guns and cartouch boxes, made for the wagon road, and did the prettiest sort of running!

After this Major Jolly and seven or eight of us, resolved upon an excursion to capture some of the baggage. We went about twelve miles, and captured two British soldiers, two negroes, and two horses laden with portmanteaus. One of the portmanteaus belonged to a paymaster in the British service, and contained gold. Jolly insisted upon my returning with the prize to camp, while he pursued a little farther. I did so. Jolly's party dashed onward, and soon captured an armorer's wagon, with which they became so much engaged that they forgot all about me. I rode along for some miles at my leisure, on my fine gray charger, talking to my prisoners, when, all at once I saw coming in advance, a party, which I soon discovered to be British. I knew it was no time to consider now; so I wheeled, put spurs to my horse, and made down the road in hopes of meeting Jolly and his party. My horse was stiff, however, from the severe exercise I had given him that morning, and I soon found that they were gaining upon me. I wheeled abruptly to the right into a cross road, but a party of three or four dashed through the woods and intercepted me. It was now a plain case, and I could no longer hope to engage one at a time. My pistol was empty, so I drew my sword and made battle. I never fought so hard in my life. I knew it was death any how, and I resolved to sell my life as dearly as possible.

In a few minutes one finger on my left hand was split open; then I received a cut on my sword arm by a parry which disabled it. In the next instant a cut from a sabre across my forehead (the scar from which I shall carry to my grave,) the skin slipped down over my eyes, and the blood blinded me so that I could see nothing. Then came a thrust in the right shoulder blade, then a cut upon the left shoulder, and a last cut (which you can feel for yourself) on the back of my head—and I fell upon my horse's neck. They took me down, bound up my wounds, and placed me again on my horse a prisoner of war.

When they joined the party in the main road, their were two tories who knew me very well—Littlefield and Kelly. Littlefield cocked his gun, and swore he would kill me. In a moment nearly twenty British soldiers drew their swords, and cursing him for a d__d coward, for wanting to kill a boy without arms and a prisoner ran him off. Littlefield did not like me, and for a very good reason. While we were at Grindall Shoals with Morgan, he once caught me out, and tried to take my gun away from me. I knocked him down with it, and as he rose I clicked it, and told him if he didn't run I'd blow him through. He did not long hesitate which of the two to choose.

I asked Kelly not to tell the British who I was, and I do not think the fellow did. Col. Tarlton sent for me, and I rode by his side for several miles. He was a very fine looking man, with rather a proud bearing, but very gentlemanly in his manners. He asked me a great many questions, and I told him one lie, which I have often thought of since. In reply to his querry whether Morgan was reinforced before the battle? I told him "he was not, but that he expected a reinforcement every minute." "He asked me how many dragoons Washington had." I replied that "he had seventy, and two volunteer companies of mounted militia—but you know they won't fight." "By G_d!" he quickly replied, "they did to-day, though!"

7. Captain Henry Connally volunteered at the request of the governor of North Carolina to command a combined company of draftees and men who had enlisted for eighteen months or who had joined for the duration. This excerpt describes his part of the action and the weather during the battle.[14]

... in December just before Christmas Gen Nathanil [sic] Greene from the north took command of us all. This was in 1780. We all by his proclamation and the orders of our Governor was placed under his command and assembled at Charlotte, from then this applicant was placed under Col Washington and marched to S Carolina to Augusta and Ninety Six, after marching in a southern direction for several days news came that Tarleton was after us. We were all now under Gen. Morgan, and a terrible conflict ensued at the Cowpens between Tarletons men and the army under Gen Morgan, at the "Cow Pens" Here the Americans were victorious and took a great many military stores & cannons baggage and six or seven hundred british and tory prisoners This was in January, 1781 it was cold weather but inclined to be rainey during the battle the company which belonged to this applicant was placed under a Col Howard on the extreme right flank of the division and this applicant commanded a company in the action our company when just about to catch up our horses which was tied about four hundred paces in the rear of the line of Battle fell upon us with great fury but we was fortunately relieved by Washingtons legion that hastened to our assistance after the engagement we all formed a junction with Gen. Greene.

8. Lieutenant Thomas Anderson compiled a journal of his service in the Delaware Regiment from 1780 to 1782. This extract describes the Cowpens campaign and battle. In many instances, the entries match verbatim those of Captain Kirkwood, of the same regiment, as if, perhaps, they had been dictated. The important difference, of course, is in his detailed description of the action of 17 January 1781.[15]

Nov 4, This day Genl Morgans Light Infantry With Col Washington's Cavalry March'd down toward Rudgeley's Within 13 miles of Camden to reconiter [sic] the Enemy and return'd to camp On the 9th Inst March'd 100

"22d This day the Maryland Division arrived here,

"27 The army under the Comd of Genl Gates march'd to Charlotte to Huts,

"28 Received Orders to hold ourselves in readyness to March at a moments warning Accordingly left Our tents Standing with all our Sick behind and March'd to 12 Mile Creek This creek is the line between North and South Carolina from thence We march'd to the Hanging Rock, Where the Infantry remain'd Whilst Col Washington With his Cavalry Went down to Col. Rudgely's and With the deception of a Pine top took the Garrison Consisting of One Coln, One Major, three Captains, four Lieuts, One hundred rank and file, From thence Return'd to Camp with the Prisoners and arrived On the 2nd Decbr (100 miles)

Dec 6th Genl. Greene took Command of the Southern army in the rom of Genl Gates Who was recall'd.

"17 march'd to Charlotte (15 miles)

"21st Was join'd With two Compys from the Maryland line Commanded by Capts Dobson, & Anderson and March'd to Biggers Ferry on the Catawba river. (15 miles)

        Crossed the River and march'd. (5 miles)

        March'd (16 miles)

        March'd (13 miles)

        March'd (8 miles)

Jany 1781

        March'd (10 miles)

        March'd to the Cowpens (12 miles)

7th.   Before day Reced Information that Col Tarlton Was Within Five Miles of us With a Strong Body of Horse and Infantry Whereon We got up and put Ourselves in Order of Battle by day Light they Hove in Sight Halted and Form'd the Line in Full View as We had no artillery to annoy them and the Genl not thinking it prudent to advance from the ground We had form'd, We look'd at each other for a Considerable time, about Sunrise they began the attack by the Discharge of two pieces of cannon and three Huzzas advancing briskly On our riflemen that Was posted in front Who Fought Well Disputing the ground that Was between them and us, Flying from One tree to another at last being forst [*sic*] to give ground they fell back in Our rear the Enemy Seeing us Standing in Such good Order Halted for Some time to dress their line Which Outflanked ours Considerably The [*sic*] then advanced On boldly under a Very heavy fire until the got Within a few yards of us but their line Was So much longer than ours the turn'd our Flanks Which Caused us to fall back Some Disstance The Enemy thinking that We Were broke set up a great Shout Charged us With their bayonets but in no Order We let them Come Within ten Or fifteen yards of us then give them a full Volley and at the Same time Charged them home. They not expecting any Such thing put them in Such Confusion that We Were in amongst them With the Bayonets Which Caused them to give ground and at last to take to the flight But We followed them up so Close that they never Could get in Order again untill We Killed and took the Whole of the Infantry Prisoners, At the Same time that We Charged, Col Washington Charged the horse Which Soon gave Way We followed them ten miles but not being able to Come up With them Returned back to the field of Battle that night and lay amongst the Dead & Wounded Very Well pleased With Our days Work

March this day 20

Jan 18, March'd off With the prisoners for the Catawba River arrived at it On the 23d Inst being, (100 miles)

Febry 1st The Enemy under the Comd of Earl Cornwallis Crossed the River below Where Genl Davidson With Some of the South Carolina Militia Was posted, Killed the Genl and Some of the men Which Caused us to March for Salisbury for fear that the [sic] Would get between us and our army Which Was on the Way for Guilford We arrived at Col Locks before day every step up to our Knees in Mud it rained On us all the Way (30 miles)

9. Sergeant Major William Seymour served in the southern campaign and at the battle of the Cowpens. The following is excerpted from his journal.[16]

[Preceding this account the author described the campaign leading to the battle. That account is reproduced in Appendix B] Next day being the seventeenth January, we received intelligence a while before day, that Colonel Tarleton was advancing in our rear in order to give us battle, upon which we were drawn up in order of battle, the men seeming to be all in good spirits and very willing to fight. The militia were dismounted and were drawn up in front of the standing troops on the right and left banks, being advanced about two hundred yards. By this time the enemy advanced and attacked the militia in front, which they stood very well for some time till being overpowered by the superior number of enemy they retreated, but in very good order, not seeming to be the least bit confused. By this time the enemy advanced and attacked our light infantry with both cannon and small arms, where meeting with a very warm reception they then thought to surround our right flank, to prevent which Captain Kirkwood with his company wheeled to the right and attacked their left flank so vigorously that they were soon repulsed, our men advancing on them so very rapidly that they soon gave way. Our left flank advanced at the same time and repulsed their right flank, upon which they retreated off, leaving us entire masters of the field, our men pursuing them for the distance of twelve miles, insomuch that all their infantry was killed, wounded, and taken prisoners. This action commenced about seven o'clock in the morning and continued till late in the afternoon.

In the action were killed of the enemy one hundred and ninty men, wounded one hundred and eighty, and taken prisoners one Major, thirteen Captains, fourteen Lieutenants, and nine Ensigns, and five hundred and fifty private men, with two field pieces and four standards of colours. Their heavy baggage would have shared the same fate, if Tarleton, who retreated with his cavalry, had not set fire to it, burning up twenty-six waggons. This victory on our side can be attributed to nothing else but Divine Providence, they having thirteen hundred in the field of their best troops, and we not eight hundred of standing troops and militia.

The troops against us were the 7th or Royal English Fuzileers, the First Battalion of the 71st, and the British Legion, horse and foot.

The courage and conduct of the brave General Morgan in this action is highly commendable, as likewise Colonel Howard, who at all times of the action rode from right to left of the line encouraging the men; and indeed all the officers and men behaved with uncommon and undaunted bravery, but more especially the brave captain Kirkwood and his company, who did that day wonders, rushing on the enemy without either dread or fear, and being instrumental in taking a great number of prisoners.

Our loss in the action were one Lieutenant wounded, and one Sergeant, and thirty-five killed and wounded, of which fourteen were of Captain Kirkwood's Company of the Delaware Regiment.

10. James Kelley, who served with Washington's cavalry, rendered this account of the battle when he applied for veteran's benefits in 1835.[17]

> ... he returned to Camden county - in a very short time he volunteerd under Col. Washington. they did not rendizvous [sic] at any particular place—there was but 2 or 3 volunteerd when he did—Washington had about 300 horse at that time—Declarant was a horseman & found his own horse he cannot recollect the name of his captains there was with Washington Col Howard & Col Pickens—all the men he thinks amounted to 300. We marched to a garrison called Rugeleys occupied by tories and some British—we got a pine log & Hacked it to look as much like a cannon as possible & put it on an old pair of Waggon wheels & run it up near the fort & sent in a Flag & Col Rugeley (a Tory) surrendered the garrison. [?] marched on to the [sic] join Genl. Morgan & did join him at the place where the battle of the Cowpens was fought & but a few days before said battle—Declarant fought under Col Washington in said battle The battle ground was part in the woods & part in an old field—the militia were in front & the regulars in the rear Washington and his men on the wing—They barely got formed before Tarlton made his charge—the militia soon run—the

British began to cut down the militia very fast & Washington & Howards men charged [?] & with the regulars of Morgan soon routed the British - Col. Washington & two or three men pursued Tarlton 18 or 15 miles & he [Kelley] understood that during this chase Washington would have been killed by one of the British but that one of Washington's men shot the fellows arm off & Washington made a hack at Tarlton & disabled Tarltons fingers & glanced his head with his sword and took a good many prisoners. Morgan took the prisoners on towards virginia. . . .

11. Cornet James Simmons, 3d Dragoons, made this statement in support of Sergeant Lawrence Everhard's petition for a pension in 1803. Apparently his statement was taken by a clerk who experienced difficulty maintaining the first person; both "I" and "you" refer to Simmons.[18]

> That about the dawn of day on the 17th of January 1781, you selected Sergeant Everhart from your Regiment and ten men, whom you sent to reconnoitre Lt. Colonel Tarletons Army. The advanced guard of this army were mounted as we understood, and believed, on some of the fleetest race horses which he had impressed from their owners in this Country, and which enabled them to take Serjeant Everhart and one of the men—but the other ten men returned, and gave you information of the approach of the enemy.
>
> Immediately after the Battle of the Cowpens commenced, you will recollect that your first charge was made on the enemy's Cavalry, (who were cutting down our Militia) and when, after a smart Action, you instantly defeated, leaving in the course of ten minutes 18 of their brave 17th Dragoons dead on the spot, and whom you will recollect were deserted by Colo. Tarleton's Legeonary Cavalry.
>
> The former wore a uniform of red and buff, with Sheep Skin, on their caps; the latter wore a Uniform of Green with black facings. In pursuit of their Cavalry you overtook their Artillery, whom you immediately made prisoners, but the Drivers of the Horses who were Galloping off with 2-3 pounders, you could not make Surrender until after Repeated Commands from you, you were obliged to order to be Shot; after securing these field peices [sic], your third Charge was made on the right wing of their Army Composed of their Legeonary [sic] Infantry, intermixed with the Battallion of the Brave 71st (under the Command of Major McArthur,) and who, under the Operation of a Universal panic, (having been successfully charged on the left of their Army by our friend Col. Howard) instantly surrendered; immediately

after Securing the Prisoners your 4th Charge was in pursuit of their Cavalry, who finding they could no longer Keep Everhart a Prisoner, Shot him with a Pistol, in the head, over one of his eyes, (I cannot remember particularly which) being then intermixed with the enemy, Everhart pointed out to me the man who shot him, and on whom a just Retaliation was exercised, and who by my order, was instantly Shot, and his horse as well as I can recollect, was given to Everhart, whom I ordered in the rear to the Surgeons. It was at this period after the Action that we sustained the greatest loss of Men, Lt Bell having previously taken off with him in pursuit of the Enemy, on our left nearly a fourth part of your Regt. The enemy were obliged to retreat, and were pursued by you 22 Miles taking several prisoners, and wounded. To the best of my recollection Sergeant Everhart was so disabled by his wound, that he was discharged from you, and he retired from the Army.

12. Private John Baldwin of Burke County, North Carolina, fought the Indians and served with Major McDowell at the Cowpens.[19]

> ... he served under Capt. Alexander Erwin in a Rifle Company & with Col. Jo. McDowell, Burke County, he says he was at the battle of the Cowpens where Genl Morgan commanded, at the commencement of this battle the attack was just made on his militia, he recalled that McDowell told his men to take aim when they fired, and as they retreated to divide to the right & left & form in the rear. Morgan defeated the British with his Regulars, after they conceived the Americans were all running, - the British as he understood lost 900 prisoners and a great many tories were taken—after this battle he returned home. ...

13. Private William Neel was a Virginian who served several years in militia units until he volunteered to go south with Captain Patrick Buchanan. This memoir is a priceless description of General Morgan.[20]

> Second Company of Militia Patrick Buchanan Capt. Lieut's name not remembered some of the non commissioned officers and privates; James Young and James Graham Sergeants, John Kerr, Nicholas Clark, Louis Courser (?), Gilbert Christian, John Bodkin, and Ephraim Bates. Genl Morgan's personal appearance to bee over Six feet high, his metle [sic] to be of much Bodily strength, with a large Scar on his Cheek wore no marks of distinction as an officer his Sword excepted, Battle at Cowpens, Tarleton's defeat, the Army paraded before day a cold morning, formed in single file with the Militia on the right of the Regulars, stood in ranks till Sun rise, at which time the battle commenced, to all this I was an Eye witness, marched off in haste with the

Prisoners, recrossed the Broad River encamped the first night on the north bank. . . .

14. Private John Thomas was a member of the Virginia Militia.[21]

On the 3rd day of October 1778 [sic] he entered the service under the Command of Capt James Winn. He was drafted for six months as a militia man. William Daring [sic] was 1st Lieutenant 1st Sergeant named Sanders John Obannion or Banyon he is not certain which was 2nd Searjeant [sic] At the time deponent entered the service there was a line of soldiers [?] to Francis Triplets the other line of battle The rifle men under the command of Genl Morgan were 200 yards to the front. the orders said that not a gun was to be fired without orders—the rifle men were to fire and passed [?] breaks in the Centre and fall off to the right and flank of the Musquet Line. They Stood in their first position for some time until the Brigadge [sic] Major rode up to Gel. Morgan and informed him that the British were in Sight. Gel. Morgan then rode down to the rifle men and gave them orders to fire. They fired five rounds and broke in the centre and flanked the right and left of the musquetry. The British then charged bayonets [?] on the musquety. The musquetry then had orders to fire but doesn't know how many times they fired before they retreated. They retreated from aboutt [sic] 80 yards and were ordered to wheele [sic] and fire. They did so, the British being within aboutt [sic] 30 steps of them. The shot & firing continued about an hour and forty minutes and then the British broke and run. The Americans took about 600 prisoners. The Americans had no cannon on that occasion, the British had two field pieces stationed aboutt the center of their division Lieutenant Dearing of the Company to which deponent belonged was wounded through his hand on this occasion and bled to death. He died the next day. The battle took place in the woods & the timber was mostly pine. The whole American Army who fought at the Cowpens started with the prisoners for Salisbury and marched to the Catawba River. There the militia from Fauquier Augusta and Rockingham Counties VA left the army. And Major Triplett (who upon the resignation of Captain James Winn was made Major and commanded both companies that marched from Fauquier.) took command of the militia detachment with them from the three before mentioned counties and conducted the prisoners to Salisbury.

15. Private James Collins served in the South Carolina militia during the campaign in the south.[22]

It was not long until it became necessary for us to seek safety by joining Morgan, who was encamped at the Cowpens, but we were not permitted to remain long idle, for Tarleton came on like a thunder storm, which soon put us to our best mettle. After the tidings of his approach came into camp,—in the night,—we were all awakened, ordered under arms, and formed in order of battle by daybreak. About sunrise on the 17th January, 1781, the enemy came into full view. The sight, to me at least, seemed somewhat imposing; they halted for a short time, and then advanced rapidly, as if certain victory. The militia under Pickins and Moffitt, was posted on the right of the regulars some distance in advance, while Washington's cavalry was stationed in the rear. We gave the enemy one fire, when they charged us with their bayonets; we gave way and retreated for our horses, Tarleton's cavalry pursued us; ("now," thought I, "my hide is in the loft;") just as we got to our horses, they overtook us and began to make a few hacks at some, however, without doing much injury. They, in their haste, had pretty much scattered, perhaps, thinking they would have another Fishing creek frolic, but in a few moments, Col. Washington's cavalry was among them, like a whirlwind, and the poor fellows began to kneel from their horses, without being able to remount. The shock was so sudden and violent, they could not stand it, and immediately betook themselves to flight; there was no time to rally, and they appeared to be as hard to stop as a drove of wild Choctaw steers, going to a Pennsylvania market. In a few moments the clashing of swords was out of hearing and quickly out of sight; by this time, both lines of the infantry were warmingly engaged and we being relieved from the pursuit of the enemy began to rally and prepare to redeem our credit, when Morgan rode up in front, and waving his sword, cried out, "Form, form, my brave fellows! give them one more fire and the day is ours. Old Morgan was never beaten." We then advanced briskly, and gained th right flank of the enemy, and they being hard pressed in front, by Howard, and falling very fast, could not stand it long. They began to throw down their arms, and surrender themselves prisoners of war. The whole army, except Tarleton and his horsemen, fell into the hands of Morgan, together with all the baggage. After the fight was over, the sight was truly melancholy. The dead on the side of the British, exceeded the number killed at the battle of King's Mountain, being if I recollect aright, three hundred, or upwards. The loss, on the side of the Americans, was only fifteen or sixteen, and a few slightly wounded. This day, I fired my little rifle five times whether with any effect or not, I do not know. Next day after receiving some small share of the plunder, and taking care to get as much powder as we could, we (the militia) were disbanded and returned to our old haunts, where we obtained a few day's rest.

16. Private Henry Wells was a soldier in the Delaware contingent of the Continental Line and fought at Trenton, Germantown, and the Brandywine. His description seems a bit fanciful.[23]

> In the Spring of 1780 Col. Hall Still commanded my Regt. and Capt. McKennan my Company, we were marched into South Carolina. . . . We left the encampment at Camden [sic] in the winter. I think about the 1st of January 1781 and marched towards the Cow Pens. An express had come for Genl. Marion aboutt [sic] the time of our leaving Camden and he and most of his cavalry left us. We pursued our march under our old officers until within about one and a half days before we arrived at the "Cowpens" when we fell in with the brave Col. Morgan and his party, and he assumed command of the detachment and Col. Washington was Second in Command. Our whole force at this time numbered Some thing less than 900 men a greater proportion of whom were militia & less than 100 horse. By this time our Delaware Rigiment [sic] were reduced at least one half—Some died on the field. Some fell by disease—and Some died from hard treatment while prisoners—Two of my Cosins [sic] fell into the hands of the enemy at Camden, and died from the Severity of their treatment—the other lived to be exchanged, but he returned with a Shattered Constitution. A few days after our junction with Col Morgan having halted for a day or two we fell in with a much Superior force of the enemy, at the Cowpens under Col. Tarleton. He outnumbered us with infantry and he had three or four times as many Cavalry Yet notwithstanding our great disparity of force we came of [sic] victorious, having killed and wounded between 4 and 500 men and taken 500 prisoners. The result of this victory is mainly owing to the Skill and bravery of Cols. Morgan & Washington, for who could refuse to follow, & fight for such leaders—The total loss of the Americans in this engagement, in killed & wounded, was considerably under 100 men I think not more than fifty—The Battle commenced about 10 or 11 Oclock A. M. and continued 'til late in the evening. At the *onset* we were much alarmed by the Superiority of the Enemy in numbers, but the powerful and trumpetlike voice of our Commander drove fear from every bosom, and gave new energies to every arm. During the day, at every turn we Seemed to gain new advantages. Washington & Morgan knew how to turn *every* circumstance to good account—they were a host within themselves - after the Battle was over it was reported in the Camp that Some Stray *fingers* were found on the field which were Said to belng to Col. Tarleton. The Bayttle was fought about the middle of January 1781. Col. Tarleton was hard run by a small detachment of American horse and barely escaped being taken prisoner. It was *generally agreed* in the Camp that Tarleton could easily

have been *Shot* by those in pursuit of him, but their object was to take him alive. In this fight I was struck across the left shoulder by one of Tarleton's Troopers, With his Sword with Such Violence, that the colar [*sic*] of my coat, my vest and my Shirt, were each cut through, and the flest & skin Sleightly [*sic*] scratched and bruised so much so that there was a considerable not [*sic*] or welt on my Sholder for a number of days,— The prisoners taken in the engagement were Sent into the interior of the Country. (The name of the place I do not now recollect) and a part of the troops were Sent to guard them, the ballance [*sic*] of us went into winter quarters, and remained near the Cowpens, . . .

17. Lieutenant Colonel Banastre Tarleton, in this reading, describes the movement of his troops to the battlefield, his analysis of the terrain, enemy dispositions, and course of action, and the deployment of his forces.[24]

Accordingly, at three o'clock in the morning on the 17th, the pickets being called in, the British troops, under the command of Lieutenant-colonel Tarleton, were directed to follow the route the Americans had taken the previous evening, and the baggage and waggons were ordered to remain upon the ground till daybreak, under the protection of a detachment of each corps. Three companies of light infantry, supported by the legion infantry, formed the advance; the 7th regiment, the guns, and the 1st battalion of the 71st, composed the center; and the cavalry and mounted infantry brought up the rear. The ground which the Americans had passed being broken, and much intersected by creeks and ravines, the march of the British troops during the darkness was exceedingly slow, on account of the time employed in examining the front and flanks as they proceeded. Before dawn, Thickelle [Thicketty][25] creek was passed, when an advanced guard of cavalry was ordered to the front. The enemy's patrole approaching, was pursued and overtaken: Two troops of dragoons, under Captain Ogilvie, of the legion, were then ordered to reinforce the advanced guard, and to harass the rear of the enemy. The march had not continued long in this manner, before the commanding officer in front reported that the American troops were halted and forming. The guides were immediately consulted relative to the ground which General Morgan the occupied, and the country in his rear. These people described both with great perspicuity: They said that the woods were open and free from swamps; that the part of Broad river, just above the place where King's creek joined the stream, was about six miles distant from the enemy's left flank, and that the river, by making a curve to the westward, ran parallel to the rear.

Lieutenant-colonel Tarleton having attained a position, which he certainly might deem advantageous, on account of the vulnerable situation of the enemy, and the supposed vicinity of the two British corps on the east and west of Broad river, did not hesitate to undertake those measures which the instructions of his commanding officer imposed, and his own judgment, under the present appearances, equally recommended. He ordered the legion dragoons to drive in the militia parties who covered the front, that General Morgan's disposition might be conveniently and distinctly inspected. He discovered that the American commander had formed a front line of about one thousand militia, and had composed his second line and reserve of five hundred continental light infantry, one hundred and twenty of Washington's cavalry, and three hundred back woodsmen. This accurate knowledge being obtained, Tarleton desired the British infantry to disencumber themselves of every thing, except their arms and ammunition: The light infantry were then ordered to file to the right till they became equal to the flank of the American front line: The legion infantry were added to their left; and, under the fire of a three-pounder, this part of the British troops was instructed to advance within three hundred yards of the enemy. This situation being acquired, the 7th regiment was commanded to form upon the left of the legion infantry, and the other three-pounder was given to the right division of the 7th: A captain, with fifty dragoons, was placed on each flank of the corps, who formed the British front line, to protect their own, and threaten the flanks of the enemy: The 1st battalion of the 71st was desired to extend a little to the left of the 7th regiment, and to remain one hundred and fifty yards in the rear. This body of infantry, and near two hundred cavalry, composed the reserve. During the execution of these arrangements, the animation of the officers and the alacrity of the soldiers afforded the most promising assurances of success.

The dispositions being completed, the front line received orders to advance; a fire from some of the recruits of the 7th regiment was suppressed, and the troops moved on in as good a line as troops could move at open files: The militia, after a short contest, were dislodged, and the British approached the continentals. The fire on both sides was well supported and produced much slaughter: The cavalry on the right were directed to charge the enemy's left: They executed the order with much gallantry, but were drove back by the fire of the reserve, and by a charge of Colonel Washington's cavalry. As the contest between the British infantry in the front line and the continentals seemed equally balanced, neither retreating, Lieutenant-colonel Tarleton thought the advance of the 71st into line, and a movement of the cavalry in reserve to threaten the enemy's right flank, would put a victorious period into the action. No time was lost in performing this manoeuvre. The 71st were desired to pass the 7th before they gave their fire, and were directed not to entangale [*sic*] their right flank with the left of the other battalion. The cavalry were ordered to incline to the left, and to form a line, which would embrace the whole of the enemy's right flank. Upon the advance of the 71st, all the infantry again moved on: The continentals and back woodsmen gave ground: The British rushed forwards: An order was dispatched to the cavalry to charge: An unexpected fire at this instant from the Americans, who came about as they were retreating, stopped the British, and threw them into confusion. Exertions to make them advance were useless. The part of the cavalry which had not been engaged fell likewise into disorder, and an unaccountable panic extended itself along the whole line. The Americans, who before thought they had lost the action, taking advantage of the present situation, advanced upon the British troops, and augmented their astonishment. A general flight ensued. Tarleton sent directions to his cavalry to form about four hundred yards to the right of the enemy, in order to check them, whilst he endeavoured to rally the infantry to protect the guns. The cavalry did not comply with the order, and the effort to collect the infantry was ineffectual: Neither promises nor threats could gain their attention; they surrendered or dispersed, and abandoned the guns to the artillery men, who defended them for some time with exemplary resolution. In this last stage of defeat Lieutenant-colonel Tarleton made another struggle to bring his cavalry to the charge. The weight of such an attack might yet retrieve the day, the enemy being much broken by their late rapid advance; but all attempts to restore order, recollection, or courage, proved fruitless. Above two hundred dragoons forsook their leader, and left the field of battle. Fourteen officers and forty horse-men were, however, not unmindful of their own reputation, or the situation of their commanding officer. Colonel Washington's cavalry were charged, and driven back into the continental infantry by this handful of brave men. Another party of the Americans, who had seized upon the baggage of the British troops on the road from the late encampment, were dispersed, and this detachment retired towards the Broad river unmolested. On the route Tarleton heard with infinite grief and astonishment, that the main army had not advanced beyond Turkey creek: He therefore directed his course to the south east, in order to reach Hamilton's ford, near the mouth of Bullock creek, whence he might communicate with Earl Cornwallis.

The number of killed and wounded, in the action at the Cowpens, amounted to near three hundred on both sides, officers and men inclusive: This loss was almost equally shared; but the Americans took two pieces of cannon, the colours of the 7th regiment, and near four hundred prisoners.[26]

18. Lieutenant Roderick Mackenzie published this letter. He was an officer of the 71st Highlanders and witness to the battle.[27]

Letter X

The defeat of the British detachment at Cowpens, which I informed you would be the subject of this letter, has been variously represented by different authors; it is a point, however, in which they all agree, that at a particular stage of the engagement the whole of the American infantry gave way, and, that the legion-cavalry, though three times the number of those of the enemy, contributed nothing to complete their [the American] confusion.

Ramsey[28] states this action as follows, Volume II, page 196: [Ramsey here notes the two field pieces, five-to-four superiority in infantry, and three-to-one superiority in cavalry, and describes the deployment (in two lines) of Morgan's troops. He describes the retirement of American militiamen, who were then rallied by their officers.].

The Marquis de Chastellus, in his Travels in North America, accounts for the defeat thus: [de Chastellux' describes Morgan's two "wings" of infantry, one of which that officer commanded to wheel to the right, retreat thirty to forty paces, and recommence firing, and credits this maneuver with the victory].

The Annual Register for 1781 gives the following account: [Herein is described the withdrawal of the militia to lure the British infantry into a deadly fire from the second line]. Our author [Tarleton] is so materially concerned, as the principal agent of this scene of ruin, that an impartial account is not to be expected from him; his statement of his own conduct on that day, if authentick, would do honour to the immortal Frederick [the Great, of Prussia]!

The Marquis's exposition of the defeat, in spite of his assertion, that it has the sanction of General Morgan, is flimsy and erroneous. The editor of the Annual Register has been deceived; consequently, of these several accounts, that given by Doctor Ramsey deserves more attention.

I was upon the detachment in question, and the narrative which I now offer has been submitted to the judgment of several respectable officers, who were also in this action, and it has met with their intire [*sic*] approbation.

Towards the latter end of December, 1780, Earl Cornwallis received intelligence, that General Morgan had advanced to the westward of the Broad River, with about one thousand men. Two-thirds of this force were militia, about one hundred of them cavalry, the rest continentals. His intention was to threaten Ninety Six, and to distress the western frontiers. To frustrate these designs, Lieutenant Colonel Tarleton was detached with the light and legion-infantry, the fusiliers, the first battalion of the 71st regiment, about three hundred and fifty cavalry, two field pieces, and an adequate proportion of men from the royal artillery; in all near a thousand strong. This corps, after a progress of some days, arrived at the vicinity of Ninety Six, a post which was then commanded by Lieutenant Colonel Allen. An offer of reinforcement from that garrison was made to Lieutenant Colonel Tarleton. The offer was rejected; and the detachment, by fatiguing marches, attained the ground which Morgan had quitted a few hours before: This position was taken about ten o'clock on the evening of the 16th of January. The pursuit re-commenced by two o'clock the next morning, and was rapidly continued through marshes and broken ground, til day light, when the enemy were discovered in front. Two of their videttes were taken soon after; these gave information that General Morgan had halted, and prepared for action; he had formed his troops as described by Ramsey, in an open wood, secured neither in front, flank, nor rear. Without the delay of a single moment, and in despite of extreme fatigue, the light-legion infantry and fusiliers were ordered to form in line. Before this order was put into execution, and while Major Newmarsh, who commanded the latter corps, was posting his officers, the line, far from complete, was led to the attack by Lieutenant Colonel Tarleton himself. The seventy-first regiment and cavalry, who had not as yet disentangled themselves from the brushwood with which Thickelle [Thicketty][29] Creek abounds, were directed to form, and wait for orders. The military valour of British troops, when not entirely divested of the powers necessary to its exertion, was not to be resisted by an American militia. They gave way on all quarters, and were pursued to their continentals: the second line, now attacked, made a stout resistance. Captain Ogilvie, with his troop, which did not exceed forty men, was ordered to charge the right flank of the enemy. He cut his way through their line, but, exposed to a heavy fire, and charged at the same time by the whole of Washington's dragoons, was compelled to retreat in confusion. The reserve, which as yet had no orders to move from its first position, and consequently remained near a mile distant, was now directed to advance. When the line felt "the advance of the seventy-first, all the infantry again moved on: the continentals and backwoods-men gave ground: the British rushed forwards: an order was dispatched to the cavalry to charge."[30] This order, however, if such was then thought of, being either not delivered or disobeyed, they stood aloof, without availing themselves of the fairest opportunity of reaping the laurels which lay before them. The infantry were not in condition to overtake the fugitives; the latter had marched thirty miles in the course of the last fortnight; the former, during that time, had been in motion day and night. A number, not less than two-thirds of the British infantry officers, had already fallen, and nearly the same proportion of privates; fatigue, however, enfeebled the pursuit, much more than loss of blood. Morgan soon discovered that the legion-cavalry did not advance, and that the infantry, though well disposed, were unable to come up with his corps; he ordered Colonel Washington, with his dragoons, to cover his retreat, and to check the pursuit. He was obeyed; and the protection thus afforded, gave him an opportunity of rallying his scattered forces. They formed, renewed the attack, and charged in their turn. In disorder from the pursuit, unsupported by the cavalry, deprived of the assistance of the cannon, which in defiance of the utmost exertions of those who had them in charge, were now left behind, the advance of the British fell back, and communicated a panick to others, which soon became general: a total route ensued. Two hundred and fifty horse which had not been engaged, fled through the woods with the utmost precipitation, bearing down such officers as opposed their flight: the cannon were soon seized by the Americans, the detachment from the train being either killed or wounded in their defence; and the infantry were easily overtaken, as the cause which had retarded the pursuit, had now an equal effect in impeding the retreat: dispirited on many accounts, they surrendered at discretion. Even at this late stage of the defeat, Lieutenant Colonel Tarleton, with no more than fifty horse, hesitated not to charge the whole of Washington's cavalry, though supported by the continentals; it was a small body of officers, and a detachment of the seventeenth regiment of dragoons, who presented themselves on this desperate occasion; the loss sustained was in proportion to the danger of the enterprise, and the whole body was repulsed.

Whether in actions of importance, or slight skirmishes, I every where can trace exaggerated accounts of this author's prowess. On his retreat after the above defeat, he says, page 218, "Another party of the Americans, who had seized upon the baggage of the British troops on the road from the late encampment, were dispersed." Earl Cornwallis, in his dispatches to the Commander in Chief, writes, that "Lieutenant Colonel Tarleton retook the baggage of the corps, and cut to pieces the detachment of the enemy who had taken possession of it; and after destroying what they could not conveniently bring off, retired with the remainder, unmolested, to Hamilton's Ford." And the Annual Register for 1781 says, that our author "had the fortune of retaking the baggage, the slender guard in whose custody it was being left cut to pieces." All these misrepresentations have originated from one and the same source; the fact however stands thus:

    A detachment from each corps, under the command of Lieutenant Fraser of the 71st regiment (who was afterwards killed at York Town), had been left at some distance to guard the baggage; early intelligence of the defeat was conveyed to this officer by some friendly Americans; what part of the baggage could not be carried off he immediately destroyed, and with his men mounted on the waggon, and spare horses, he retreated to Earl Cornwallis unmolested; nor did he, on this occasion, see any of the American horse or foot, or of the party then under our author's directions. This was the only body of infantry that escaped, the rest were either killed or made prisoners. The dragoons joined the army in two separate divisions; one arrived in the neighborhood of the British encampment upon the evening of the same day, at which time his Lordship had the mortification to learn the defeat of his detachment; the other, under Lieutenant Colonel Tarleton, appeared the next morning.
        I am, etc.

19. Alexander Chesney was a Tory who lived in the vicinity of the Cowpens. Chesney enlisted in the Loyalist militia in June 1780 and fought in a number of skirmishes. He was wounded with Ferguson at King's Mountain. He led a company of militia and served as a guide to Tarleton at the Cowpens.[31]

    Tarleton came into Ninety-Six district to go in quest of General Morgan [January 1781] and sent to the garrison for guides acquainted with Morgan's situation which was then convenient to my house on Pacholet [sic]; I joined Col Tarleton and marched to Fair-forest having failed to get intelligence of Morgan's situation he sent me out [January 16] to endeavour to do so and make mills grind for the Army: when I reached the Pacholet river I swam my horse over a private ford not likely to be guarded, leaving the man behind me to go on more quietly & reconnoitre the same. I found the fires burning but no one there, on which I rode to my father's who said Morgan was gone to the Old-fields about an hour before; my wife said the same and that they had used or destroyed my crop & took away almost every thing. I immediately returned to Col Tarleton and found he had marched to the Old fields. I overtook them before 10 oclock near the Cowpens on Thickety Creek where we suffered a total defeat by some dreadful bad management. The Americans were posted behind a rivulet with Riflemen as a front line and Cavarly [sic] in the rear so as to make a third line; Col Tarleton charged at the head of his Regiment of Cavalry called the British Legion which was filled up from the prisoners taken at the battle of Camden; the Cavalry supported by a detachment of the 71st Regt under Major McArthur broke the Riflemen without difficulty, but the prisoners on seeing their own Regt opposed to them in the rear would not proceed against it and broke; the remainder charged but were repulsed—this gave time to the front line to rally and go in from the rear of their Cavalry which immediately charged and broke in the rear of the 71st (then unsupported) making many prisoners: The rout was almost total. I was with Tarleton in the charge who behaved bravely but imprudently the consequence was his force disperced [sic] in all directions the guns and many prisoners fell into the hands of the Americans.

NOTES
Appendix C

1. James Graham, *The Life of General Daniel Morgan of the Virginia Line of the Army of the United States* (New York: Derby and Jackson, 1856), 467–70. A somewhat abbreviated version appears in Daniel Morgan, *Cowpens Papers, Being the Correspondence of General Morgan and the Prominent Actors*, comp. Theodorus Bailey Myers (Charleston, SC: News and Courier, 1881), 24–26.

2. Lynda Worley Skelton, ed., *General Andrew Pickens: An Autobiography* (Clemson, SC: Pendleton District Historical and Recreational Commission, 1976), 17–18; Bailey, *Heroes*, 24–35.

3. He refers to Thomas Usher Charlton, *The Life of Major General James Jackson* (Augusta, GA, 1809).

4. Colonel John Eager Howard. Skelton inaccurately inserts parenthetically that Howard commanded the Virginia militia. These troops were under his operational control during the battle but only because Howard, from the Maryland Line, was the senior Continental officer remaining.

5. Garden, *Anecdotes*, 60.

6. Lee, Henry, Jr., *The Campaign of 1781 in the Carolinas* (Chicago: Quadrangle Books, 1969), 96–99. This account can also be found in Hugh F. Rankin, *The American Revolution* (New York: G. P. Putnam's Sons, 1964), 270–72. The original account was not broken into paragraphs.

7. A copy of this letter may be found in the holdings of The Cowpens National Battlefield marked Howard to ?? MS 102, Box 4.

8. As a consequence of the greater time required to load the rifle.

9. Joseph Johnson, *Traditions and Reminiscences Chiefly of the American Revolution in the South* (Spartanburg, SC: Walker & James, 1972), 507, 512, 526–32. This text is a reprint of an 1851 edition published in Charleston, SC, by Walker & James, Moss, *Patriots*, 128.

10. James Hodge Saye, *Memoirs of Major Joseph McJunkin: Revolutionary Patriot* (Greenwood, SC: Greenwood Index-Journal, 1925), 32–34, reprinted from the Richmond, VA, *Watchman and Observer* of 1817. See also Bailey, *Heroes*, 216–49.

11. Major McAuthur was more than forty at the time.

12. James Kelley was probably one of these men. See James Kelley in this appendix.

13. Young, "Memoir," 88, 100–102.

14. RWPA, 1 August 1833, W8188, M804/627, Moss, *Patriots*, 61.

15. Thomas Anderson, "Journal of Lieutenant Thomas Anderson of the Delaware Regiment, 1780–1782," *Historical Magazine*, 2d ser., 1 (1867):208, 209. Like Captain Kirkwood, Lieutenant Anderson kept a record of the miles he marched during the campaign. At the end of his published journal, he had accounted for 4,513 miles and had participated in the battles of the Cowpens, Guilford Court House (15 February 1781), and Eutaw Springs (8 September 1781), 211.

16. Seymour, *Journal*, 10–15.

17. RWPA, 28 April 1835, M804/1466.

18. RWPA, 7 April 1834, S25068, M804/944. It is reprinted in Balch, *Maryland Line*, 45.

19. RWPA, S6565, M804/123, Moss, *Patriots*, 15.

20. RWPA, supplementary statement, 19 March 1836, S15945, M804/1804, Moss, *Patriots*, 217–18. See Appendix B for Neel's description of the campaign.

21. RWPA, 9 August 1832, S16271, M804/2370, Moss, *Patriots*, 284.

22. James Collins, *Autobiography of a Revolutionary Soldier* (Clinton, LA: Feliciana Democrat, 1859), 56–58, Moss, *Patriots*.

23. RWPA, S11712, M804/2529, Moss, *Patriots*, 304, 405.

24. Tarleton, *Campaigns*, 220–24.

25. Tarleton may be calling the creek "Thickelle" because of the label of that stream on a 1770 map of the area. The original of the map may be found in the Caroliniana Library.

26. Compare these figures with those offered by Brigadier General Morgan or Sergeant Major Seymour.

27. Mackenzie, *Strictures*, 91–103. I have summarized Mackenzie's lengthy quotations from Tarleton's work.

28. He refers to David Ramsay, *The History of the Revolution in South Carolina* (Trenton, NJ, 1785).

29. Hanger insists that the 71st was but 300 yards behind the line in which the other units were deploying, Hanger, *Address*, 104, 107, 116.

30. Here Mackenzie quotes Tarleton's *Campaigns*, 217. In the 1787 edition, this passage is on page 223.

31. Jones, *Journal*, 21–22.

APPENDIX D

Correspondence Pertaining to the Campaign of The Cowpens, 1 December 1780 to 20 January 1781

Contents

Page

1. Correspondence between Morgan and Nathanael Greene............................ 162

2. Correspondence between Tarleton and Cornwallis 172

3. Miscellaneous correspondence of Cornwallis 179

4. Correspondence from David George to Tarleton.. 182

1. Greene assumed command of the Southern Army from General Horatio Gates in December 1780. These letters between Greene and Morgan (whom he appointed in Letter 1 to command the expedition that met Tarleton a month later at the Cowpens) demonstrate both Morgan's anxiety and Greene's optimism.

Letter 1:

To Brig. Genl. Morgan[1]

Sir–

You are appointed to the command of a corps of Light Infantry, a detachment of militia, and Lt. Col. Washington's Regiment of Light Dragoons. With these troops you will proceed to the West side of the Catawba river, where you will be joined by a body of Volunteer Militia under the command of Brig. Genl. Davidson of this State, and by the militia lately under the command of Brig. Genl. Sumter. This force, and such others as may join you from Georgia, you will employ against the enemy on the West side of the River, either offensively or defensively as your own prudence and discretion may direct, acting with caution, and avoiding surprizes by every possible precaution. For the present I give you the entire command in that quarter, and do hereby require all Officers and Soldiers engaged in the American cause to be subject to your orders and command. The object of this detachment is to give protection to that part of the country and spirit up the people—to annoy the enemy in that quarter—collect the provisions and forage out of the way of the enemy, which you will have formed into a number of small magazines, in or near the position you might think proper to take. You will prevent plundering as much as possible, and be as careful of your provisions and forage as may be, giving receipts for whatever you take to all such as are friends to the independence of America. Should the enemy move in force towards the Pedee, where this Army will take a position, you will move in such direction as to enable you to join me if necessary, or to fall upon the flank or into the rear of the enemy as the occasion may require. You will spare no pains to get good intelligence of the Enemy's situation, and keep me constantly advertised of both your and their movements. You will appoint for the time being a Quarter Master, Commissary and Forage Master, who will follow your instructions in their several lines.

Confiding in your abilities and activity, I entrust you with this command, being persuaded you will do everything in your power to distress the enemy and afford protection to the country.

Given under my hand at Charlotte, this 16th of December 1780.

    Nath. Green

Letter 2:

    Camp on the Cheraws, on the east side of the Pedee[2]
    Dec. 29th, 1780

Dear Sir: We arrived here the 26th inst., after a very tedious and disagreeable march, owing to the badness of the roads and the poor and weak state of the teams. Our prospects with regard to provisions are mended, but this is no Egypt.

I have this moment received intelligence that Gen. Leslie has landed at Charleston, and is on his way to Camden. His force is about two thousand, perhaps something less. I am also informed that Lord Cornwallis has collected his troops at Camden. You will watch their motions very narrowly, and take care and guard against a surprise. Should they move in force this way, you will endeavor to cross the river and join us. Do not be sparing of your expresses, but let me know as often as possible, of your situation. I wish to be fully informed of your prospect respecting provisions, and also the number of militia that has joined you.

A large number of tents and hatchets are on the road. As soon as they arrive you shall be supplied. Many other articles necessary for this army, particularly shoes, are coming on.

    I am, sir, your most obedient servant,
    Nathanael Greene

Letter 3:

This letter informs Morgan of the arrival of General Leslie and suggests that Morgan is the object of the British movements.[3]

    Camp Hicks's Creek, on Pedee, Dec. 30th, 1780.

Dear General: I inclose you a number of letters, by a sergeant of Lieut. Col. Washington's regiment, which I hope will arrive safe. We are at present in a camp of repose, and the general is exerting himself, and everybody else, to put his little army in a better condition. Tents in sufficient numbers for a larger army than ours, are coming from Philadelphia; they are expected to arrive early in January. We also expect a number of shoes, shirts, and some other articles essentially necessary.

Col. Marion writes the general, that General Leslie landed in Charleston, with his command, on the 20th inst., and that he had advanced as far as Moncks's Corner. You know Lord Cornwallis has collected his force at Camden—probably they mean to form a junction, and attempt to give a blow to a part of our force while we are divided, and most probably that blow will be aimed at you, as our position in the centre of a wilderness is less accessible than your camp. I know your discretion renders all caution from me unnecessary; but my friendship will plead an excuse for the impertinence of wishing you to run no risk of a defeat. May your laurels flourish when your locks fade, and an age of peace reward your toils in war. My love to every fellow soldier, and adieu.

Yours, most truly,
O. H. Williams

Letter 4:

In this letter, General Morgan interprets British movements differently from Williams.[4]

Camp on Pacolet Creek, Dec. 31st 1781

Dear General: After an uninteresting march, I arrived at this place on the 25th of December. On the 27th, I received intelligence that a body of Georgia tories, about two hundred and fifty in number, had advanced as far as Fair Forest, and were insulting and plundering the good people in this neighborhood. On the 29th, I dispatched Lieut. Col. Washington, with his own regiment and two hundred militia horse, who had just joined me, to attack them. Before the colonel could overtake them, they had retreated upwards of twenty miles. He came up with them next day, about twelve o'clock, at Hammond's store-house, forty miles from our camp. They were alarmed and flew to their horses. Lieut. Col. Washington extended his mounted riflemen on the wings, and charged them in front with his own regiment. They fled with the greatest precipitation, without making any resistance. One hundred and fifty were killed and wounded, and about forty taken prisoners. What makes this success more valuable, it was attained without the loss of a man. This intelligence I have just received by the Baron de Glaubec, who served in the expedition as a volunteer. To guard against any misfortune, I have detached two hundred men to cover the retreat of the fortunate party. When I obtain a more particular account, I shall transmit it to head-quarters, and recommend those men who have distinguished themselves on this occasion.

The militia are increasing fast, so that we cannot be supplied in this neighborhood more than two or three days at farthest. Were we to advance, and be constrained to retreat, the consequence would be very disagreeable; and this must be the case should we lay near the enemy, and Cornwallis reinforce, which he can do with the greatest facility.

General Davidson has brought in one hundred and twenty men, and has returned to bring forward a draft of five hundred more. Col. Pickens has joined me with sixty. Thirty or forty of the men who came out with him have gone into North Carolina to secure their effects, and will immediately repair to my camp.

When I shall have collected my expected force, I shall be at a loss how to act. Could a diversion be made in my favor by the main army, I should wish to march into Georgia. To me it appears an advisable scheme, but should be happy to receive your directions on this point, as they must be the guide of my actions. I have consulted with General Davidson and Col. Pickens, whether we could secure a safe retreat, should we be pushed by a superior force. They tell me it can be easily effected by passing up the Savannah and crossing over the heads of the rivers along the indian line.

To expedite this movement, should it meet with your approbation, I have sent for one hundred swords, which I intend to put into the hands of expert riflemen, to be mounted and incorporated with Lieut. Col. Washington's corps. I have also written to the quarter-master to have one hundred packsaddles made immediately—should be glad if you would direct him to be expeditious. Packsaddles ought to be procured, let our movements be what they may, for our wagons will be an impediment, whether we attempt to annoy the enemy or provide for our own safety. It is incompatible with the nature of light troops to be encumbered with baggage.

I would wish to receive an answer to this proposition as soon as possible. This country has been so exhausted, that the supplies for my detachment have been precarious and scant ever since my arrival, and in a few days will be unattainable; so that a movement is unavoidable. At my particular request, Col. Malmady has been so obliging as to undertake the delivery of these dispatches. He will be able to give you a just idea of our situation and prospects.

I have the honor to be, &c.,
Daniel Morgan

N. B.—Should this expedition be thought advisable, a profound secrecy will be essentially necessary, as you know the soul of the enterprise. Col. Lee's corps would ensure its success.

  D. M.

Letter 5:

Camp on Pacolet, Jan. 4, 1781[5]

Dear Sir: As soon as I could form a just judgment of your situation and prospects, I dispatched Col. Malmady to give you the necessary information, and I flatter myself he has done it to your satisfaction. The account he brings you of Lieut. Col. Washington's success at Hammond's store is as authentic as any I have been able to collect. It was followed by some small advantages. Gen. Cunningham, on hearing of Water's defeat, prepared to evacuate Fort Williams, and had just marched out with the last of his garrison, as a party, consisting of about forty militia horsemen under Col. Hays, and ten dragoons under Mr. Simmonds, arrived with an intention of demanding a surrender. The enemy's force was so superior to theirs, that they could effect nothing more than the demolition of the fort.

Sensible of the importance of guarding against surprise, I have used every precaution on this head. I have had men who were recommended as every way calculated for the business, continually watching the motions of the enemy; so that unless they deceive me, I am in no danger of being surprised.

I have received no acquisitions of force since I wrote you; but I expect in a few days to be joined by Cols. Clark's and Twigg's regiments. Their numbers I cannot ascertain. The men on the north side of Broad river I have not yet ordered to join me; but have directed their officers to keep notice. I intend these as a check on the enemy, should they attempt anything against my detachment.

My situation is far from being agreeable to my wishes or expectations. Forage and provisions are not to be had. Here we cannot subsist, so we have but one alternative, either to retreat or move into Georgia. A retreat will be attended with the most fatal consequences. The spirit which now begins to pervade the people, and call them into the field, will be destroyed. The militia who have already joined will desert us, and it is not improbable but that a regard for their own safety will induce them to join the enemy.

I shall wait with impatience for your directions on the subject of my letter to Col. Malmady, as till then my operations must be suspended.

I am, sir, truly yours,
Daniel Morgan

Letter 6:

This letter responds to Morgan's letter of the 31st.[6]

Camp South Carolina, at Kurshadt's Ferry, east side of Pedee, Jan. 8th, 1781.

Dear Sir: Col. Malmady arrived here yesterday, with your letter of the 31st December. Nothing could have afforded more pleasure than the successful attack of Lieut. Col. Washington upon the tories. I hope it will be attended with a happy influence upon both whig and tory, to the reclaiming of one, and the encouragement of the other. I wish you to forward to me an official report as soon as possible, that I may send it to the northward.

I have maturely considered your proposition of an expedition into Georgia, and cannot think it warrantable in the critical situation our army is in. I have no small reason to think, by intelligence from different quarters, that the enemy have a movement in contemplation, and that in all probability it will be this way, from the impudence of the tories, who are collecting in different quarters, in the most inaccessible swamps and morasses. Should you go into Georgia, and the enemy push this way, your whole force will be useless. The enemy having no object there but what is secure in their fortifications, will take no notice of your movement, but serve you as General Prevost did General Lincoln, oblige you to return by making a forward movement themselves; and you will be so far in the rear that you can do them no injury. But if you continue in the neighborhood of the place you are now at, and they attempt to push forward, you may interrupt their communications with Charleston, or harass their rear, both of which will alarm the enemy not a little.

If you employ detachments to interrupt supplies going to Ninety-six, and Augusta, it will perplex the enemy much. If you think Ninety-six, Augusta, or even Savannah can be surprised, and your force will admit of a detachment for the purpose, and leave you a sufficiency to keep up a good countenance, you may attempt it. But don't think of attempting either, unless by surprise, for you will only beat your heads against the wall without success. Small parties are better to effect a surprise than large bodies, and the success will not greatly depend upon the numbers, but on the secrecy and spirit of the attack.

I must repeat my caution to you to guard against a surprise. The enemy and the tories both will try to bring you into disgrace, if possible, to prevent your influence upon the militia, especially the weak and wavering.

I cannot pretend to give you particular instructions respecting a position. But somewhere between the Saluda and the north branch of Broad river appears to be the most favorable for annoying the enemy, interrupting their supplies, and harassing their rear, if they should make a movement this way.

If you could detach a small party to kill the enemy's draft horses and recruiting cavalry, upon the Congaree, it would give them almost as deadly a blow as a defeat. But this matter must be conducted with great secrecy and dispatch.

Lieut. Col. Lee has just arrived with his legion, and Col. Green is within a few days' march of this, with a reinforcement.

> I am, dear sir, truly yours,
> Nathanael Greene

Letter 7:

Greene wrote this letter to Morgan to answer his letter of the 4th.

Camp on the Pedee Jan. 13th, 1781

Dear Sir: I am at this moment favored with your letter of the 4th inst. Col. Malmady also delivered me your dispatches of the 31st of December, which I answered on the 8th inst., wherein I informed you that I cannot think an expedition into Georgia eligible at this time. Since I wrote you I have received letters from Virginia, informing me of the arrival of Gen. Phillips, with a detachment of 2,500 men from New York. This circumstance renders it still more improper for you to move far to the southward. It is my wish also that you should hold your ground if possible; for I foresee the disagreeable consequences that will result from a retreat. If moving as far as Ninety-six, or anywhere in the neighborhood of it, will contribute to the obtaining more ample supplies, you have my consent. Col. Tarleton is said to be on his way to pay you a visit. I doubt not but he will have a decent reception and a proper dismission. And I am happy to find you have taken every proper precaution to avoid a surprise.

I wish you to be more particular respecting your plan and object in paying a visit to Georgia.

Virginia is raising 3,000 men to recruit this army.

I am, &c.,
Nathanael Greene

Letter 8:

Camp at Burr's Mill on Thicketty Creek, 15 January 1781.[7]

Dear General: Your letters of the 3rd and 8th instant, came to hand yesterday just as I was preparing to change my position, was therefor obliged to detain the express until this evening.

The accounts I have transmitted to you of Lieutenant Colonel Washington's success, accord with his opinion. The number killed and wounded on the part of the tories must depend on conjecture, as they broke on the first charge, scattered through the woods and were pursued in every direction. The consequences attending this defeat will be fatal to the disaffected. They have not been able to embody.

Sensible of the importance of having magazines of forage and provisions established in this country, I have left no means in my power unassayed to effect this business. I dispatched Captain Chitty, (whom I have appointed as commissary of purchases for my command), with orders to collect and store all the provisions that could be obtained between the Catawba and Broad rivers. I gave him directions to call on Colonel Hill, who commands a regiment of militia in that quarter, to furnish him with a proper number of men to assist him in the execution of this commission, but he, to my great surprise, had just returned without effecting any thing. He tells me that his failure proceeded from the want of the countenance and assistance of Colonel Hill, who assured him that General Sumpter directed him to obey no orders from me, unless they came through him.

I find it impracticable to procure more provisions in this quarter than is absolutely necessary for our own immediate consumption: indeed it has been with the greatest difficulty that we have been able to effect this. We have to feed such a number of horses that the most plentiful country must soon be exhausted. Nor am I a little apprehensive that no part of this state accessible to us, can support us long. Could the militia be persuaded to change their fatal mode of going to war, much provision might be saved, but the custom has taken such deep root that it cannot be abolished.

Upon a full and mature deliberation, I am confirmed in the opinion that nothing can be effected by my detachment in this country which will balance the risks I will be subjected to by remaining here. The enemy's great superiority of numbers and our distance from the main army, will enable Lord Cornwallis to detach so superior a force against me, as to render it essential to our safety to avoid coming to action; nor will this always be in my power. No attempt to surprise me will be left untried by them, and situated as we must be, every possible precaution may not be sufficient to secure us. The scarcity of forage makes it impossible for us to be always in a compact body; and were this not the case, it is beyond the art of man to keep the militia from straggling. These reasons induce me to request that I may be recalled with my detachment; and that General Davidson and Colonel Pickens may be left with the militia of North and South Carolina and Georgia. They will not be so much the object of the enemy's attention, and will be capable of being a check on the disaffected, which is all I can effect.

Colonel Pickens is a valuable discreet, and attentive officer, and has the confidence of the militia.

My force is inadequate to the attempts you have hinted at. I have now with me only two hundred South Carolina and Georgia, and one hundred and forty North Carolina, volunteers. Nor do I expect to have more that two-thirds of these to assist me, should I be attacked, for it is impossible to keep them collected.

Though I am convinced that were you on the spot, the propriety of my proposition would strike you forcibly; should you think it unadvisable to recall me, you may depend on my attempting every thing to annoy the enemy, and to provide for the safety of the detachment. I shall cheerfully acquiesce in your determinations.

Col. Tarleton has crossed the Tyger at Musgrove's Mill; his force we cannot learn. It is more than probable we are his object. Cornwallis, by last accounts, was at the cross-roads near Lee's old place.

[As a result of last-minute intelligence, Morgan added] We have just learned that Tarleton's force is from eleven to twelve hundred British.

> I am, dear general,
> Truly yours,
> Daniel Morgan

Letter 9:

Camp on Pedee, Jan. 19th, 1781.[8]

Dear Sir: Your favor of the 15th was delivered me last evening about 12 o'clock. I am surprised that Gen. Sumter should give such an order as that you mention to Col. Hill, nor can I persuade myself but that there must be some mistake in the matter; for though it is the most military to convey orders through the principal to the dependents, as well from propriety as respect, yet this may not always be convenient, or even practicable; and therefore to give a positive order not to obey, was repugnant to reason and common sense. As the head was subject to your orders, consequently the dependents are also. I will write Gen. Sumter on the subject; but it is better to conciliate than aggravate matters, where everything depends so much upon voluntary principles, I wish you to take no notice of the matter, but endeavor to influence his conduct to give you all the aid in his power. Write to him frequently, and consult with him freely. He is a man of great pride and considerable merit, and should not be neglected. If he had given such orders, I am persuaded he will see the impropriety of the matter and correct it in the future, unless personal glory is more the object than public good, which I cannot suppose is the case with him, or any other man who fights in the cause of liberty.

I was informed of Lord Cornwallis' movement before the receipt of your letter, and agree with you in the opinion that you are the object. And from his making so general a movement, it convinces me he feels a great inconvenience from your force and situation. Gen. Leslie has crossed the Catawba to join him. He would never harness his troops to remove you, if he did not think it an object of some importance; nor would he put his collective force in motion if he had not some respect for your numbers. I am sensible your situation is critical, and requires the most watchful attention to guard against surprise. But I think it is of great importance to keep up a force in that quarter; nor can I persuade myself that the militia alone will answer the same valuable purposes as when joined by the continental troops.

It is not my wish you should come to action unless you have a manifest advantage and a moral certainty of succeeding. Put nothing to the hazard. A retreat may be disagreeable, but it is not disgraceful. Regard not the opinions of the day. It is not our business to risk too much, our affairs are in too critical a situation, and require time and nursing to give them a better tone.

If General Sumpter and you could fix a plan for him to hold the post which you now occupy, and he to be joined by the militia under General Davidson, and you with your force and the Georgia and Virginia militia, to move towards Augusta or into that quarter, I should have no objection, provided you think it will answer any valuable purpose, and can be attempted with a degree of safety. I am unwilling to recall you if it can be avoided, but I had rather recall you than expose you to the hazard of a surprise.

Before we can possibly reach you I imagine the movements of Lord Cornwallis and Colonel Tarleton will be sufficiently explained, and you obliged to take some decisive measures. I shall be perfectly satisfied if you keep clear of misfortune; for though I wish you laurels, I am not willing to expose the common cause to give you an opportunity to acquire them.

As the rivers are subject to sudden and great swells, you must be careful that the enemy do not take a position to gain your rear, where you can neither retreat by your flanks or front. The Pedee rose twenty-five feet last week in thirty hours. I am preparing boats to move always with the army; would one or two be of use to you? They will be put on four wheels, and made to move with little more difficulty than a loaded wagon.

General Davidson is desired to receive orders, and in conjunction with Gen. Sumter, to consult with you a plan for a combined attack upon one of the divisions of Lord Cornwallis's army, and also respecting your movements into Georgia.

I am, with great esteem, &c.,
Nathanael Greene

2. This exchange of letters includes all available correspondence between Cornwallis and Tarleton written during the latter's movement to the Cowpens.

Letter 1:

Cornwallis discovered that Morgan's army had entered South Carolina in mid-December 1780. He dispatched this letter to inform Tarleton of the development.[9]

Wynnesborough, Dec. 18th, 1780

Dear Tarleton,

Lord Rawdon has received intelligence, which, however, he does not credit, that Morgan's Corps and the Cavalry had passed the Catawba. I have sent out everybody that I could engage to go, but the friends here are so timid & stupid that I can get no intelligence. I have heard nothing from 96, but a man who came here from Broad River says that Gen'l Cunningham has beat Clarke and wounded him mortally. I shall be glad to hear a confirmation of this. I apprehend we must first dislodge Lacey etc. from Turkey Creek & then march up the West Side of Catawba to some of the fords above Tuckaseege. I wish you would take pains to inform yourself as thoroughly as possible of the state of the roads, Provisions, forage, Mills, etc. I hear a good account of the Recruits in general. I hope to march from here 3500 fighting men barring those I mentioned to you upon the frontier.

Lord Rawdon very readily agreed to undertake Watson so we shall be relieved of that plague.

I trust you will make every possible shift rather than go much further back, as I should in that case be uneasy about McArthur, and as soon as you have been able to get information about the Country, I should be glad to see you to talk over our march.

> I am Dear Tarleton
> Very Sincerely Yours
> Cornwallis

Letter 2:

Cornwallis sent two letters to Tarleton on 26 December 1780. They express the concern Cornwallis felt about Morgan's movements and hint at the urgency of defeating him before the French could cut British lines of communications between Wilmington and Charleston.[10]

[To Tarleton]

A man came this morning from Charlotte town; his fidelity, however, very doubtful; he says, that Greene marched on Wednesday last toward Cheraws, to join General Caswell, and that Morgan, with his infantry and one hundred and twenty-four of Washington's light horse, crossed Bigger's ferry, on Thursday and Friday last, to join Lacey. I expect more intelligence before night, when you shall hear from me again.

Letter 3:

[To Tarleton]

I sent you the reports of the day. First, Morgan and Washington have passed Broad river; secondly, a brig from Cork says, that a packet had arrived there from England, and that accounts were brought, that six regiments were under orders for embarkation, *supposedly* to be destined for Carolina; thirdly, and worst report of all, if true, that one thousand French are got into Cape Fear, who will probably fortify themselves at Wilmington, and stop our water communication with Charles town with provisions; fourthly, that an embarkation was taking place, under General Phillips, from New York, said to be destined for the Cheaspeak.

Lord Rawdon mentions, that by a letter from M'Kinnon to England, he is afraid that the accoutrements for the 17th Dragoons are coming up by the slow process of General Leslie's corps. Try to get all possible intelligence of Morgan.

Letter 4:

In this letter to Tarleton dated Wynnesborough, 2 January 1780, seven o'clock a.m., Cornwallis directs aggressive pursuit and discounts the report that Morgan's force has artillery.[11]

Dear Tarleton,

I send Haldane to you last night, to desire you would pass Broad river, with the legion and the first battalion of the 71st, as soon as possible. If Morgan is still at Williams', or any where within your reach, I should wish you to push him to the utmost: I have not heard, except from M'Arthur, of his having cannon; nor would I believe it, unless he has it from very good authority: It is, however, possible, and Ninty Six is of so much consequence, that no time is to be lost.

        Yours sincerely,
        Cornwallis

Let me know if you think that the moving of a whole, or a part of my corps, can be of use.

Letter 5:

In this exchange of letters (5 and 6), Tarleton asks his commander for information and reinforcements; Cornwallis replies with speculation and assurances that troops are forthcoming.[12]

[To Cornwallis]

Somers Plantation
Jan'y 3 1/2 past 6 a. m.

My Lord,

I am well here—I move *directly toward Monses Mill* a proper course *as I have no intelligence*

    I have the Honor
      to be
        Your Lordships
          Most Devoted Serv't
            Ban. Tarleton

If the 7th or 71st
Battalion was at Byerly's
it would be well

Letter 6:

[To Tarleton]

I received yours of this morning. I suspect the enemy are retired. If so, I would lose no time. Which side of Broad River do you think it best for you to march? The 7th regt are ordered to Byerly's.

Be quite sure that 96 is safe. 7th reg't will take your old gun to Ninety Six.

Letter 7:

In this letter of 4 January 1781 to Cornwallis, Tarleton reports the presence of Morgan and proposes how to prevent an attack on Ninety Six.[13]

[To Cornwallis]

Morse's Mill
Jan'y 4 2 p.m.

Morgan, with upwards of one thousand two hundred men, being on this side of the Broad river, to threaten Ninty Six, and evade your lordship's army whenever you may move, I beg leave to offer my opinion how his design may be prevented.

I must draw my baggage, the 71st and legion's are deposited at my old camp, to me. I wish it to be escorted by the 17th light dragoons, for whom horses are ready; by the yagers, if to be spared; and by the 7th regiment. The 7th I will send, as soon as I reach Ennoree, with the field piece, to Ninty Six. My encampment is now twenty miles from Brierley's, in a plentiful forage country, and I can lay in four days flour for a move.

When I advance, I must either destroy Morgan's corps, or push it before me over the Broad river, towards King's mountain. The advance of the army should commence (when your lordship orders this corps to move) onwards for King's mountain. Frequent communication by letter can pass the Broad river. I feel myself bold in offering my opinion, as it flows from zeal for the public service, and well-grounded enquiry concerning the enemy's designs and operations.

I have directed Captain M'Pherson, the bearer of this letter, who is going on the recruiting service, to deliver a letter to Lieutenant Munroe, whom I left at my camp, to bring up my baggage, but no women.

If your lordship approves of this plan, Captain M'Pherson may give my order to Lieutenant Munroe to escort to me three puncheons of rum, and some salt; and, upon their arrival, I will move.

>I have the Honour
>to be
>Your Lordships
>Most Devoted Serv't
>Ban. Tarleton

Letter 8:

In this letter and the next (Letter 9), Cornwallis responds to Tarleton's request to chase Morgan across the Broad River.[14]

>January 5, 1781

Dear Tarleton,

I received your letter sent yesterday 7 o'clock a. m. I have ordered the baggage of your Corps to Byerley's Ferry, under the care of the 7th Regt. I propose marching on Tuesday next. You will continue to correspond with me, keeping on my left Flank, either on the east or west of Broad River, as you will judge best according to the intelligence you may receive. McArthur will of course march with you.

>Yrs.
>Cornwallis

Letter 9:

Wynnesborough, January 5th,
eight o'clock P. M.

Dear Tarleton,

Since I wrote to you this morning, I received yours, dated yesterday, two P.M. You have exactly done what I wished you to do, and understood my intentions perfectly. Lest my letter of this morning should miscarry, I repeat the most material paragraph.

Your baggage is ordered to Brierley's, under care of the seventh regiment. I propose to march on Sunday.[15]

Yours sincerely,
Cornwallis

Letter 10:

To Colonel Tarleton, 6 January:[16]

I received yours of yesterday. You will see that some parts of your wishes are already anticipated. I am that you have already received three of the Q'r, Master Genl's waggons at Byerleys. Isent another two loaded with rum and salt; you will easily conceive that we have not many to spare. I shall march on Monday & direct my course for Bullock Creek. Leslie will march on Teusday by the river road for the same place. I approve of your proposal relative to the 7th reg't. I shall send orders to the comm'g officer accordingly.

Letter 11:

McAlister's Plantation
January 8th, 1781 7 P.M.

Dear Tarleton,

I have just received yours, 7th January, three o'clock P. M. I shall remain here tomorrow, march to cross roads on Wednesday, halt Thursday, and reach Bullock's creek meeting house Saturday.

I have no news.

Yours very sincerely,
Cornwallis

Letter 12:

M'Alister's, January 9, 1781
three P.M.

Dear Tarleton,

Nothing new since yesterday; some of Washington's cavalry, who had been escorting prisoners to Charlotte town, returned over Broad river. I have taken every means in my power to find out Morgan's movements, and whether he repasses Broad river.

I received yours January 8th.

Yours very sincerely,
Cornwallis

Letter 13:

Bull Run, Jan'y 14th, 1780, 10 P. M.

Dear Tarleton,

I received yesterday morning your letter dated Duggins, Indian Creek, Jan'y 11th, 5 a. m. By report however of the man who brought it I conceive it ought to have been dated Jan'y 12 as he assures me that he left you on Friday morning.

I shall march tomorrow to the head of Tardy River & the next day to Hillhouse near Bullock Creek Meeting House. Leslie is at last got out of the swamps & reached this day the neighborhood of Rocky Mount. I have not heard of Morgan's moving, but conclude he will now cross Broad River, as I hear it has fallen very much.

Yrs. sincerely
Cornwallis

Letter 14:

To Colonel Tarleton, from Hillhouse Plantation on Turkey Creek, 16 January 1781:

I have not heard from you since the 11. I fear Morgan has too much the start of you. I have ordered meal to be ground & propose marching in three or four days to Beatty's Ford. Leslie will join me tomorrow or Thursday.

Letter 15:

This was Tarleton's last letter to Cornwallis before the battle.[17]

> Pacolet Jan'y 16th
> 8 a. m.
>
> My Lord
>
> I have been most cruelly retarded by the waters.
> Morgan is in force and gone for Cherokee Ford.
> I am now on my march. I wish he could be stopped.
>
> I have the Honor
> to be Your most Devoted Serv't
> Ban. Tarleton

Letter 16:

Cornwallis apparently lost no confidence in his brash young field commander because of his defeat at the hands of Morgan. See Mackenzie's assessment (Appendix E) for another interpretation of Cornwallis' motive.[18]

> Lieutenant Colonel Tarleton,
>
> You have forfeited no part of my esteem as an officer, by the unfortunate event of the action of the seventeenth instant; the means you used to bring the enemy to action, were able and masterly, and must ever do you honor; your disposition was unexceptionable; the total misbehavior of the troops could alone have deprived you of the glory which was justly your due.
>
> Lord Cornwallis

3. These letters represent miscellaneous correspondence from Cornwallis concerning the Cowpens campaign.[19]

Letter 1:

9 January 1781 (?)

To Lord Rawdon:

I think it prudent to remain here a day or two longer, otherwise by the corps on my flanks being so far behind, I should be in danger of losing my communications. I have not heard from Tarleton this day, nor am I sure whether he has passed the Ennoree.

Letter 2:

12 January 1781

To General Leslie:

I have not heard from Tarleton since Tuesday, I believe he is as much embarrassed with the waters as you are.

Letter 3:

12 January 1781

To Lord Balfour:

The Rains have put a total stop to Tarleton and Leslie, & I do not think it right to advance too far with a large train of provision waggons and so small a corps.

Letter 4:

12 January 1781

To Lord Rawdon:

The Rains have impeded all operations on both sides. Morgan is at Scull's Shoals on Pacolet, & Tarleton I believe still on the south of Ennoree unable to pass either that River or the Tyger. The Broad River is so high that it is with difficulty a canoe can pass. If Leslie had not been likewise detained, I might have tried to stop Morgan's retreat, but the Corps I have with me altho' very good, will not afford a strong detachment to take care of Baggage & Provisions.

Letter 5:

On 18 January 1781, Cornwallis reported the results of the battle to his superior, Sir Henry Clinton.[20]

Camp on Turkey Creek, Broad River,
18th January, 1781

Sir:

In my letter of the sixth of this month, I had the honor to inform your Excellency, that I was ready to begin my March for North Carolina, having been delayed some days by a diversion made by the Enemy towards Ninty Six. General Morgan remained on the Pacolet, his Corps by the best accounts I could get, consisted of about five hundred men, Continentals & Virginia State Troops, & one hundred Cavalry under Colonel Washington, & six or seven hundred Militia, but that Body is so fluctuating, that it is impossible to ascertain its number, within some hundreds, for three days following Lieut. Colonel Tarleton with the Legion & Corps annexed to it, consisting of about 300 Cavalry & as Many Infantry, & the 1st Battalion of the 71st Regiment, and one three pounder, had already passed the Broad River, for the Relief of Ninty Six. I therefor directed Lieut. Colonel Tarleton to march on the West of Broad River, to endeavor to strike a blow at General Morgan, & in all events, to oblige him to repass the Broad River. I likewise ordered that he should take with him the 7th Regiment, and one three pounder, which were marching to reinforce the garrison of Ninty Six, as long as he should think their Services could be useful to him. The Remainder of the Army marched between the Broad River and the Catauba. As General Greene had quitted Mecklenburg County, & crossed the Pedee, I made not the least doubt that General Morgan would retire on our advancing. The Progress of the Army was greatly impeded by heavy Rains, which swelled the Rivers & Creeks; yet Lieut. Col. Tarleton conducted his march so well & got so near to General Morgan, who was retreating before him, as to make it dangerous for him to pass the Broad River, and came up with him at 8:00 AM on the 17th instant. Everything now bore the most promising Aspect. The Enemy were drawn up in an open wood and, having been lately joined by some Militia, were more numerous; but the different Quality of the Corps under Lieut. Col. Tarleton's Command, and his great superiority in cavalry, left him no room of doubt of the most brilliant Success. The attack was begun by the first Line of Infantry, consisting of the 7th Regiment, the Infantry of the Legion & Corps of Light Infantry annexed to it; & Troop of Cavalry was placed on each Flank: the 1st Battalion of the 71st, and the Remainder of the Cavalry, formed the reserve. The Enemy's Line soon gave way, & their Militia quitted the Field; but, on our Troops having been thrown in some disorder by the pursuit, General Morgan's Corps faced about & gave them a heavy fire. This unexpected event, occasioned the utmost confusion in the first

Line. The 1st Battalion of the 71st & the cavalry were successively ordered up; but neither the exertions, entreaties, or Example of Lieut. Colonel Tarleton could prevent the panic from becoming general; the two three pounders were taken, & I fear the Colors of the seventh Regiment shared the same fate. In justice to the Detachment of the Royal Artillery, I must here observe that no terrors could induce them to abandon their Guns, & they were all either killed or wounded in defense of them. Lieut. Colonel Tarleton with difficulty assembled fifty of his Cavalry, who having had time to recollect themselves, & being animated by the Bravery of the Officer who had so often led them to victory, charged & repulsed Colonel Washington's Horse, retook the Baggage of the Corps, & cut to pieces the detachment of the Enemy who had taken possession of it, & after destroying what they could not conveniently bring off, retired with the Remainder, unmolested, to Hamilton's Ford, near the Mouth of Bullock's Creek. The Loss of our Cavalry is inconsiderable, but I fear, about 400 of the Infantry are either killed or wounded, or taken. I will transmit the particular account of the Loss, as soon as it can be ascertained.

It is impossible to foresee all the consequences, that this unexpected & extraordinary event may produce, but your Excellency may be assured, that nothing but the most absolute necessity shall induce me to give up the important object of the Winter's Campaign. I shall direct Lieut. Colonel Balfour to transmit a Copy of this Letter, by the first opportunity, to the Secretary of State.

I have the Honor to be Your most obedt. & most humb. Servt.

Cornwallis

4. These letters from a British sympathizer in South Carolina, David George, with erroneous information, served to alarm and mislead Tarleton. The letters arrived at Tarleton's camp in the late afternoon of 1 January 1781.[21]

Letter 1:

My Wifes sister Last Night came to my house out of strong Rebel Settlement up at Princes fort; by her I have heard the Design & Intention of the Rebels; as far as their Captains have any Knowledge; as she came she Informs me that she got into some of their Camps on the south side of the Pacolate River at one Grimes Mill about Ten or Twelve Miles below the Iron Works on Lasons Fork—she understood from Captain Francis Princes and Henry Princes Wives; That they were waiting for Colonel Morgan & Colonel Washington who was on their March; in order to Join Them Morgan with five or six Hundred Light horse had Crossed broad River at Smiths ford a few Dayes agoe; and Washington with their artillery and foot men was to Cross broad River at the same ford yesterday; That they intended to march against Ninety Six and agusta; they say they will have Three Thousand men; tho go against Them places: but I have always observed that they alwayes make the Most of There men.

Letter 2:

I have sot [*sic*] down to acquaint you with what I have Heard a few Moments agoe Morgan & Washington Had Joind the party that Lay at Grimes Mill yesterday & they all moved to Colonel Henderson Plantation about a mile this side of the mill and I am well Informed that they Intend to March as fast as they can to Ninty Six I don't believe they have as many men at it is Reported to my Wifes Sister.

NOTES

Appendix D

1. Morgan, *Papers*, 9–10.

2. Graham, *Life*, 271.

3. Graham, *Life*, 272.

4. Graham, *Life*, 267–69. Obviously Morgan or Graham has misdated this letter; it should read 31 December 1780.

5. Graham, *Life*, 274–75. An abbreviated version can be found in Bass, *Dragoon*, 146.

6. Graham, *Life*, 272–74.

7. Johnson, *Correspondence*, 370–71; and Graham, *Life*, 285–86.

8. Graham, *Life*, 287–88. In Johnson, *Correspondence*, 373–74, this letter is dated incorrectly as 9 January.

9. Bass, *Dragoon*, 139–40.

10. Bass, *Dragoon*, 141.

11. Tarleton, *Campaigns*, 250–51. The original letter was misdated 1780 instead of 1781. Tarleton recognizes the error in his history, 250. Quoted in Bass, *Dragoon*, 143; and Edwards, *Morgan*, 97.

12. Bass, *Dragoon*, 144.

13. Tarleton, *Campaigns*, 251–52.

14. Letter 8 is reproduced in Bass, *Dragoon*, 145. Letter 9 is from Bass, *Dragoon*, 146; and Tarleton, *Campaigns*, 252–53.

15. The sentence in italics was encoded in the original message. Tarleton, *Campaigns*, 253.

16. Letters 10–14 may be found in Bass, *Dragoon*, 147, 150.

17. Bass, *Dragoon*, 151.

18. Reprinted in William Moultrie, *Memoirs of the American Revolution so far as it is related to the States of North and South Carolina, and Georgia* (New York: David Longworth, 1802), 257–58. General Moultrie served in the Revolution

and afterwards was elected governor of South Carolina. Mackenzie dismisses this letter as "goodness of his heart," *Strictures*, 105. George Hanger, who had served as a major with the Legion in South Carolina but was not present at the Cowpens, insists that this letter is a genuine reflection of Cornwallis' sentiment toward Tarleton and not a mere consolation, Hanger, *Address*, 91.

19. Bass, *Dragoon*, 148–49.

20. Clark, *State Records*, vol. 17, 981–82.

21. Bass, *Dragoon*, 142.

APPENDIX E

Miscellaneous Writings Pertaining to the Campaign of The Cowpens

Contents

Page

1. Tarleton's assessment of the battle of the Cowpens, 1787............................ 188

2. Lieutenant Roderick Mackenzie's letter published in the
   London *Morning Chronicle*, 9 August 1782 190

3. Mackenzie's assessment of Tarleton, 1787... 190

1. Tarleton's assessment of the Battle of the Cowpens.[1]

A diffuse comment upon this affair would be equally useless and tiresome: Two observations will be sufficient: One will contain the general circumstances which affected the plan of the campaign, and the other the particular incidents of the action. It appears that Earl Cornwallis intended to invade North Carolina: Before his march commenced, an irruption was made by the enemy into the western part of South Carolina: In order to expel hostility from that quarter, he directed Lieutenant-colonel Tarleton to proceed with a corps, and "push the enemy to the utmost"[2]; at the same time desiring to know if any movement by the main army would be useful. Tarleton, finding the Americans not so far advanced as was reported, halted his troops, that he might convey his opinion, by letter, to his commanding officer. He proposed that the army under Earl Cornwallis, and the corps of light troops, should commence their march at the same time for King's mountain, and that he would endeavour to destroy the enemy, or push them over the Broad river to that place. Earl Cornwallis replied, that Tarleton perfectly understood his intentions [Letter 8, Miscellaneous Correspondence, Appendix D]. After three days move from Wynnesborough, his lordship sent intelligence that General Leslie was retarded by the waters, and that he imagined the light troops must be equally impeded. Tarleton shortened his marches till he heard that the reinforcement was out of the swamps, though he had more difficulties of that nature to struggle against than could possibly be found between the Catawba and Broad rivers: This delay being occasioned by General Leslie's corps, rather astonished him, because the troops under that officer's command were not mentioned in the first proposal; and if they were deemed necessary for the combination, one forced march would have brought them from the banks of the Catawba to the middle road, which Earl Cornwallis was then moving on, between the two great rivers, and where no creeks or waters could obstruct their advance towards Tryon county. On the 14th Earl Cornwallis informed Tarleton that Leslie had surmounted his difficulties, and that he imagined the enemy would not pass the Broad river, though it had fallen very much. Tarleton then answered, that he would try to cross the Pacolet to force them, and desired Earl Cornwallis to acquire as high a station as possible, in order to stop their retreat. No letter, order, or intelligence, from head quarters, reached Tarleton after this reply, previous to the defeat on the 17th, and after that event he found Earl Cornwallis on Turkey creek, near twenty-five miles below the place where the action had happened. The distance between Wynnesborough and King's mountain, or Wynnesborough and Little Broad river, which would have answered the same purpose, does not exceed sixty-five miles: Earl Cornwallis commenced his march on the 7th or 8th of January. It would be mortifying to describe the advantages that might have resulted from his lordship's arrival at the concerted point, or to expiate upon the calamities which were produced by this event. If an army is acting where no co-operation can take place, it is necessary for the commander in chief to keep as near as possible to his detachments, if such a proceeding does not interfere with a manoeuvre which in itself would decide the events of the campaign. A steady adherence to that line of conduct would prevent the misfortunes which detachments are liable to, or soften their effects. Earl Cornwallis might have conceived, that, by attending to the situation of the enemy, and of the country, and by covering his light troops, he would, in all probability, have alternately brought Generals Morgan and Greene into his power by co-operative movements: He might also have concluded, that all his parties that were beaten in the country, if they had no corps to give them instant support or refuge, must be completely destroyed. Many instances of this nature occurred during the war. The fall of Ferguson [at King's Mountain] was a recent and melancholy example: That catastrophe put a period to the first expedition into North Carolina; and the affair of the Cowpens overshadowed the commencement of the second.

The particular incidents relative to the action arise from an examination of the orders, the march, the comparative situation of Morgan and Tarleton, the disposition, and the defeat. The orders were positive. The march was difficult, on account of the number of creeks and rivers; and circuitous, in consequence of such impediments: The Pacolet was passed by strategem: The Americans to avoid an action, left their camp, and marched all night: The ground where General Morgan had chosen for the engagement, in order to cover his retreat to Broad river, was disadvantageous for the Americans, and convenient for the British: An open wood was certainly as proper a place for action as Lieutenant-colonel Tarleton could desire; America does not produce many more suitable to the nature of the troops under his command. The situation of the enemy was desperate in case of misfortune; an open country, and a river in their rear, must have thrown them entirely into the power of a superior cavalry; whilst the light troops, in case of repulse, had the expectation of a neighboring force to protect them from destruction. The disposition was planned with coolness, and executed without embarrassment. The defeat of the British must be ascribed either to the bravery or good conduct of the Americans; to the loose manner of forming which had always been practiced by the King's troops in America; or to some unforeseen event, which may throw terror into the most disciplined soldiers, or counteract the best-concerted designs.

The extreme extension of the files exposed the British regiments and corps, and would, before this unfortunate affair, have been attended with detrimental effect, had not the multiplicity of lines with which they generally fought rescued them from such imminent danger. If infantry who are formed very open, and only one or two deep, meet with opposition, they can have no stability: But when they experience an unexpected shock, confusion will ensue, and flight, without immediate support, must be the inevitable consequence. Other circumstances, perhaps, contributed to so decisive a rout, which, if the military system admitted the same judicious regulation as the naval, a court martial would, perhaps, have disclosed. Public trials of commanding officers after unfortunate affairs are as necessary to one service as another, and might, in some instances, be highly beneficial to the military profession. Influenced by this idea, Lieutenant-colonel Tarleton, some days after the action, required Earl Cornwallis's approbation of his proceedings, or his leave retire till inquiry could be instituted, to investigate his conduct. The noble earl's decided support of Lieutenant-colonel Tarleton's management of the King's troops, previous to and during the action, is fully expressed in a letter from his lordship.

2. Lieutenant Roderick Mackenzie served in the 71st (Frasier's) Highlanders at the battle of the Cowpens. After his return to England, he attacked his former commander, Tarleton, in the press. This letter appeared in the *London Morning Chronicle* on 9 August 1782.[3]

> You got yourself and your party completely ambuscaded, completely surrounded, upon all sides, by Mr. Morgan's rifle men. What was the consequence? The two detachments of British were made prisoners after a great slaughter was made among them, your legion dragoons were so broke by galling fire of rifle shot that your charging was in vain, till prudence, on your side, with about twenty men who were well mounted, made your retreat good, by leaving the remains of the poor blended legion in the hands of Mr. Morgan who I must say, though an enemy, showed great masterly abilities in this manoeuver.
>
> Thus fell, at one blow, all the Provincial Legion, with about *three hundred* veterans [italics in Commager edition]![4]

3. Mackenzie's Assessment of Tarleton.

Letter XI

My dear sir,

As a circumstantial detail of the action at Cowpens was given to you in my last letter, observations upon the causes of that disaster shall be the subject of this.

You have already my opinion, that Earl Cornwallis is incapable of wilful [sic] misrepresentation; leaving then to the judgment of others, the propriety of producing a confidential letter[5], written by his Lordship in the goodness of his heart, evidently with design to console our author under a severe misfortune, and never meant for publication; I only contend, that this letter, is altogether inadequate to the purpose to which this journalist [Tarleton] has converted it, that of transferring the blame from himself to the troops.

It has been before shewn, that the dispatches of Earl Cornwallis, with respect to the action of Blackstocks, had bestowed a laurel on Lieutenant Colonel Tarleton, which should have adorned the brows of General Sumpter, but then, as now, his Lordship drew his information from a corrupted fountain. That the "unqualified decision" of that nobleman in favour of our author, in regard to the action of Cowpens, was "made without any opportunity of personal observation" has been happily noticed by others.[6] It is a transcript of Lieutenant Colonel Tarleton's report, and therefore, like the evidence of a man in his own cause, totally inadmissable.

Our author, through the whole of his narrative, seems to have Julius Caesar in view; but Caesar's mind was above any occasion for recourse to vanity, ostentation, or detraction. It was his pride to bestow due praise on deserving officers, while this journalist distinguishes himself by lavishing reproaches directly on his General, and obliquely on others who had the misfortune of serving under his command. As an individual on this detachment, credit may be given to me for an acquaintance with every circumstance which is here described. If to be disinterested is necessary for the investigation of truth, I come so far qualified for this talk. Unconnected with party, devoid of spleen, and too unimportant to be affected by general reflections on collective bodies of military men, candour and impartiality may be allowed me—But to proceed.

The first error in judgment to be imputed to Lieutenant Colonel Tarleton, on the morning of the 17th of January, 1781, is, the not halting of his troops before he engaged the enemy. Had he done so, it is evident that the following advantages would have been the result of his conduct. General Morgan's force and situation might have been distinctly viewed, under cover of a superior cavalry; the British infantry, fatigued with rapid marches, day and night, for some time past, as has been already observed, might have had rest and refreshment; a detachment from the several corps left with the baggage, together with batt-men, and officers servants, would have had time to come up. and join in the action. The artillery all this time might have been playing on the enemy's front, or either flank, without risk of insult; the commandants of regiments, Majors M'Arthur and Newmarsh, officers who held commissions long before our author was born, and who had reputations to this day unimpeached, might have been consulted, and, not to dwell on the enumeration of all the advantages which would have accrued from so judicious a delay, time would have been given for the approach of Earl Cornwallis to the preconcerted point, for the unattainment of which he has been so much and so unjustly censured.

The second error was, the un-officer-like impetuosity of directing the line to advance before it was properly formed, and before the reserve had taken its ground; in consequence of which, as might have been expected, the attack was premature, confused, and irregular.

The third error in this ruinous business, was the omission of giving discretional powers to that judicious veteran M'Arthur, to advance with the reserve, at the time the front line was in pursuit of the militia, by which means the connection so necessary to troops engaged in the field was not preserved.

His fourth error was, ordering Captain Ogilvie, with a troop, to charge, before any impression was made on the continentals, and before Washington's cavalry had been engaged.

The next, and the most destructive, for I will not pretend to follow him through all his errors, was in not bringing up a column of cavalry, and completing the rout, which, by his own acknowledgement, had commenced through the whole American infantry.

After what has been said, there may not, perhaps, be a better criterion to judge the conduct of those corps, upon whom Lieutenant Colonel Tarleton has stamped the charge of "total misbehaviour," than by an examination of the state of discipline they were then under, of their general conduct upon every former occasion, and of the loss which they sustained on this.

The fusiliers had served with credit in America from the commencement of the war, and under an excellent officer, General Clarke, had attained the summit of military discipline; they had at this time, out of nine officers who were in the action, five[7] killed or wounded.

The first battalion of the 71st regiment, who had landed in Georgia in the year 1778, under the command of Archibald Campbell, had established their reputation in the several operations in that province, at Stone Ferry, at the sieges of Savannah and Charlestown, and at the battle of Camden. Now, not inferior to the 7th regiment in discipline, they were led by an officer of great experience, who had come into the British service from the Scottish Dutch brigade: Out of sixteen officers [including the light company of the 2nd battalion] which they had in the field, nine[8] were killed or wounded.

The battalion of light infantry had signalized themselves separately on many occasions. The company of the 16th regiment[9] was well known by its services in the army commanded by Major General Prevost; those of the seventy-first regiment were distinguished under Sir James Baird at the serprise of General [Anthony] Wayne in Pennsylvania, of Baylor's dragoons in New Jersey, at Briar Creek in Georgia, at the capture and subsequent defence of Savannah, at the battle near Camden under Earl Cornwallis; and even Lieutenant Colonel did them justice at the defeat of Sumpter, just after the last mentioned action.

The light infantry company of the Prince of Wales's American regiment,[10] when but newly raised and indifferently disciplined, acquired reputation under General Tryon at Danbury; their only officer [Lieutenant Lindsay] was here wounded.

The infantry of the legion had seen much service, and had always behaved well: this our author will surely not deny.

The troops of the seventeenth regiment of dragoons, when ordered into action, displayed that gallantry with which they had stamped their character on every former occasion. They had here but two officers, both of whom were wounded, one mortally.[11] The detachment of artillery was totally annihilated.

Such were the troops whom this journalist has so severely stigmatized. Few corps, in any age or country, will be found to have bled more freely.

It is an established custom in armies for the commanding officer, whether victorious or vanquished, to account for the loss which he has sustained. In the present instance it requires no extraordinary sagacity to discover, that Lieutenant Colonel Tarleton had his own particular reasons for withholding such an account; and it is evident that had this loss of officers, to which that of the soldiers probably bore a near proportion, been faithfully published, the veracity of our author's account might have been justly called in question, and the cause of the defeat, instead of being left to a "*perhaps*," [italics original] might have been reduced to a certainty.

In describing the particular incidents of this action, our journalist says, page 221, "The extreme extension of the files always exposed the British regiments and corps, and would, before this unfortunate affair, have been attended with detrimental effect, had not the multiplicity of lines with which they generally fought, rescued them from such imminent danger." He still continues to furnish argument against himself; if his files were too extensive, why did he not contract them? for he says, in the same page, that "the disposition was planned with coolness, and executed without embarrassment." Any other mode of attack, or disposition, therefore, which he might have planned, would doubtless have been executed with equal promptitude. The latter part of this quotation is not less inconsistent. I would ask Lieutenant Colonel Tarleton in what action, during the campaign of which he treats, did the multiplicity of lines rescue the British troops from imminent danger? and on what occasion did their front line, or any part thereof, give way I believe it will be found that it fell to Lieutenant Colonel Tarleton alone to lead the troops of Britain into a situation, from which they could be driven by an equal; or even by double or treble their number.

When Earl Cornwallis fought the memorable battle near Camden, his force, considerably under two thousand men, was opposed by upwards of six thousand. At Guilford, his Lordship, with not one third of the enemy, obtained a glorious victory over General Greene, the best commander in the American service; and Lord Rawdon upon Hobkirk's Hill, routed the same General, who had now added experience to his other talents, and this, though his numbers compared with his enemy, did not bear the last mentioned proportion. Many other proofs could be brought of the fallacy of our author's reasoning, but these which have been adduced will, I trust, sufficiently shew the impossibility of forming a multiplicity of lines, with so manifest an inferiority of numbers; nay, I venture to affirm, that the disparity of force at Cowpens was smaller that it had been in any engagement during the southern campaigns, consequently, Lieutenant Colonel Tarleton had it in his power to engage with greater advantages than occurred either previous to his defeat or since.

Ramsey has well observed, Volume II, p. 203,

Whilst Lord Cornwallis was anticipating, in imagination, a rich harvest of glory, from a rapid succession of victories, he received the intelligence, no less unwelcome than unexpected, of the complete overthrow of the detachment led by Lieutenant Colonel Tarleton. So contemptible, from their conduct at Camden, was his Lordship's opinion of the American militia—so unlimited was his confidence in the courage and abilities of Lieutenant Colonel tarleton, that, of all improbable events, none seemed to him more improbable, than that an inferior force, two-thirds militia, should gain such a decisive advantage over his favourite hero.

I have now done with the action at Cowpens, and on this occasion confess that I am not without my feelings as an individual for so wanton an attack on characters and entire corps, whose conduct had been, til then, unsullied. There is not an officer who survived that disastrous day, who is not far beyond the reach of slander and detraction; and with respect to the dead, I leave to Lieutenant Colonel Tarleton all the satisfaction which he can enjoy, from reflecting that he led a number of brave men to destruction, and then used every effort in his power to damn their fame with posterity.

I am, etc.

NOTES
Appendix E

1. Tarleton, *Campaigns*, 225–28.

2. See Letter 4, Cornwallis to Tarlton, Appendix E, 174.

3. Henry Steele Commager and Richard B. Morris, eds., *The Spirit of 'Seventy-Six*, vol. 2 (Indianapolis IN: Bobbs-Merrill, 1958), x.

4. Mackenzie, *Strictures*, 104–18. I have summarized Mackenzie's lengthy quotations from Tarleton's work.

5. Mackenzie cites a letter from Cornwallis to Tarleton reproduced in Appendix D, 179.

6. Mackenzie cites the *Critical Review* of May 1787.

7. Mackenzie lists Captain Helyar and Lieutenant Marshal killed, Major Newmarsh (the commander) and Lieutenants Harling and L'Estrange wounded, *Strictures*, 110).

8. Mackenzie lists Lieutenants Macleod and Chisholm killed and Lieutenants Grant, Mackintosh, Flint, Mackenzie (the author), Sinclair, Forbes, and Macleod wounded, *Strictures*, 111.

9. Sir Frederick Maurice tells us that the 16th Foot was with Cornwallis at the time of Tarleton's defeat, in *The 16th Foot* (London: Constable & Company, 1931), 67. Returns of 15 January 1781 indicate that the army contained only three companies of the 16th, totaling only forty-one rank and file present for duty, Clark, *State Records*, vol. 17, 1009.

10. This is the only mention of the presence of the Prince of Wales' American Regiment, raised in June 1777. In some accounts, it is described merely as "the light company"; in others, it may be lumped in with the British Legion, Raymond, *Loyalists*, 209.

11. These were Lieutenant Nettles and Cornet Patterson. Patterson was mortally wounded, *Strictures*, 113.

BIBLIOGRAPHY

Primary Sources

Anderson, Thomas. "Journal of Lieutenant Thomas Anderson of the Delaware Regiment, 1780–1782." *Historical Magazine*, 2d ser., 1 (1867):207–11.

Balch, Thomas. *Papers Relating Chiefly to the Maryland Line During the Revolution*. Philadelphia: T. K. and P. G. Printers, 1857.

Beatty, William. "The Journal of Captain William Beatty, of the Maryland Line, 1776–1781." *Maryland Historical Magazine*, 2d ser., 1 (1867):79–85, 147–50.

Clinton, Sir Henry. *The American Rebellion*. Edited by William B. Willcox. New York: Archon Books, 1971.

Collins, James. *Autobiography of a Revolutionary Soldier*. Clinton, LA: Feliciana Democrat, 1859.

Ewald, Captain Johann. *Diary of the American War: A Hessian Journal*. Translated by and edited by Joseph P. Tusten. New Haven, CT: Yale University Press, 1979.

Fitzpatrick, John C., ed. *The Writings of George Washington*. 39 vols. Washington, DC: Government Printing Office, 1931–44.

Garden, Alexander. *Anecdotes of the Revolutionary War in America*. Charleston, SC: A. E. Miller, 1822.

Greene, Nathanael. *The Papers of General Nathanael Greene*. Edited by Richard K. Showman, et al. Chapel Hill: University of North Carolina Press, 1976.

Hanger, George. *An Address to the Army in Reply to the Strictures by Roderick Mackenzie*. London: James Ridgeway, 1789.

Jones, E. Alfred, ed. *The Journal of Alexander Chesney*. Columbus, OH: Ohio State University, 1921.

Kirkwood, Robert. *The Journal and Order Book of Captain Robert Kirkwood of the Delaware Regiment of the Continental Line*. Edited by Joseph Brown Turner. Wilmington: Historical Society of Delaware, 1910.

Lee, Henry, Jr. *Campaign of 1781 in the Carolinas*. Chicago: Quadrangle Books, 1969.

_____. *Memoirs of the Southern Department of the United States*. Edited by Robert E. Lee. New York: University Publishing, 1870.

Lloyd, H. *Continuation of the History of the Late War in Germany Between the King of Prussia and the Emperor of Germany and Her Allies*. Part II. London: S. Hooper, 1781.

Mackenzie, Roderick. *Strictures on Lt. Col Tarleton's History of the Campaign of 1780 and 1781 in the Southern Provinces of North America*. London, 1787.

Morgan, Daniel. *Cowpens Papers, Being the Correspondence of General Morgan and the Prominent Actors*. Compiled by Theodorus Baily Myers. Charleston, SC: News and Courier, 1881.

_____. *Papers of Daniel Morgan, Relating to the Revolution*. Compiled by Theodorus Baily Myers. New York: Ottawa, 1887.

Moultrie, William. *Memoirs of the American Revolution so far as it is related to the States of North and South Carolina, and Georgia*. New York: David Longworth, 1802.

Pickens, Andrew L. *Skyagunsta, The Border Wizard Owl, Major General Andrew Pickens (1739–1817)*. Greenville, SC: Observer Print, c. 1934.

Revolutionary War Pension Applications and Bounty-Land-Warrant Application Files. Record Group 15, M804. National Archives, Washington, D.C. Copies at the Visitor's Center, Cowpens National Battlefield, transliterated and donated by Professor Lawrence E. Babits.

Saxe, Field Marshal Count. *Reveries or Memoirs upon the Art of War*. Westport, CT: Greenwood Press, 1971.

Saye, James Hodge. *Memoirs of Major Joseph McJunkin: Revolutionary Patriot*. 2d ed. Greenwood, SC: Greenwood Index-Journal, 1925.

Seymour, William. *A Journal of the Southern Expedition 1780–1783*. Wilmington: Historical Society of Delaware, 1896.

Skelton, Lynda Worley, ed. *General Andrew Pickens: An Autobiography*. Clemson, SC: Pendleton District Historical and Recreational Commission, 1976.

Von Steuben, Frederick W. *Regulations for the Order and Discipline of the Troops of the United States*. New York: J. McLean, 1784.

Tarleton, Banastre. *A History of the Campaigns of 1780 and 1781 in the Southern Provinces of North America*. Dublin: T. Cadell, 1787.

Wolfe, Major General James. *Instructions to Young Officers*. London, Museum Restoration Service, 1967.

Young, Thomas. "Memoir of Major Thomas Young, a Revolutionary Patriot of South Carolina." *The Orion* 3 (October-November 1843):88, 100–102.

Secondary Sources

Alden, John Richard. *General Charles Lee Traitor or Patriot?* Baton Rouge: Louisiana State University, 1951.

Army War College Historical Section. *Historical Statements Concerning the Battle of Kings Mountain and the Battle of the Cowpens, South Carolina.* Washington, DC: U.S. Government Printing Office, 1928.

Asprey, Robert B. *War in the Shadows.* 2 vols. Garden City, NY: Doubleday & Company, 1975.

Atkinson, Christopher T. "British Forces in North America 1774–1781: Their Distribution and Strength." *Journal of the Society for Army Historical Research* 20 (1941):208–23.

Babits, Lawrence E. *Cowpens Battlefield A Walking Tour.* Johnson City, TN: Overmountain Press, 1993.

Bailey, J. D. *Some Heroes of the American Revolution.* Spartanburg, SC: Bond & White Printers, 1924.

Barnes, R. Money. *The History of the Regiments & Uniforms of the British Army.* London: Seeley Service & Co., 1964.

Bartholomees, James Boone, Jr. "Fight or Flee: The Combat Performance of the North Carolina Militia in the Cowpens-Guilford Court House Campaign, January to March, 1781." Ph.D. diss., Duke University, 1978.

Bass, Robert D. *The Green Dragoon.* Columbia, SC: Sandlapper Press, 1957.

Bearss, Edwin C. *The Battle of the Cowpens.* Washington, DC: Office of Archeology and Historical Preservation, U.S. Department of the Interior, 1967.

Bendiner, Elmer. *The Virgin Diplomats.* New York: Knopf, 1976.

Boatner, Mark Mayo III. *Encyclopedia of the American Revolution.* New York: David McKay Company, 1976.

Boorstin, Daniel J. *The Americans: The Colonial Experience.* New York: Random House, 1958.

Bowler, Arthur. *Logistics and the Failure of the British Army in America 1775–1783.* Princeton, NJ: Princeton University Press, 1975.

Browne, James Alex. *Englands Artillerymen.* London: Hall, Smart and Allen, 1865.

Buchholz, Arden. *Moltke, Schlieffen and Prussian War Planning.* New York: St. Martin's Press, 1991.

Caruana, Adrien. *Grasshoppers and Butterflies: The Light 3-Pounders of Patterson and Townshend*. Bloomfield, Ontario, 1979.

Chandler, David. *The Art of Warfare in the Age of Marlborough*. New York: Hippocrene Books, 1976.

Clark, Walter. *State Records of North Carolina*. 16 vols. Goldsboro, NC: Nash Bros., 1896.

Clausewitz, Carl von. *On War*. Edited by and translated by Michael Howard and Peter Paret. Princeton, NJ: Princeton University Press, 1984.

Commager, Henry Steele, and Richard B. Morris, eds. *The Spirit of 'Seventy Six*. 2 vols. Indianapolis: Bobbs-Merrill, 1958.

Conrad, Dennis Michael. "Nathanael Greene and the Southern Campaign." Ph.D. diss. Duke University, 1979.

Curtis, Edward E. *Organization of the British Army in the American Revolution*. New Haven, CT: Yale University Press, 1926.

Dann, John C., ed. *The Revolution Remembered: Eyewitness Accounts of the War for Independence*. Chicago: University of Chicago Press, 1980.

Darling, Anthony D. *Red Coat and Brown Bess*. Alexandria Bay, NY: Museum Restoration Service, 1987.

Davidson, Chalmers Gaston. *Piedmont Partisan: The Life and Times of Brigadier-General William Lee Davidson*. Davidson, NC: Davidson College Press, 1951.

Davis, Burke. *The Cowpens-Guilford Courthouse Campaign*. Philadelphia: J. B. Lippencott, 1962.

Dederer, John Morgan. *Making Bricks Without Straw: Nathanael Greene's Southern Campaign and Mao Tse Tung's Mobile War*. Manhattan, KS: Sunflower University Press, 1983.

Delbrück, Hans. *History of the Art of War Within the Framework of Political History*. Translated by Walter J. Renfroe, Jr. Westport, CT: Greenwood Press, 1975.

Dictionary of American Biography. 20 vols. New York: Scribner, 1928–37.

Douwes, William F. "Logistical Support of the Continental Light Dragoons." *Military Collector and Historian* 24 (1972):101–6.

Draper, Lyman. *King's Mountain and its Heroes*. Cincinnati, OH: Peter G. Thompson, 1881.

Duffy, Christopher. *The Army of Frederick the Great*. New York: Hippocrene Books, 1974.

Duncan, Captain Francis. *History of the Royal Regiment of Artillery.* 2 vols. 3d ed. London: John Murray, 1872–73; 1879.

Edwards, William Waller. "Morgan and his Riflemen." *William and Mary Quarterly*, 1st ser., 23 (1914):73–106.

Esposito, Vincent, ed. *West Point Atlas of American Wars.* 2 vols. New York: Praeger, 1959.

Fortescue, John W. *A History of the 17th Lancers.* London: Macmillan, 1895.

Fuller, J. F. C. *A Military History of the Western World.* 3 vols. New York: Minerva Press, 1955.

Gibbes, Robert W. *Documentary History of the American Revolution.* 3 vols. Columbia, SC: Banner Steam-Power Press, 1853–57.

Graham, James. *The Life of General Daniel Morgan of the Virginia Line of the Army of the United States.* New York: Derby and Jackson, 1856.

Greene, George Washington. *The Life of Nathanael Greene.* 3 vols. New York: Hurd & Houghton, 1867–71.

Groves, Percy, Lieutenant-Colonel. *Historical Records of the 7th or Royal Regiment of Fusiliers (The City of London Regiment) 1685–1903.* Guernsey: Frederick B. Guerin, 1903.

Gruber, Ira D. *The Brothers Howe in the American Revolution.* New York: Atheneum, 1972.

Heinl, Robert Debs, Jr. *Dictionary of Military and Naval Quotations.* Annapolis, MD: United States Naval Institute, 1966.

Heitman, Francis B., ed. *Historical Register of Officers of the Continental Army During the Revolution: April, 1775 to December, 1782.* Washington, DC: Lowdermilk, 1890.

Henry, Robert. *Narratives of the Battle of Cowan's Ford.* Greensboro, NC: D. Schenck, Sr., 1891.

Hibbert, Christopher. *Redcoats and Rebels.* New York: W. W. Norton, 1990.

Higginbotham, Don. *Daniel Morgan, Revolutionary Rifleman.* Chapel Hill: University of North Carolina Press, 1961.

Higginbotham, Don, ed. *Military Analysis of the Revolutionary War.* Millwood, NY: KTO Press, 1977.

———. *Reconsiderations of the Revolutionary War.* Westport, CT: Greenwood Press, 1978.

Higgins, W. Robert, ed. *The Revolutionary War in the South: Power, Conflict, and Leadership*. Durham, NC: Duke University Press, 1979.

Hill, Jim Dan. *The Minute Man in Peace and War*. Harrisburg, PA: Stackpole 1964.

Huffstettler, Joel W. "Henry Lee and Banastre Tarleton: How Historians Use Their Memoirs." *Southern Historian* 6 (1985):12–19.

Johnson, Joseph. *Traditions and Reminiscences Chiefly of the American Revolution in the South*. Charleston, SC: Walker & James, 1851.

Johnson, William. *Sketches of the Life and Correspondence of Nathanael Greene*. 2 vols. Charleston, SC: A. E. Miller, 1822.

Katcher, Philip R. N. *Encyclopedia of British, Provincial, and German Army Units 1775–1783*. Harrisburg, PA: Stackpole, 1973.

Ketchum, Richard M. "Men of the American Revolution XVI: Daniel Morgan." *American Heritage* 27 (1976):34–35, 97.

Ketchum, Richard M., ed. "New War Letters of Banastre Tarleton." *The New-York HistoricalSociety Quarterly* 51 (January 1967):61–81.

Kyte, George W. "Victory in the South: An Appraisal of General Greene's Strategy in the Carolinas." *North Carolina Historical Review* 37 (1960):321–47.

Lambert, Robert Stansbury. *South Carolina Loyalists in the American Revolution*. Columbia: University of South Carolina Press, 1987.

Livy. *The War with Hannibal*. Translated by Aubrey de Sélincourt and edited by Betty Radice. Baltimore, MD: Penguin Books, 1968.

Lloyd, E. M. E. *A Review of the History of Infantry*. Westport, CT: Greenwood Press, 1976.

Lunt, James. *John Burgoyne of Saratoga*. New York: Harcourt Brace Jovanovich, 1975.

Mahler, Michael D. "190th Anniversary—The Battle at Cowpens." *Military Review* 51, no. 1 (1971):56–63.

Mahon, John K. *History of the Militia and the National Guard*. New York: Macmillan, 1983.

Martin, James Kirby, and Mark Edward Lender. *A Respectable Army: The Military Origins of the Revolution 1763–1789*. Arlington Heights, IL: Harlan Davidson, 1982.

Maurice, F. *The 16th Foot*. London: Constable & Company, 1931.

McGrady, Edward. *The History of South Carolina in the Revolution, 1780–1783*. New York, 1902.

Meschutt, David. "Portraits of Daniel Morgan, Revolutionary War General." *American Art Journal* 17, no. 3 (1985):34–43.

Montross, Lynn. "America's Most Imitated Battle." *American Heritage* 7, no. 3 (1956):35–37, 100–101.

Moss, Bobby Gilmer. *The Patriots at the Cowpens*. Greenville, SC: Scotia Press, 1985.

Nelson, Paul David. "British Conduct of the American Revolutionary War: A Review of Interpretations." *Journal of American History* 65 (December 1978):623–53.

———. "Horatio Gates in the Southern Department, 1780: Serious Errors and a Costly Defeat." *North Carolina Historical Review* 50 (1973):256–72.

Palmer, Dave R., and James W. Stryker. *Early American Wars and Military Institutions*. West Point, NY: U.S. Military Academy, 1977.

———. *The Way of the Fox*. Westport, CT: Greenwood, 1975.

Pancake, John S. *This Destructive War The British Campaign in the Carolinas 1780–1781*. University: University of Alabama Press, 1985.

Peckham, Howard H., ed. *Sources of American Independence*. Chicago, 1978.

Peterkin, Ernest W. *The Exercise of Arms in the Continental Infantry*. Alexandria Bay, NY: Museum Restoration Service, 1989.

Peterson, Harold L. *The Book of the Continental Soldier*. Harrisburg, PA: Stackpole, 1968.

Pohler, Johannes. *Bibliotheca Historico-Militaris*. 4 vols. New York: Burt Franklin, n.d.

Pugh, Robert C. "The Cowpens Campaign and the American Revolution." Ph.D. diss., University of Illinois, 1951.

———. "The Revolutionary Militia and the Southern Campaign, 1780–1781." *William and Mary Quarterly* 14, 3d ser. (April 1957):154–75.

Radabaugh, Jack S. "The Militia of Colonial Massachusetts." *Military Affairs* 18 (Spring 1954):1–18.

Raddall, Thomas H., Dr. "Tarleton's Legion." *Collections of the Nova Scotia Historical Society*. Vol. 28. Halifax, NS: Allen Print Limited, 1949.

Ramsay, David. *The History of the American Revolution*. 2 vols. Edited by Lester H. Cohen. Indianapolis, IN: Liberty Classics, 1990.

———. *The History of the Revolution in South Carolina*. Trenton, NJ: Isaac Collins, 1785.

Rankin, Hugh F. *The American Revolution.* New York: G. P. Putnam's Sons, 1964.

___. "Cowpens: Prelude to Yorktown." *North Carolina Historical Review* 31 (July 1954):336–69.

___. "Greene and Cornwallis: The Campaign in the Carolinas, 1780–1781." M.A. Thesis, University of North Carolina, 1950.

___. *The North Carolina Continentals.* Chapel Hill: University of North Carolina Press, 1971.

Raymond, W. O. *Loyalists in Arms.* St. John, N.B.: Sun Printing, 1904. (In New Brunswick Historical Society Collections.)

Read, Elizabeth. "John Eager Howard." *The Magazine of American History.* Vol. 7. New York: A. S. Baird & Company, 276–82.

Roberts, Kenneth. *The Battle of the Cowpens: The Great Morale Builder.* Garden City, NY: Doubleday & Co., 1958.

Robertson, William G. *The Staff Ride.* Washington, DC: U.S. Army Center of Military History, 1987.

Ross, Steven. *From Flintlock to Rifle: Infantry Tactics, 1740–1866.* Rutherford, NJ: Fairleigh Dickinson University Press, 1979.

Sabine, Lorenzo. "The Tory Contingent in the British Army in America in 1781." *Historical Magazine* 8 (1864):321–26, 354–59, 389–92.

Sanchez-Saavedna, E. M. *A Guide to Virginia Military Organizations in the American Revolution 1774–1787.* Richmond: Virginia State Library, 1978.

Scheer, George F., and Hugh F. Rankin. *Rebels and Redcoats.* New York: The World Publishing Company, 1977.

Schenck, David. *North Carolina, 1780–81, Being a History of the Invasion of the Carolinas by the Army under Lord Cornwallis.* Raleigh, NC: Edwards and Broughton, 1889.

Von Schlieffen, Generalfeldmarschall Graf. *Cannae.* Berlin: E. S. Mittler, 1913.

Shy, John W. "A New Look at Colonial Militia." *The William and Mary Quarterly* 20, 3d ser. (1963):175–85.

Singleton, William N. "Cowpens: 'The Patriots' Best-Fought Battle." *Daughters of the American Revolution Magazine* 111, no. 5 (1977):473–81.

Smith, Derek. "Cowpens, 1781: The Defeat of 'Bloody Banny.'" *Army* (August 1944):40–52.

Sparks, Jared, ed. *Correspondence of the American Revolution.* 4 vols. Boston: Little, Brown & Co., 1853.

Spiller, Roger S., ed. *American Military Leaders*. New York: Praeger, 1989.

Steuart, Rieman. *A History of the Maryland Line in the Revolutionary War, 1775–1783*. Society of the Cincinnati of Maryland, 1969.

Stevens, Benjamin Franklin, comp. and ed. *The Campaign in Virginia, 1781: The Clinton-Cornwallis Controversy*. London, 1888.

Stewart, David. *Sketches of the Character, Manners and Present State of the Highlanders of Scotland*. 3d ed. Vol. 2. Edinburgh: Archibald Constable, 1825.

Thane, Elswyth. *The Fighting Quaker: Nathanael Greene*. New York: Hawthorn Books, 1972.

Thayer, Theodore. *Nathanael Greene: Strategist of the American Revolution*. New York: Twayne, 1960.

Treasy, M. F. *Prelude to Yorktown: The Southern Campaign of Nathanael Greene, 1780–1781*. Chapel Hill: University of North Carolina Press, 1963.

Trotter, William R. "Advantages Found in Retreat." *Military History* 6 (December 1989):38–45.

Ultee, Maarten, ed. *Adapting to Conditions: War and Society in the Eighteenth Century*. University: University of Alabama Press, 1986.

Wallach, Jehuda L. *The Dogma of the Battle of Annihilation*. Westport, CT: Greenwood Press, 1986.

Ward, Christopher. *The Delaware Continentals, 1776–1783*. Wilmington: Historical Society of Delaware, 1941.

Waring, Alice N. *The Fighting Elder: Andrew Pickens, 1739–1817*. Columbia: University of South Carolina Press, 1982.

Weigley, Russell. *The American Way of War*. New York: Macmillan, 1973.

_____. *History of the United States Army*. New York: Macmillan, 1967.

Weller, Jac. "Irregular but Effective: Partisan Weapons Tactics in the American Revolution, Southern Theatre." *Military Affairs* 21, no. 3 (1957):118–31.

Wheaton, W. *Historical Record of the Seventh or Royal Regiment of Fusiliers*. Leeds, 1875.

Wheeler, E. Milton. "Development and Organization of the North Carolina Militia." *North Carolina Historical Review* 61 (1964):307–23.

White, Arthur S. *Bibliography of Regimental Histories of the British Army*. London: Society for Army Historical Research, 1965.

Wickwire, Franklin B., and Mary Wickwire. *Cornwallis: The American Adventure.* Boston: Houghton Mifflin, 1970.

Willcox, William B. *The American Rebellion.* New Haven, CT: Yale University Press, 1954.

_____. "The British Road to Yorktown: A Study in Divided Command." *American Historical Review* 52 (1946):1–35.

_____. "British Strategy in America, 1778." *Journal of Modern History* 19 (1947):97–121.

_____. *Portrait of a General: Sir Henry Clinton in the War of Independence.* New York: Knopf, 1964.

Woodham-Smith, Cecil. *The Reason Why.* New York: E. P. Dutton, 1960.

Wright, John W. "The Corps of Light Infantry in the Continental Army." *American Historical Review* 31 (1926):454–61.

Wright, Robert K. *The Continental Army.* Washington, DC: U.S. Army Center of Military History, 1983.